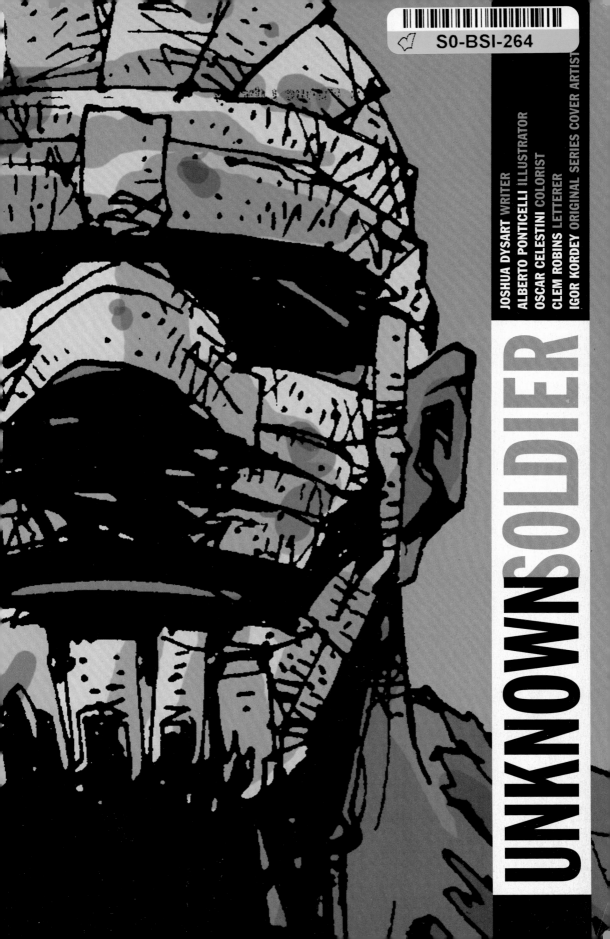

JOSHUA DYSART WRITER
ALBERTO PONTICELLI ILLUSTRATOR
OSCAR CELESTINI COLORIST
CLEM ROBINS LETTERER
IGOR KORDEY ORIGINAL SERIES COVER ARTIST

UNKNOWNSOLDIER

KAREN BERGER SVP – EXECUTIVE EDITOR PORNSAK PICHETSHOTE EDITOR - ORIGINAL SERIES GEORGE BREWER VP - DESIGN & DC DIRECT CREATIVE
BOB HARRAS GROUP EDITOR - COLLECTED EDITIONS SEAN MACKIEWICZ EDITOR ROBBIN BROSTERMAN DESIGN DIRECTOR – BOOKS

DC COMICS
PAUL LEVITZ PRESIDENT & PUBLISHER RICHARD BRUNING SVP – CREATIVE DIRECTOR
PATRICK CALDON EVP – FINANCE & OPERATIONS AMY GENKINS SVP – BUSINESS & LEGAL AFFAIRS
JIM LEE EDITORIAL DIRECTOR – WILDSTORM GREGORY NOVECK SVP – CREATIVE AFFAIRS
STEVE ROTTERDAM SVP – SALES & MARKETING CHERYL RUBIN SVP – BRAND MANAGEMENT

Cover by Igor Kordey
Publication design by Robbie Biederman

DC Comics, 1700 Broadway, New York, NY 10019. A Warner Bros. Entertainment Company. Printed by World Color Press, Inc, Montréal, QC, Canada. 08/26/09. Second Printing.
ISBN: 978-1-4012-2311-3

SUSTAINABLE
FORESTRY
INITIATIVE

Certified Fiber
Sourcing

www.sfiprogram.org

Fiber used in this product line meets the sourcing requirements
of the SFI program. www.sfiprogram.org PWC-SFICOC-260

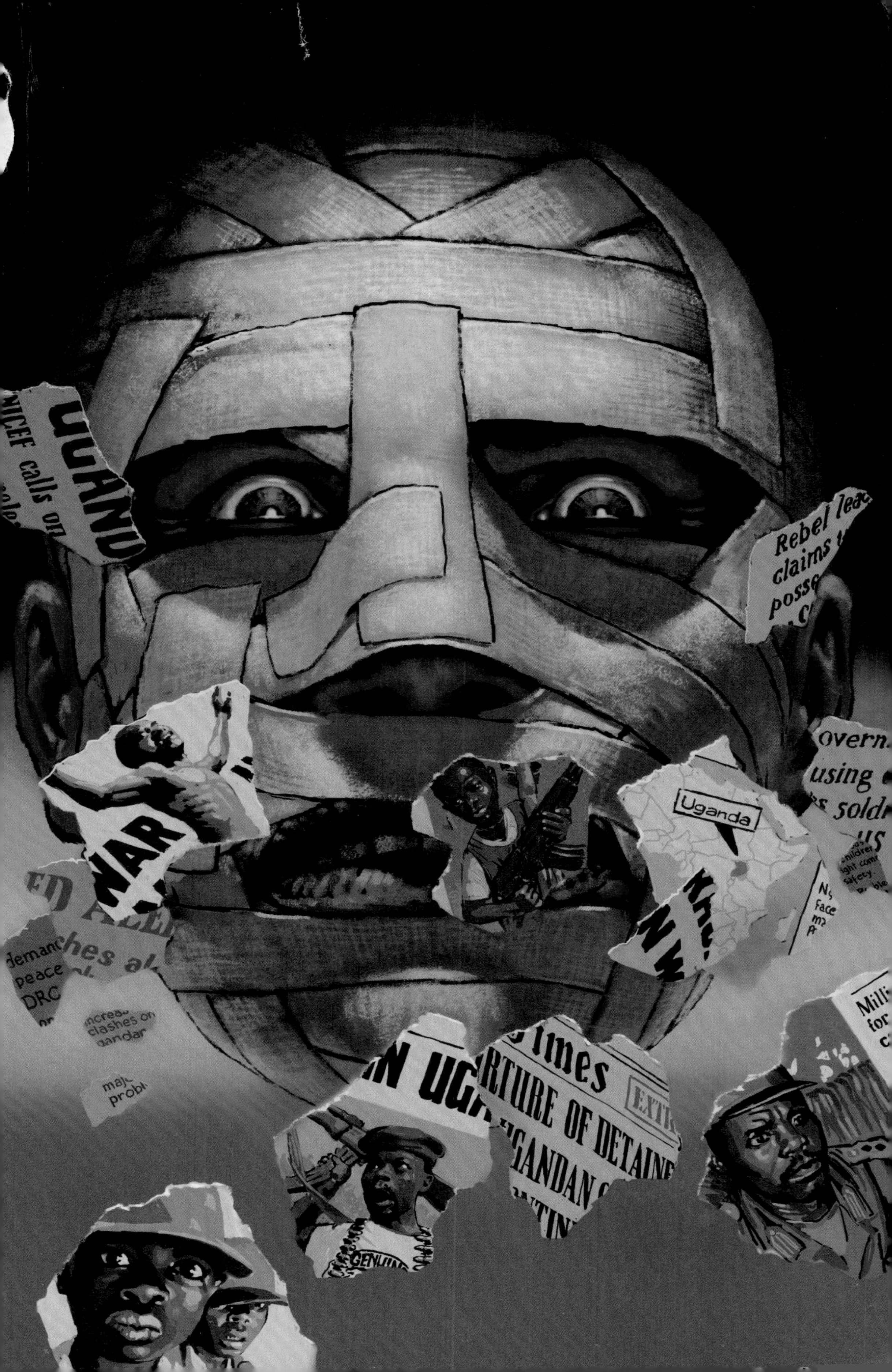

UGAND
NICEF calls on
Rebel lea
claims t
posse
overn
using
s soldi
Uganda
WAR
demanches al
peace
DRC
increa
clashes on
gandan
maj
probl
N UG
Times
RTURE OF DETAINE
GANDAN
EXTR
Milli
GENUIN

VARIANT BY RICHARD CORBEN

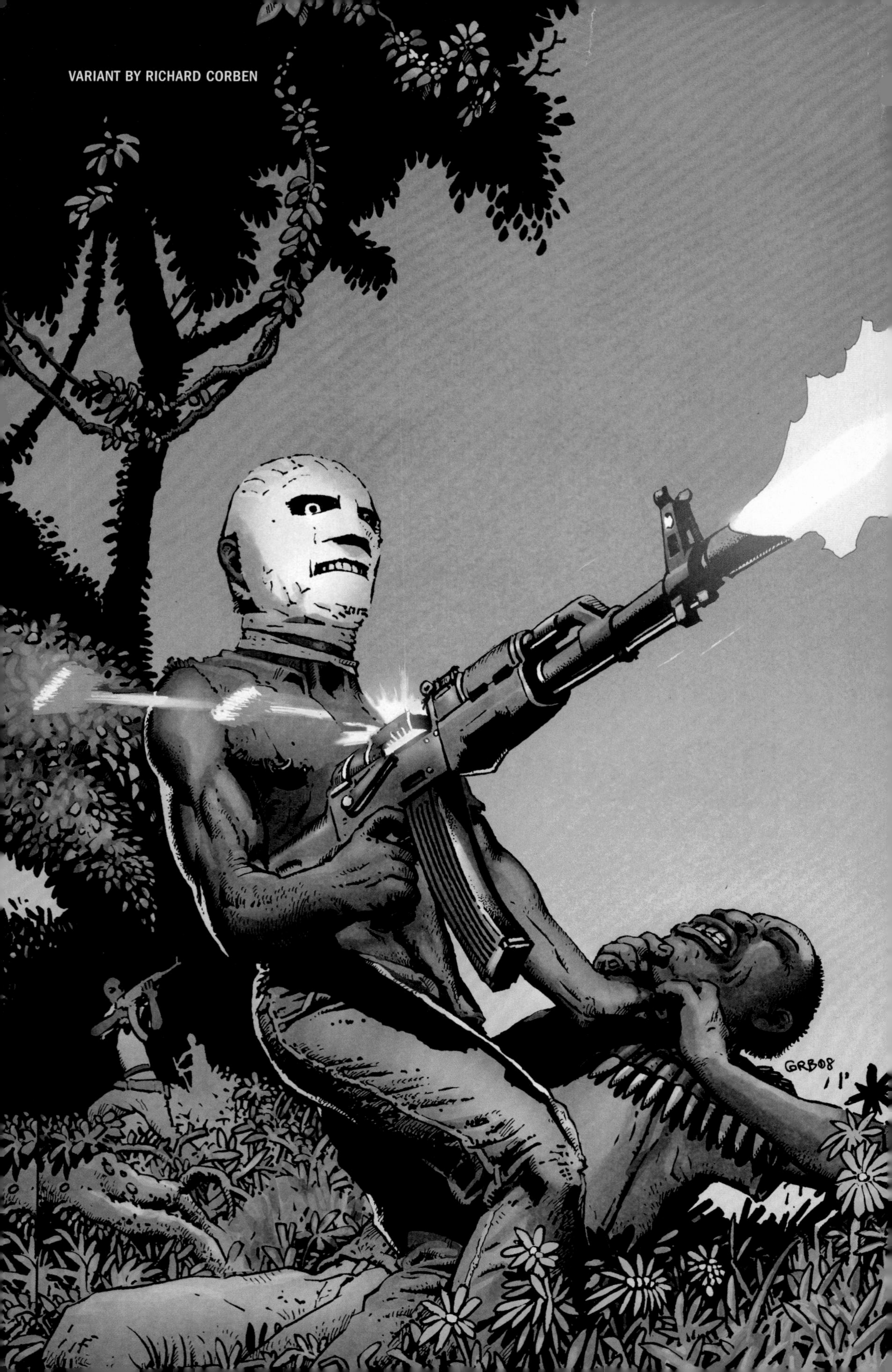
CRB08

NORTHERN UGANDA. SOMEWHERE BETWEEN GULU TOWN AND THE SUDAN BORDER.

KACKKACK KACKACK

NOVEMBER, 2002.

NHA!

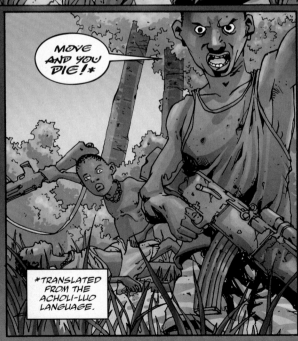

MOVE AND YOU DIE!*

*TRANSLATED FROM THE ACHOLI-LUO LANGUAGE.

YOU WANT TO DIE!?

"IN 1978, SIX MONTHS BEFORE TANZANIAN SOLDIERS AND UGANDAN EXILES ENDED THE DICTATORIAL RULE OF *IDI AMIN DADA OUMEE*..."

"MY FATHER GAVE EVERYTHING WE OWNED TO A *CABINET MINISTER* WHO THREATENED TO MAKE HIM SMOKE HIS OWN *PENIS*."

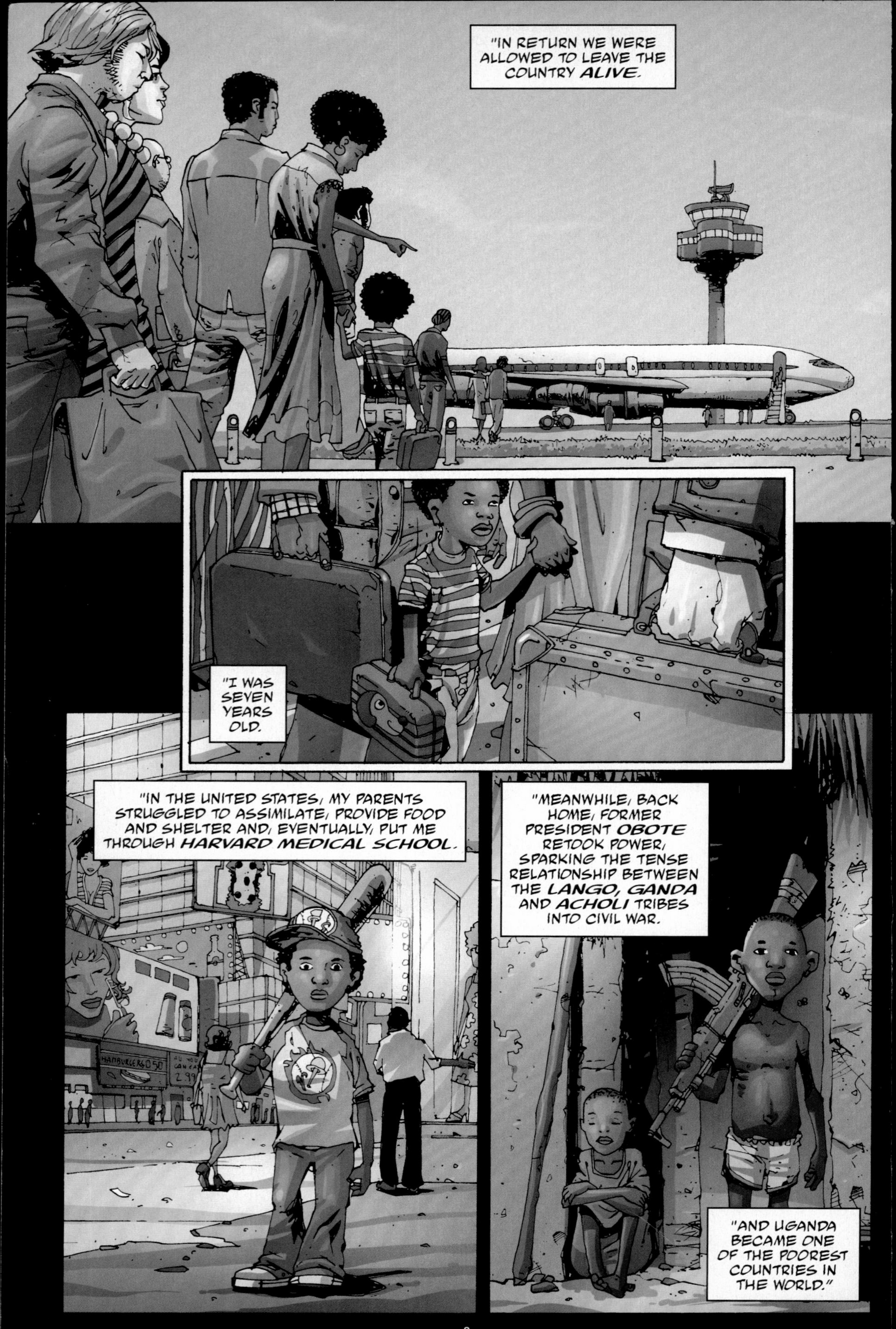
"IN RETURN WE WERE ALLOWED TO LEAVE THE COUNTRY ALIVE.
"I WAS SEVEN YEARS OLD.
"IN THE UNITED STATES, MY PARENTS STRUGGLED TO ASSIMILATE, PROVIDE FOOD AND SHELTER AND, EVENTUALLY, PUT ME THROUGH HARVARD MEDICAL SCHOOL.
"MEANWHILE, BACK HOME, FORMER PRESIDENT OBOTE RETOOK POWER, SPARKING THE TENSE RELATIONSHIP BETWEEN THE LANGO, GANDA AND ACHOLI TRIBES INTO CIVIL WAR.
"AND UGANDA BECAME ONE OF THE POOREST COUNTRIES IN THE WORLD."

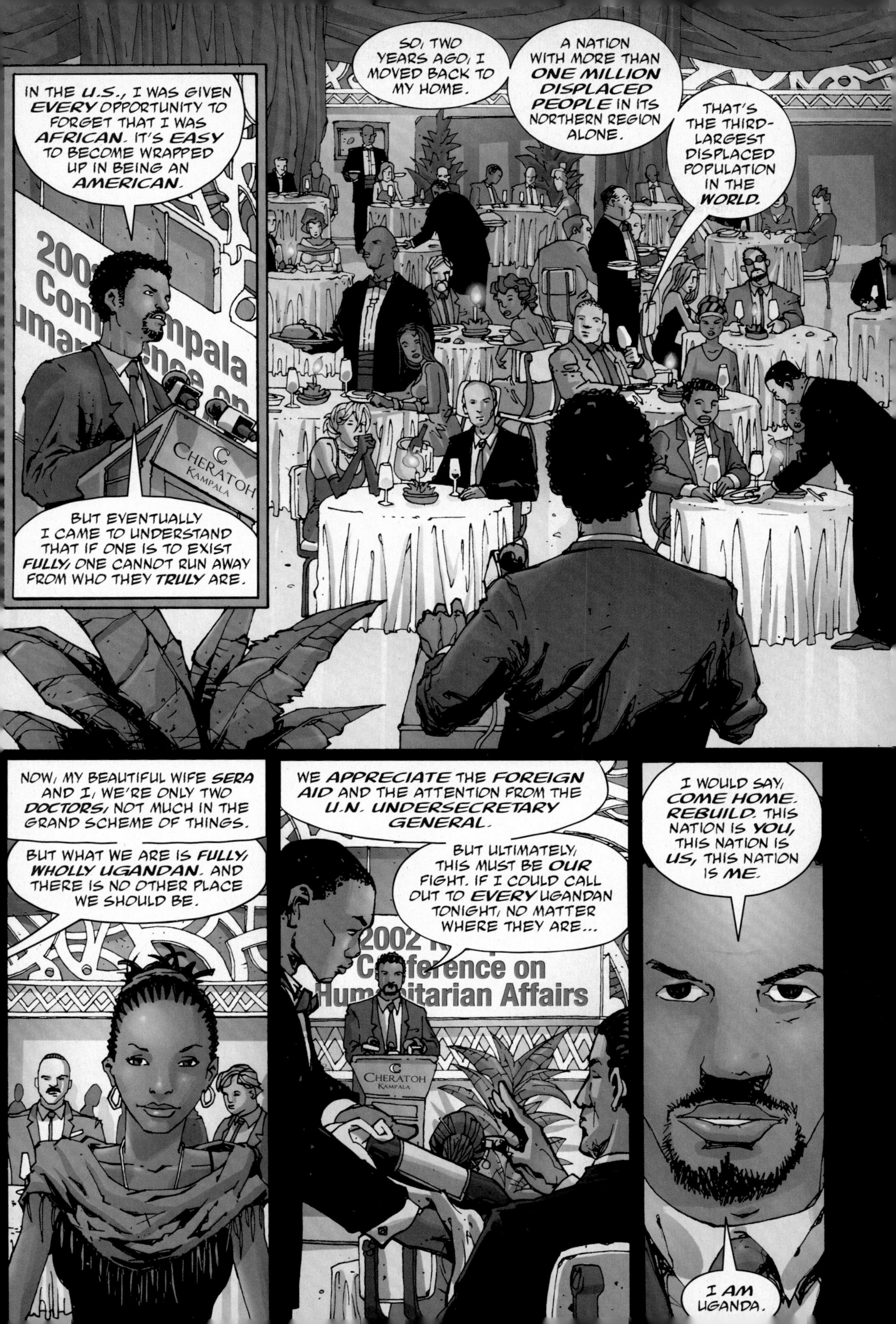
IN THE U.S., I WAS GIVEN EVERY OPPORTUNITY TO FORGET THAT I WAS AFRICAN. IT'S EASY TO BECOME WRAPPED UP IN BEING AN AMERICAN.
BUT EVENTUALLY I CAME TO UNDERSTAND THAT IF ONE IS TO EXIST FULLY, ONE CANNOT RUN AWAY FROM WHO THEY TRULY ARE.
CHERATOH
KAMPALA
SO, TWO YEARS AGO, I MOVED BACK TO MY HOME.
A NATION WITH MORE THAN ONE MILLION DISPLACED PEOPLE IN ITS NORTHERN REGION ALONE.
THAT'S THE THIRD-LARGEST DISPLACED POPULATION IN THE WORLD.
NOW, MY BEAUTIFUL WIFE SERA AND I, WE'RE ONLY TWO DOCTORS, NOT MUCH IN THE GRAND SCHEME OF THINGS.
BUT WHAT WE ARE IS FULLY, WHOLLY UGANDAN. AND THERE IS NO OTHER PLACE WE SHOULD BE.
WE APPRECIATE THE FOREIGN AID AND THE ATTENTION FROM THE U.N. UNDERSECRETARY GENERAL.
BUT ULTIMATELY, THIS MUST BE OUR FIGHT. IF I COULD CALL OUT TO EVERY UGANDAN TONIGHT, NO MATTER WHERE THEY ARE...
Conference on
Affairs
CHERATOH
KAMPALA
I WOULD SAY, COME HOME. REBUILD. THIS NATION IS YOU, THIS NATION IS US, THIS NATION IS ME.
I AM UGANDA.

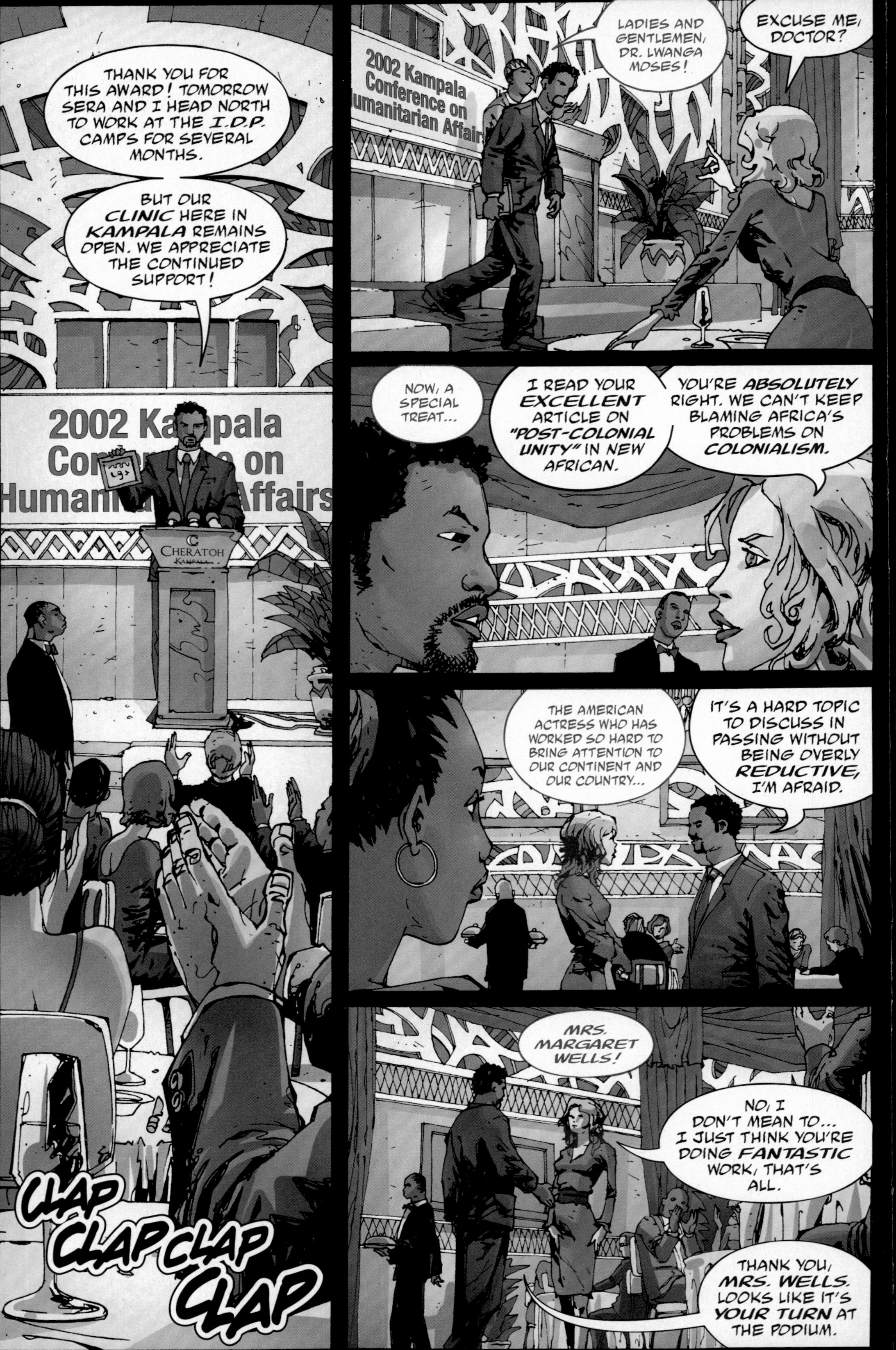
THANK YOU FOR THIS AWARD! TOMORROW SERA AND I HEAD NORTH TO WORK AT THE I.D.P. CAMPS FOR SEVERAL MONTHS.
BUT OUR CLINIC HERE IN KAMPALA REMAINS OPEN. WE APPRECIATE THE CONTINUED SUPPORT!
2002 Kampala Conference on Humanitarian Affairs
CHERATOH KAMPALA
CLAP CLAP CLAP CLAP CLAP
2002 Kampala Conference on Humanitarian Affairs
LADIES AND GENTLEMEN, DR. LWANGA MOSES!
EXCUSE ME, DOCTOR?
NOW, A SPECIAL TREAT...
I READ YOUR EXCELLENT ARTICLE ON "POST-COLONIAL UNITY" IN NEW AFRICAN.
YOU'RE ABSOLUTELY RIGHT. WE CAN'T KEEP BLAMING AFRICA'S PROBLEMS ON COLONIALISM.
THE AMERICAN ACTRESS WHO HAS WORKED SO HARD TO BRING ATTENTION TO OUR CONTINENT AND OUR COUNTRY...
IT'S A HARD TOPIC TO DISCUSS IN PASSING WITHOUT BEING OVERLY REDUCTIVE, I'M AFRAID.
MRS. MARGARET WELLS!
NO, I DON'T MEAN TO... I JUST THINK YOU'RE DOING FANTASTIC WORK, THAT'S ALL.
THANK YOU, MRS. WELLS. LOOKS LIKE IT'S YOUR TURN AT THE PODIUM.

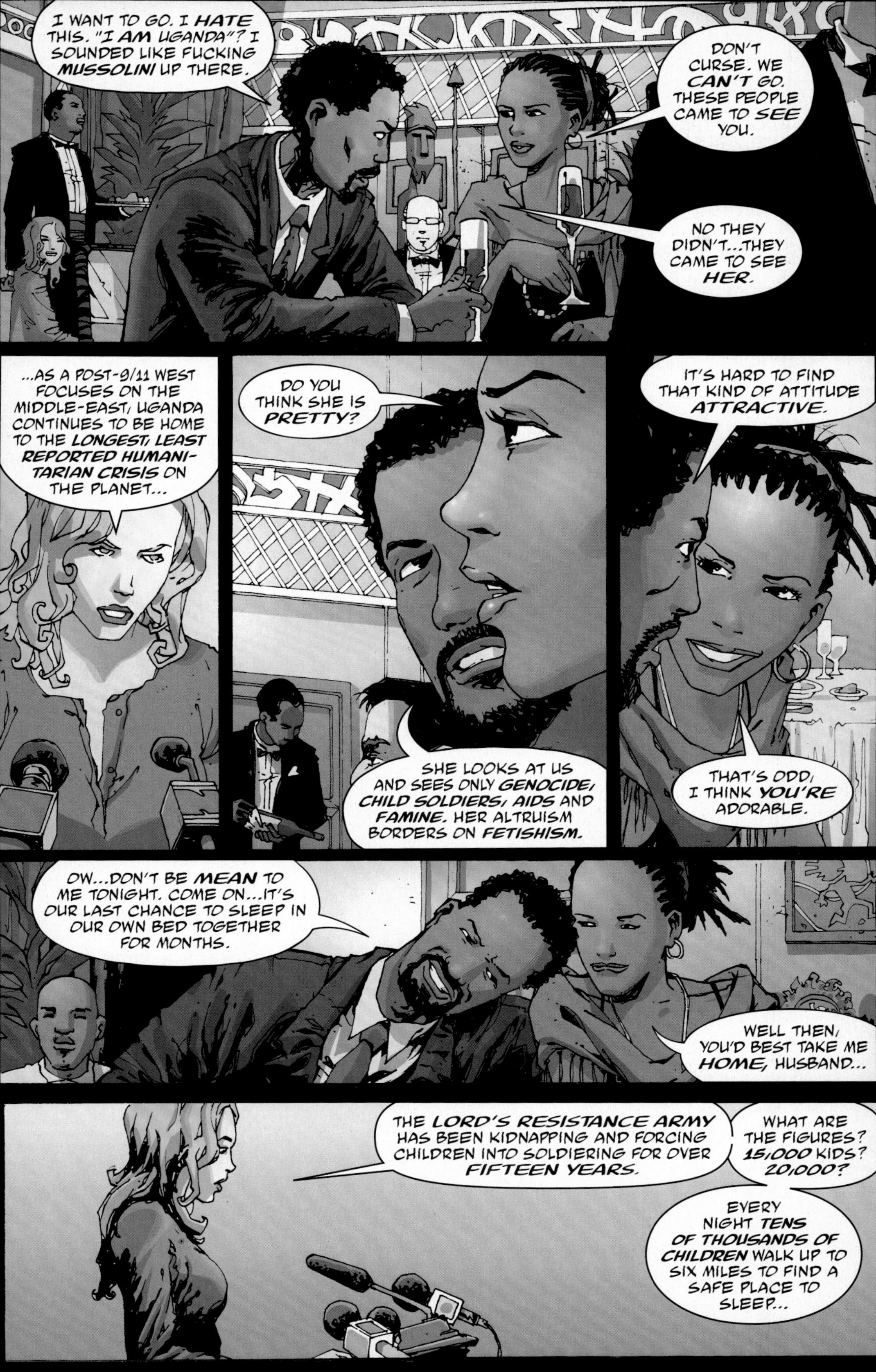

I WANT TO GO. I HATE THIS. "I AM UGANDA"? I SOUNDED LIKE FUCKING MUSSOLINI UP THERE.
DON'T CURSE. WE CAN'T GO. THESE PEOPLE CAME TO SEE YOU.
NO THEY DIDN'T...THEY CAME TO SEE HER.
...AS A POST-9/11 WEST FOCUSES ON THE MIDDLE-EAST, UGANDA CONTINUES TO BE HOME TO THE LONGEST, LEAST REPORTED HUMANITARIAN CRISIS ON THE PLANET...
DO YOU THINK SHE IS PRETTY?
SHE LOOKS AT US AND SEES ONLY GENOCIDE, CHILD SOLDIERS, AIDS AND FAMINE. HER ALTRUISM BORDERS ON FETISHISM.
IT'S HARD TO FIND THAT KIND OF ATTITUDE ATTRACTIVE.
THAT'S ODD, I THINK YOU'RE ADORABLE.
OW...DON'T BE MEAN TO ME TONIGHT. COME ON...IT'S OUR LAST CHANCE TO SLEEP IN OUR OWN BED TOGETHER FOR MONTHS.
WELL THEN, YOU'D BEST TAKE ME HOME, HUSBAND...
THE LORD'S RESISTANCE ARMY HAS BEEN KIDNAPPING AND FORCING CHILDREN INTO SOLDIERING FOR OVER FIFTEEN YEARS.
WHAT ARE THE FIGURES? 15,000 KIDS? 20,000?
EVERY NIGHT TENS OF THOUSANDS OF CHILDREN WALK UP TO SIX MILES TO FIND A SAFE PLACE TO SLEEP...

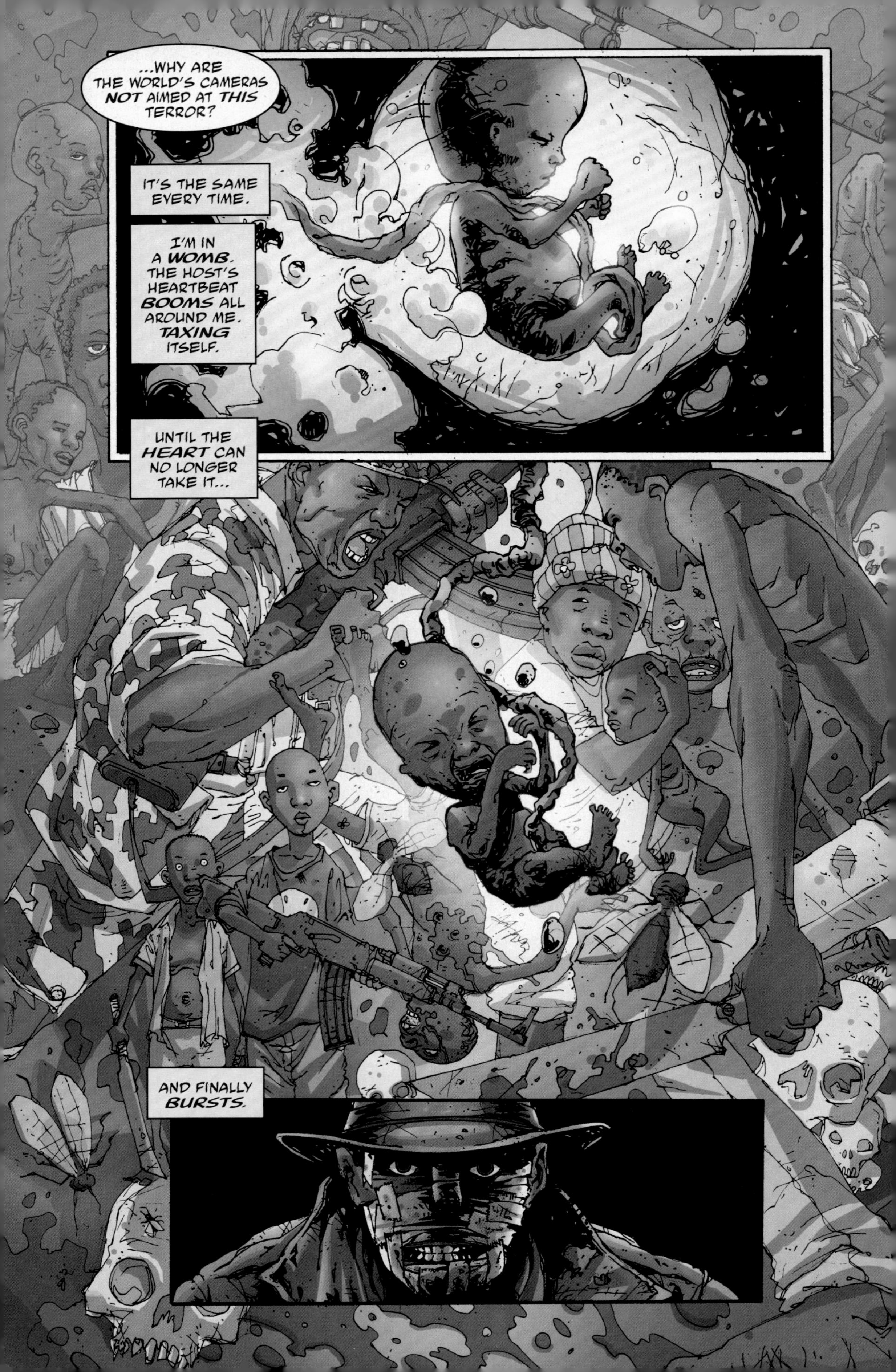
...WHY ARE THE WORLD'S CAMERAS NOT AIMED AT THIS TERROR?
IT'S THE SAME EVERY TIME.
I'M IN A WOMB. THE HOST'S HEARTBEAT BOOMS ALL AROUND ME. TAXING ITSELF.
UNTIL THE HEART CAN NO LONGER TAKE IT...
AND FINALLY BURSTS.

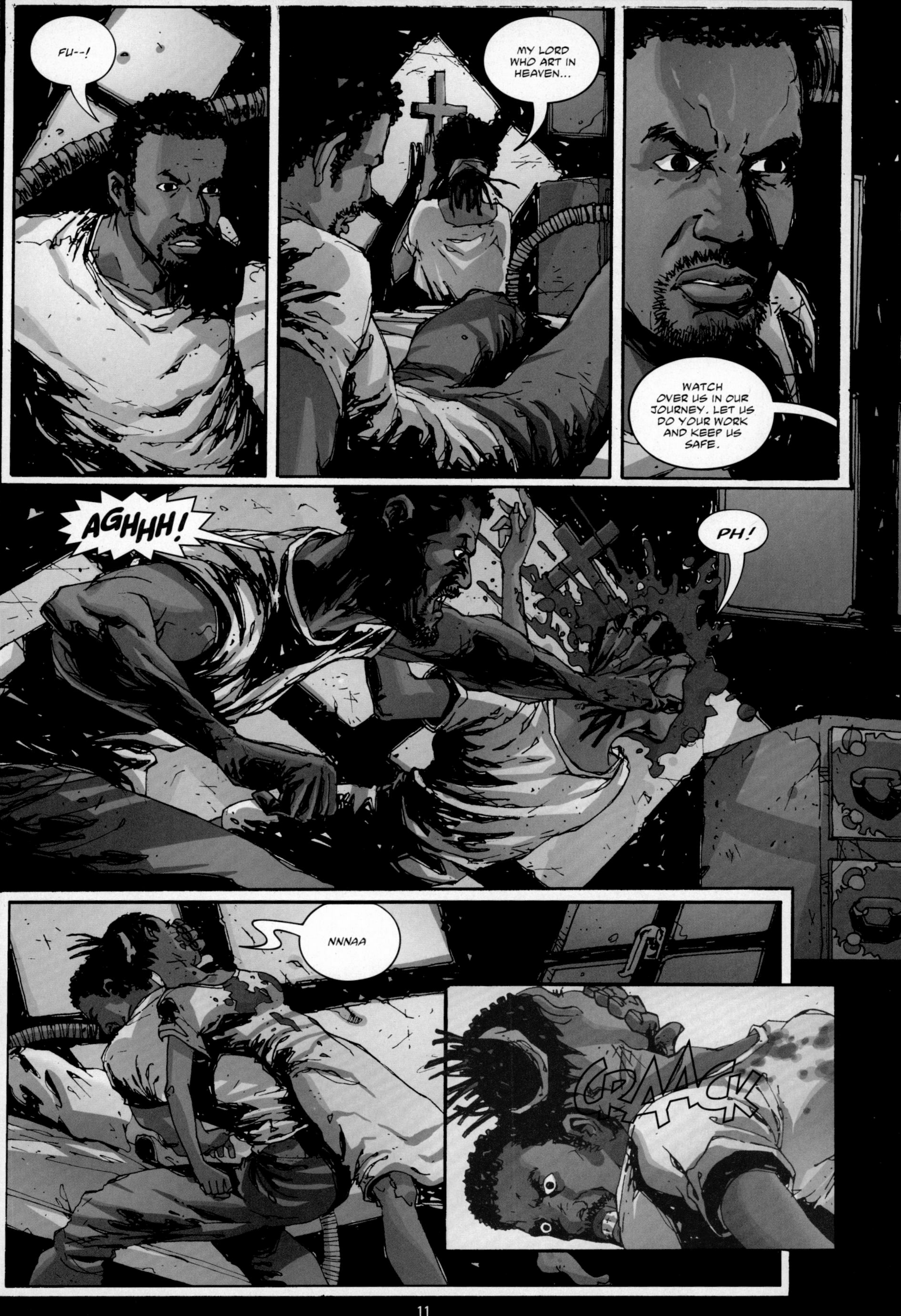
FU--!
MY LORD WHO ART IN HEAVEN...
WATCH OVER US IN OUR JOURNEY. LET US DO YOUR WORK AND KEEP US SAFE.
AGHHH!
PH!
NNNAA
CRACK

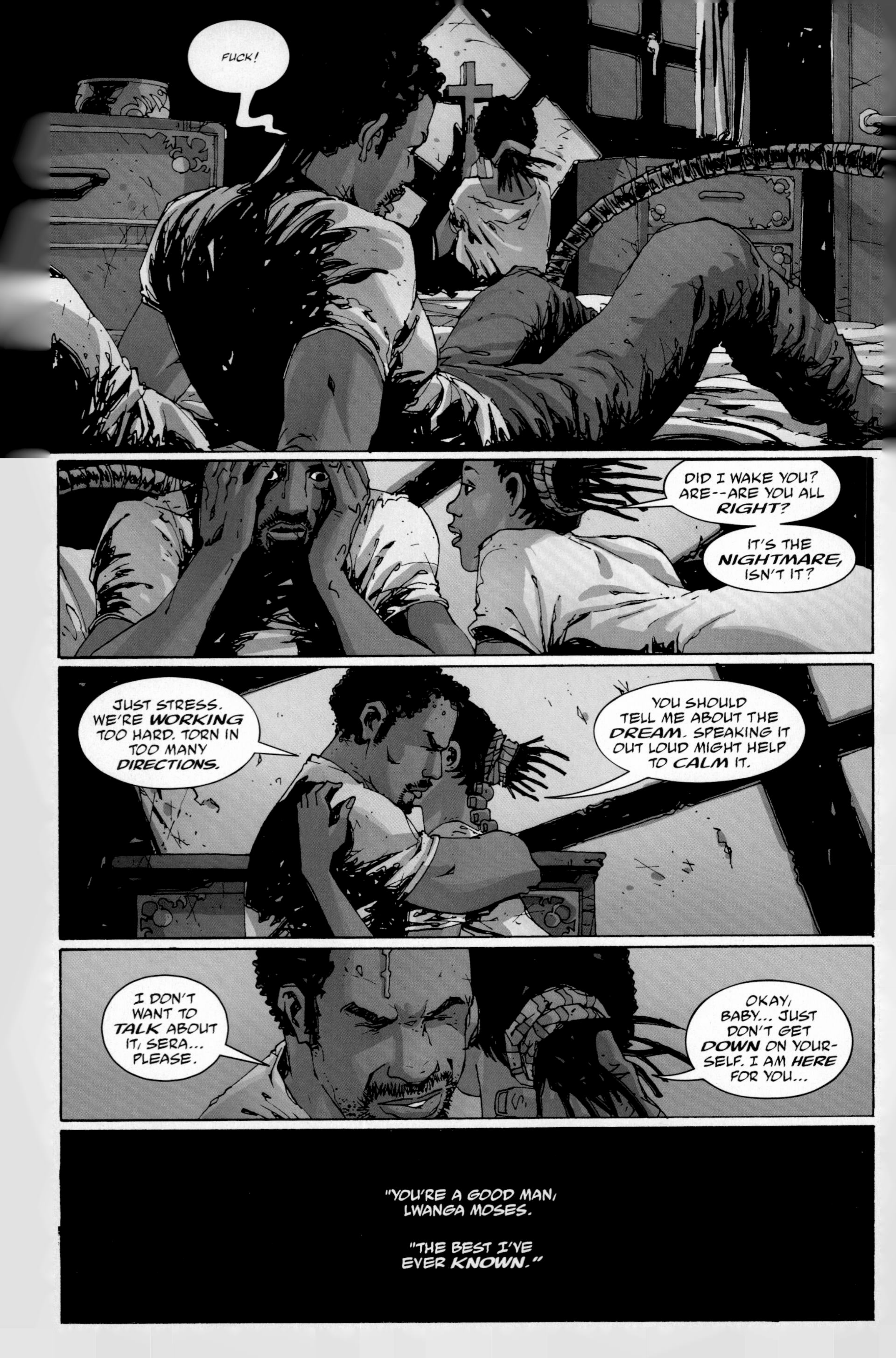
FUCK!
DID I WAKE YOU? ARE--ARE YOU ALL RIGHT?
IT'S THE NIGHTMARE, ISN'T IT?
JUST STRESS. WE'RE WORKING TOO HARD. TORN IN TOO MANY DIRECTIONS.
YOU SHOULD TELL ME ABOUT THE DREAM. SPEAKING IT OUT LOUD MIGHT HELP TO CALM IT.
I DON'T WANT TO TALK ABOUT IT, SERA... PLEASE.
OKAY, BABY... JUST DON'T GET DOWN ON YOURSELF. I AM HERE FOR YOU...
"YOU'RE A GOOD MAN, LWANGA MOSES.
"THE BEST I'VE EVER KNOWN."

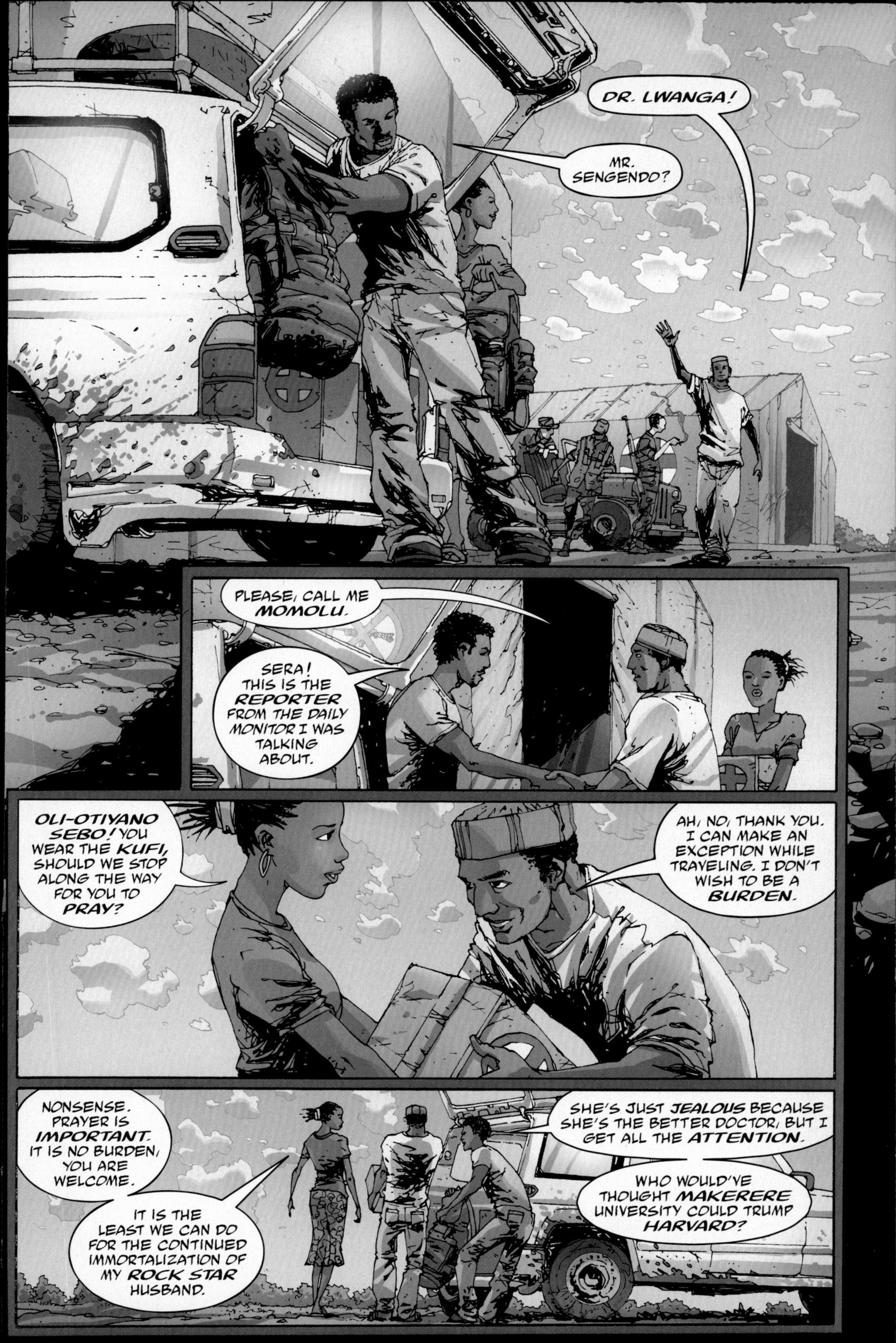
DR. LWANGA!
MR. SENGENDO?
PLEASE, CALL ME MOMOLU.
SERA! THIS IS THE REPORTER FROM THE DAILY MONITOR I WAS TALKING ABOUT.
OLI-OTIYANO SEBO! YOU WEAR THE KUFI, SHOULD WE STOP ALONG THE WAY FOR YOU TO PRAY?
AH, NO, THANK YOU. I CAN MAKE AN EXCEPTION WHILE TRAVELING. I DON'T WISH TO BE A BURDEN.
NONSENSE. PRAYER IS IMPORTANT. IT IS NO BURDEN, YOU ARE WELCOME.
IT IS THE LEAST WE CAN DO FOR THE CONTINUED IMMORTALIZATION OF MY ROCK STAR HUSBAND.
SHE'S JUST JEALOUS BECAUSE SHE'S THE BETTER DOCTOR, BUT I GET ALL THE ATTENTION.
WHO WOULD'VE THOUGHT MAKERERE UNIVERSITY COULD TRUMP HARVARD?

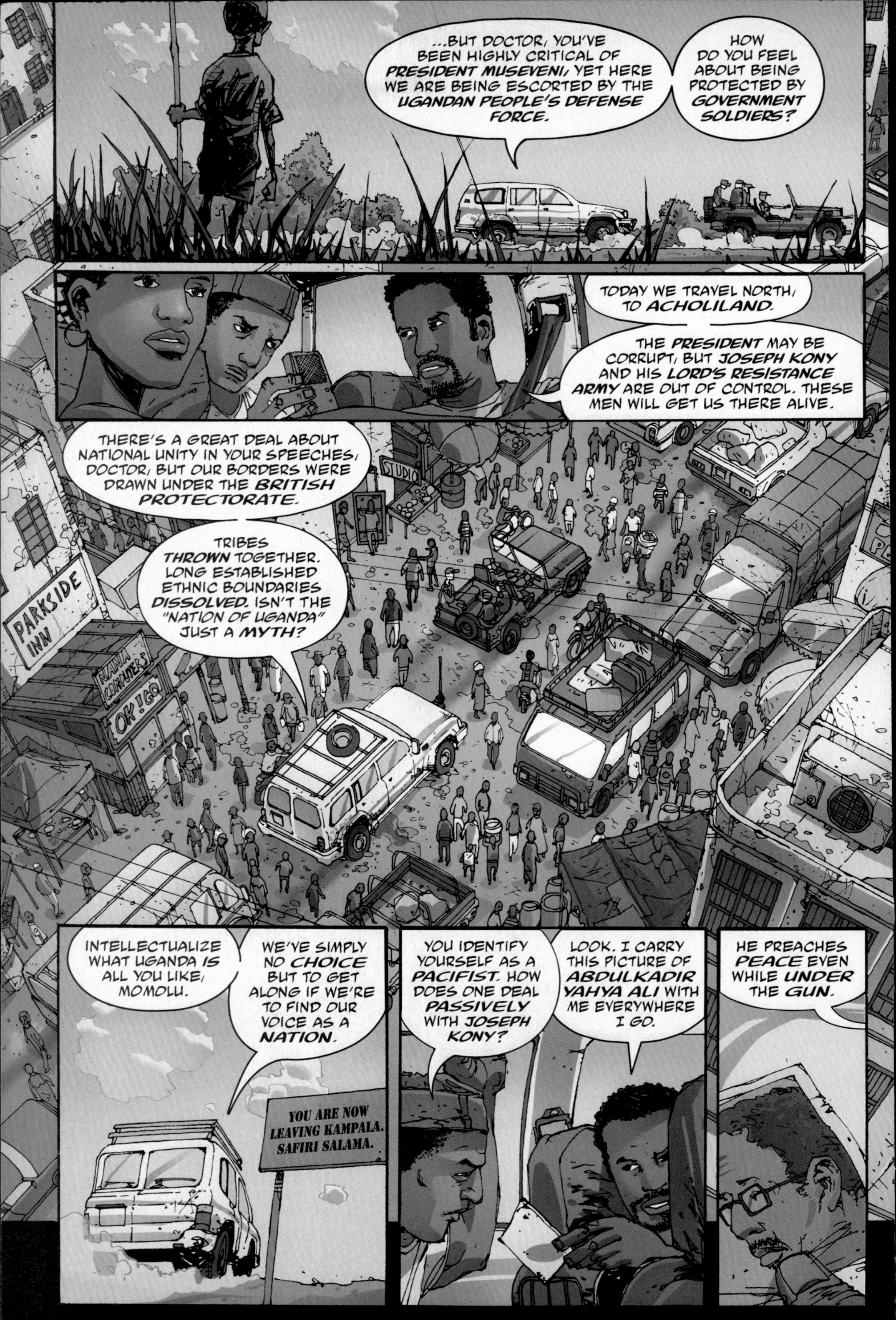

...BUT DOCTOR, YOU'VE BEEN HIGHLY CRITICAL OF PRESIDENT MUSEVENI, YET HERE WE ARE BEING ESCORTED BY THE UGANDAN PEOPLE'S DEFENSE FORCE.
HOW DO YOU FEEL ABOUT BEING PROTECTED BY GOVERNMENT SOLDIERS?
TODAY WE TRAVEL NORTH, TO ACHOLILAND.
THE PRESIDENT MAY BE CORRUPT, BUT JOSEPH KONY AND HIS LORD'S RESISTANCE ARMY ARE OUT OF CONTROL. THESE MEN WILL GET US THERE ALIVE.
THERE'S A GREAT DEAL ABOUT NATIONAL UNITY IN YOUR SPEECHES, DOCTOR, BUT OUR BORDERS WERE DRAWN UNDER THE BRITISH PROTECTORATE.
TRIBES THROWN TOGETHER. LONG ESTABLISHED ETHNIC BOUNDARIES DISSOLVED. ISN'T THE "NATION OF UGANDA" JUST A MYTH?
STUDIO
PARKSIDE INN
NAIA COMPUTERS
OK! GO
INTELLECTUALIZE WHAT UGANDA IS ALL YOU LIKE, MOMOLU.
WE'VE SIMPLY NO CHOICE BUT TO GET ALONG IF WE'RE TO FIND OUR VOICE AS A NATION.
YOU ARE NOW LEAVING KAMPALA. SAFIRI SALAMA.
YOU IDENTIFY YOURSELF AS A PACIFIST. HOW DOES ONE DEAL PASSIVELY WITH JOSEPH KONY?
LOOK. I CARRY THIS PICTURE OF ABDULKADIR YAHYA ALI WITH ME EVERYWHERE I GO.
HE PREACHES PEACE EVEN WHILE UNDER THE GUN.

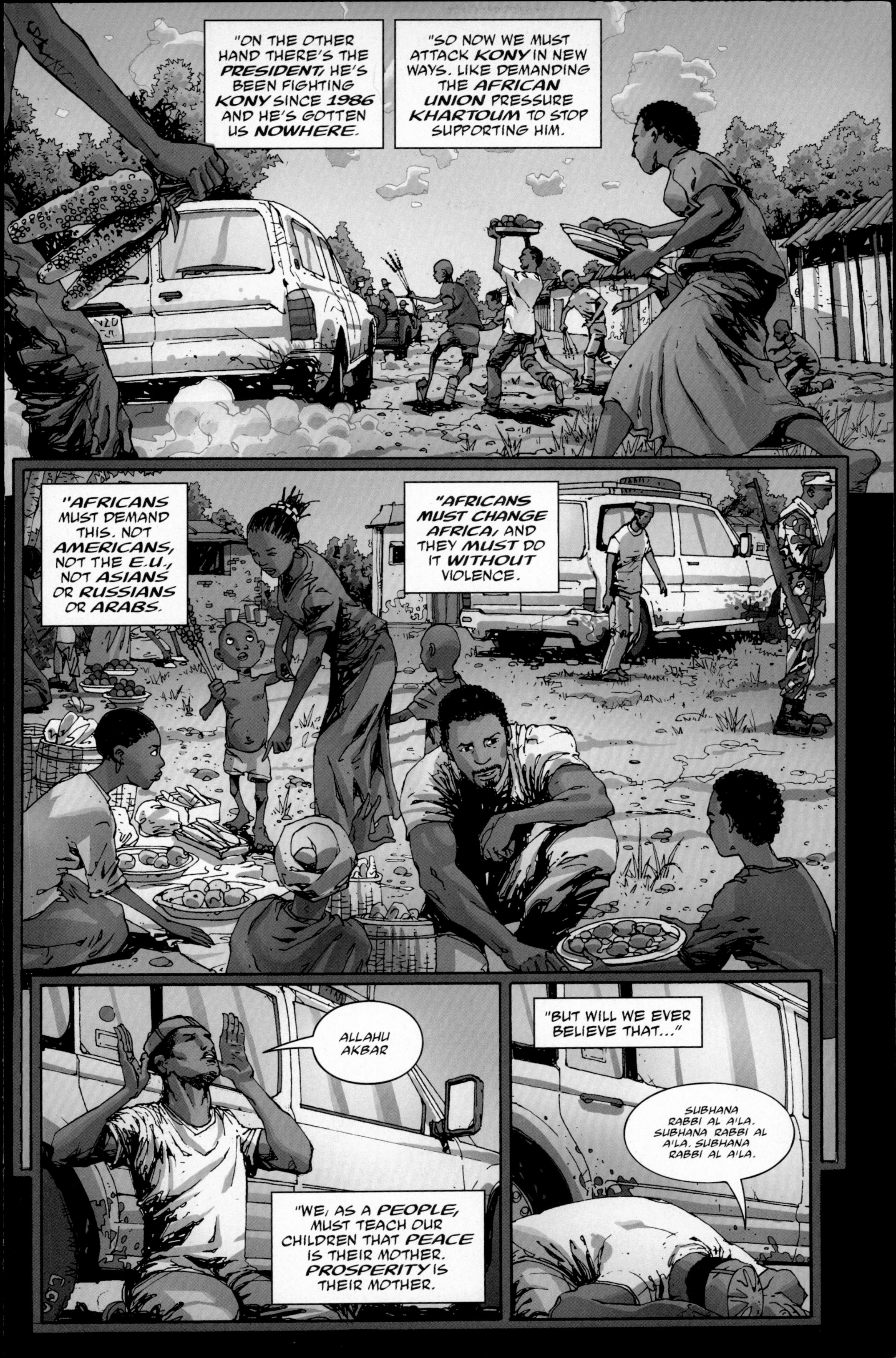
"ON THE OTHER HAND THERE'S THE PRESIDENT, HE'S BEEN FIGHTING KONY SINCE 1986 AND HE'S GOTTEN US NOWHERE.
"SO NOW WE MUST ATTACK KONY IN NEW WAYS. LIKE DEMANDING THE AFRICAN UNION PRESSURE KHARTOUM TO STOP SUPPORTING HIM.
"AFRICANS MUST DEMAND THIS. NOT AMERICANS, NOT THE E.U., NOT ASIANS OR RUSSIANS OR ARABS.
"AFRICANS MUST CHANGE AFRICA, AND THEY MUST DO IT WITHOUT VIOLENCE.
ALLAHU AKBAR
"WE, AS A PEOPLE, MUST TEACH OUR CHILDREN THAT PEACE IS THEIR MOTHER. PROSPERITY IS THEIR MOTHER.
"BUT WILL WE EVER BELIEVE THAT..."
SUBHANA RABBI AL A'LA. SUBHANA RABBI AL A'LA. SUBHANA RABBI AL A'LA.

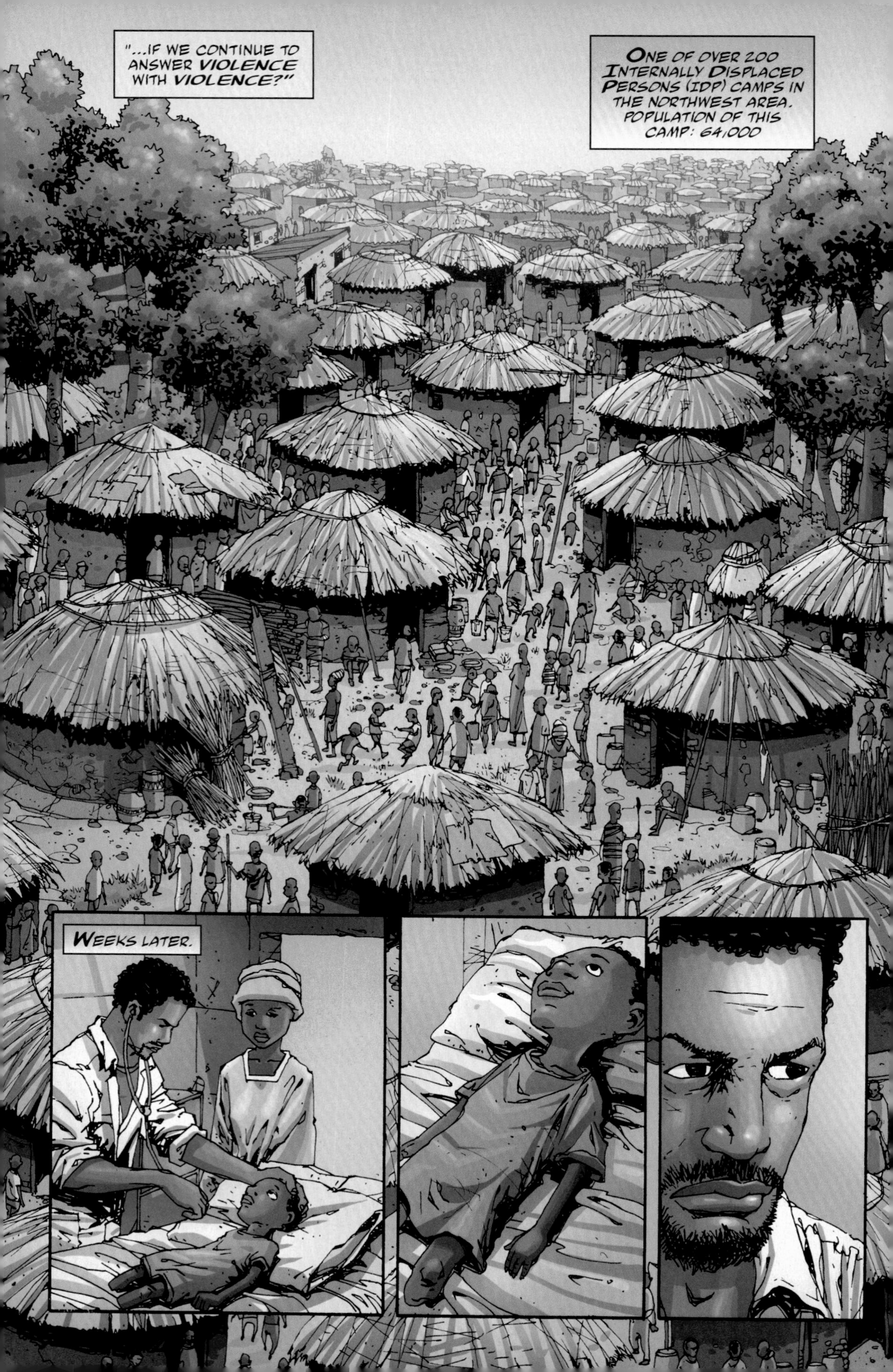
"...IF WE CONTINUE TO ANSWER VIOLENCE WITH VIOLENCE?"
ONE OF OVER 200 INTERNALLY DISPLACED PERSONS (IDP) CAMPS IN THE NORTHWEST AREA. POPULATION OF THIS CAMP: 64,000
WEEKS LATER.

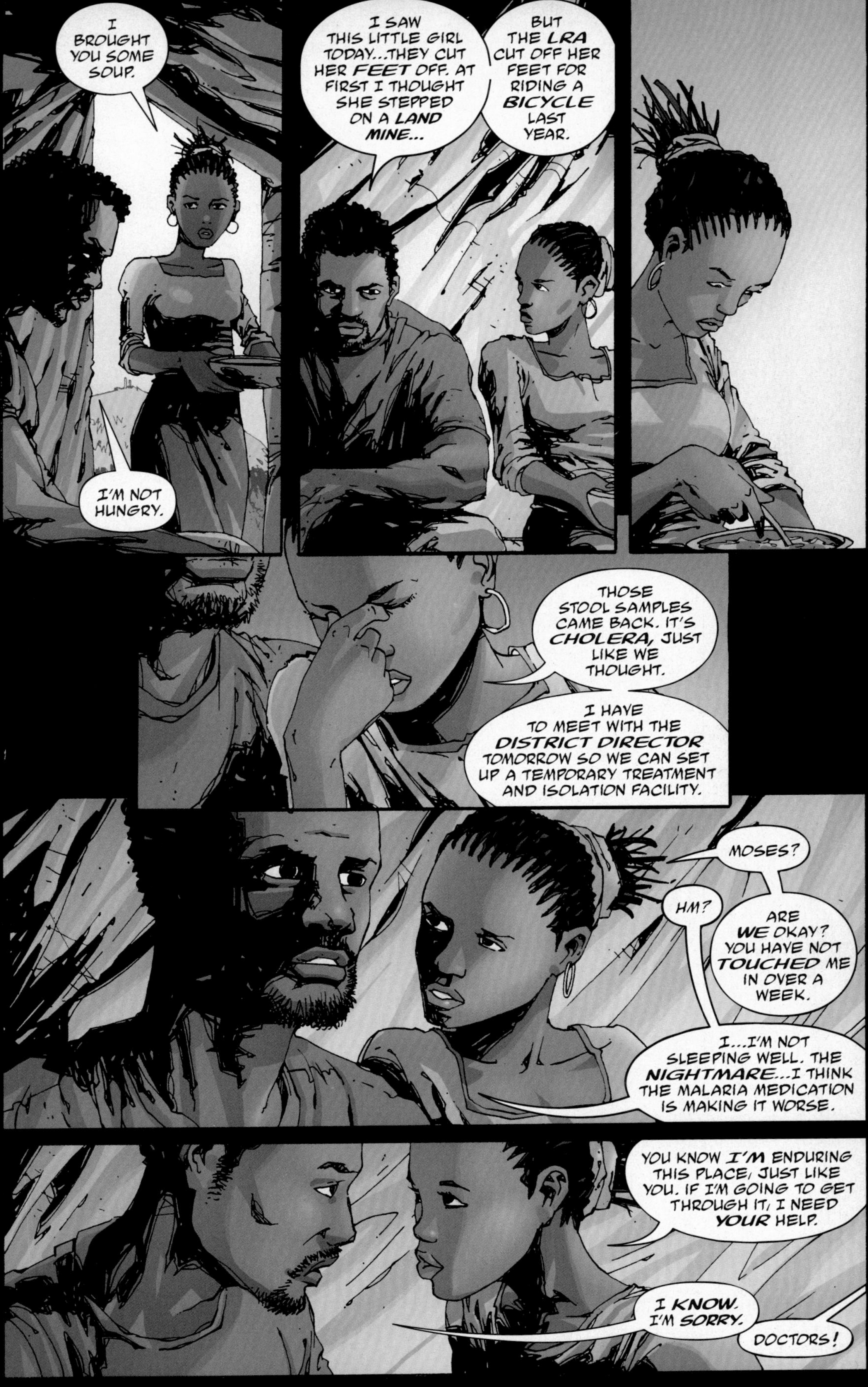
I BROUGHT YOU SOME SOUP.
I'M NOT HUNGRY.
I SAW THIS LITTLE GIRL TODAY...THEY CUT HER FEET OFF. AT FIRST I THOUGHT SHE STEPPED ON A LAND MINE...
BUT THE LRA CUT OFF HER FEET FOR RIDING A BICYCLE LAST YEAR.
THOSE STOOL SAMPLES CAME BACK. IT'S CHOLERA, JUST LIKE WE THOUGHT.
I HAVE TO MEET WITH THE DISTRICT DIRECTOR TOMORROW SO WE CAN SET UP A TEMPORARY TREATMENT AND ISOLATION FACILITY.
MOSES?
HM?
ARE WE OKAY? YOU HAVE NOT TOUCHED ME IN OVER A WEEK.
I...I'M NOT SLEEPING WELL. THE NIGHTMARE...I THINK THE MALARIA MEDICATION IS MAKING IT WORSE.
YOU KNOW I'M ENDURING THIS PLACE, JUST LIKE YOU. IF I'M GOING TO GET THROUGH IT, I NEED YOUR HELP.
I KNOW. I'M SORRY.
DOCTORS!

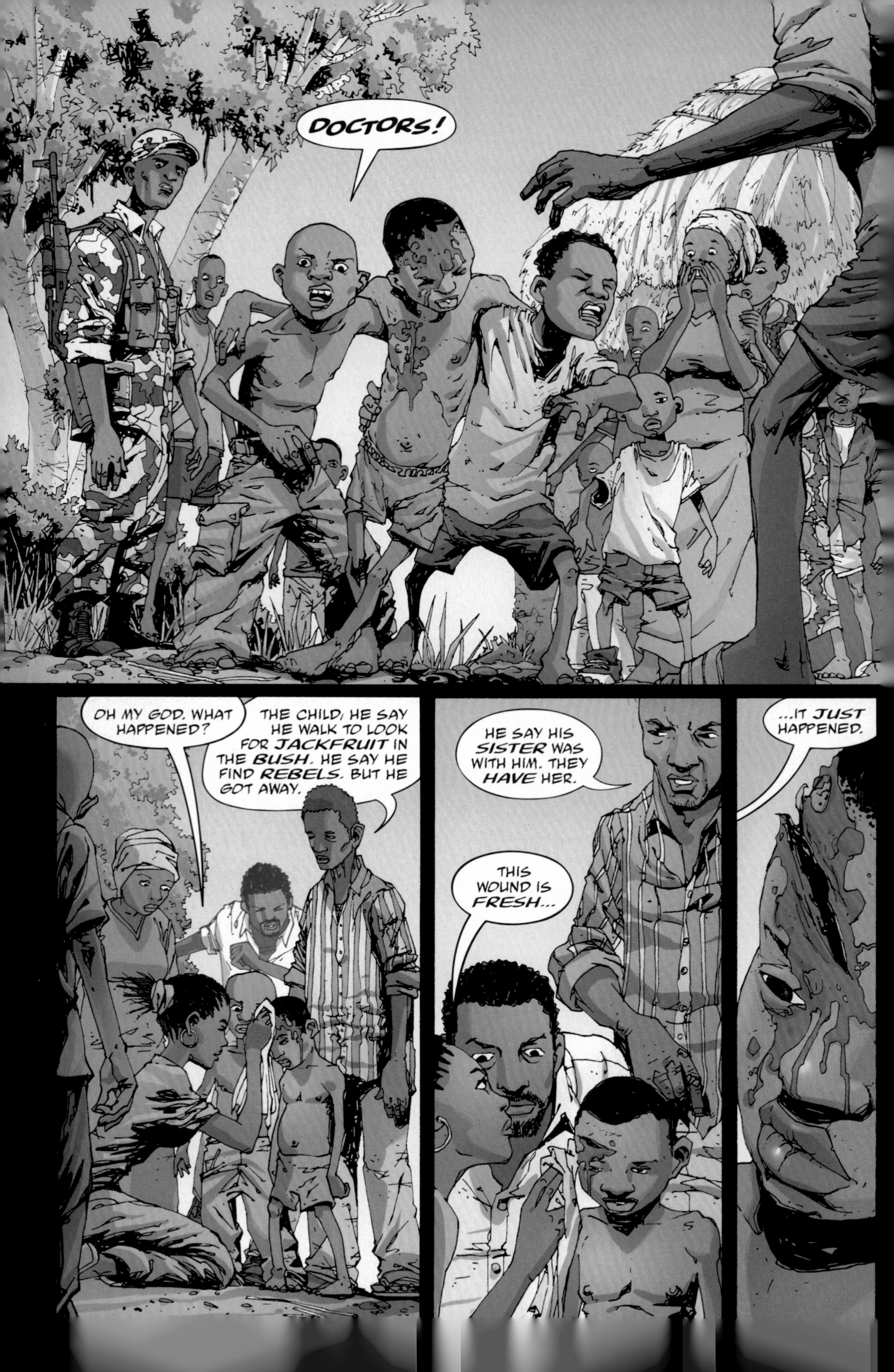
DOCTORS!
OH MY GOD. WHAT HAPPENED?
THE CHILD, HE SAY HE WALK TO LOOK FOR JACKFRUIT IN THE BUSH. HE SAY HE FIND REBELS. BUT HE GOT AWAY.
HE SAY HIS SISTER WAS WITH HIM. THEY HAVE HER.
THIS WOUND IS FRESH...
...IT JUST HAPPENED.

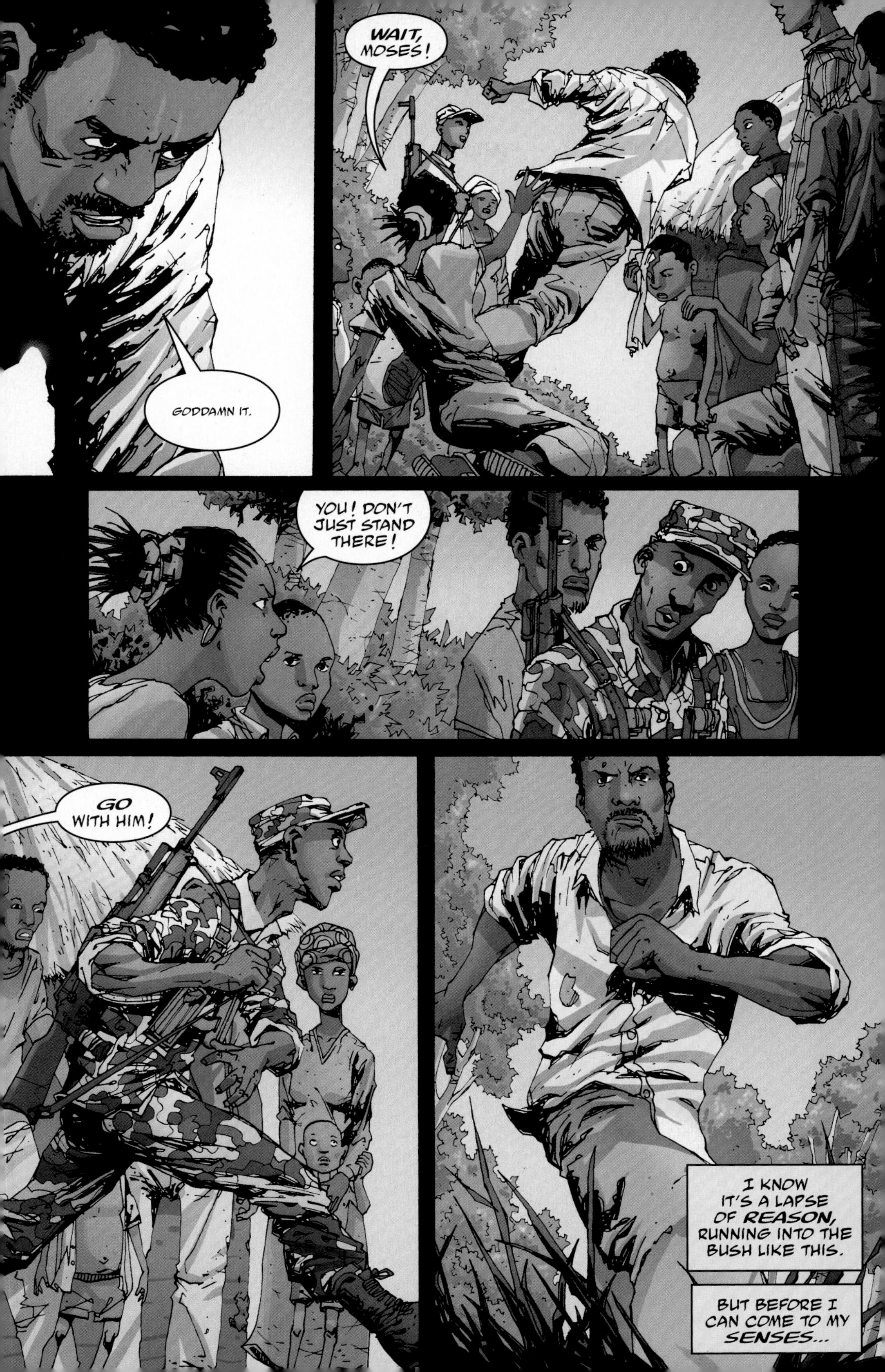
GODDAMN IT.
WAIT, MOSES!
YOU! DON'T JUST STAND THERE!
GO WITH HIM!
I KNOW IT'S A LAPSE OF REASON, RUNNING INTO THE BUSH LIKE THIS.
BUT BEFORE I CAN COME TO MY SENSES...

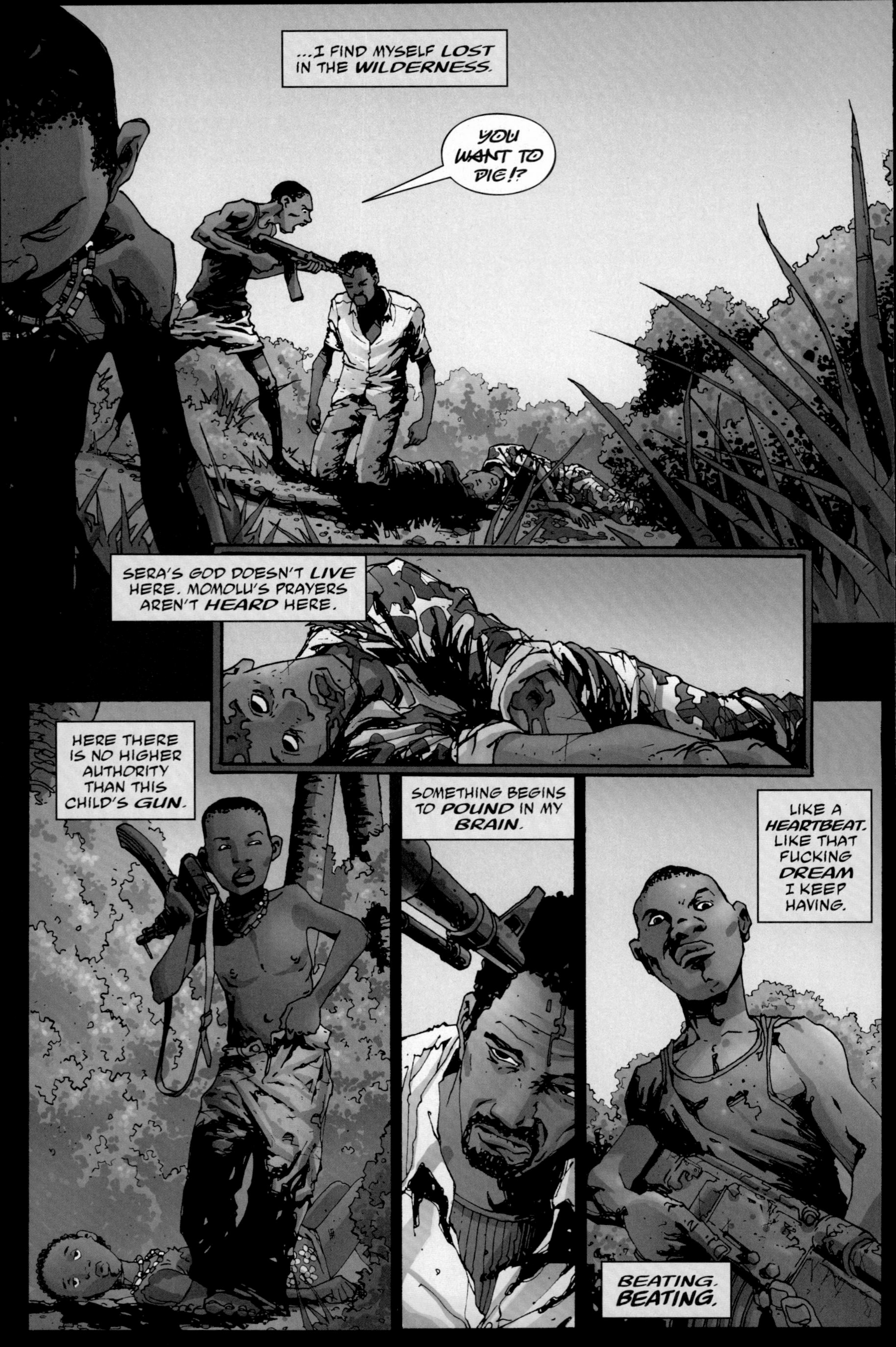
...I FIND MYSELF LOST IN THE WILDERNESS.
YOU WANT TO DIE!?
SERA'S GOD DOESN'T LIVE HERE. MOMOLU'S PRAYERS AREN'T HEARD HERE.
HERE THERE IS NO HIGHER AUTHORITY THAN THIS CHILD'S GUN.
SOMETHING BEGINS TO POUND IN MY BRAIN.
LIKE A HEARTBEAT. LIKE THAT FUCKING DREAM I KEEP HAVING.
BEATING. BEATING.

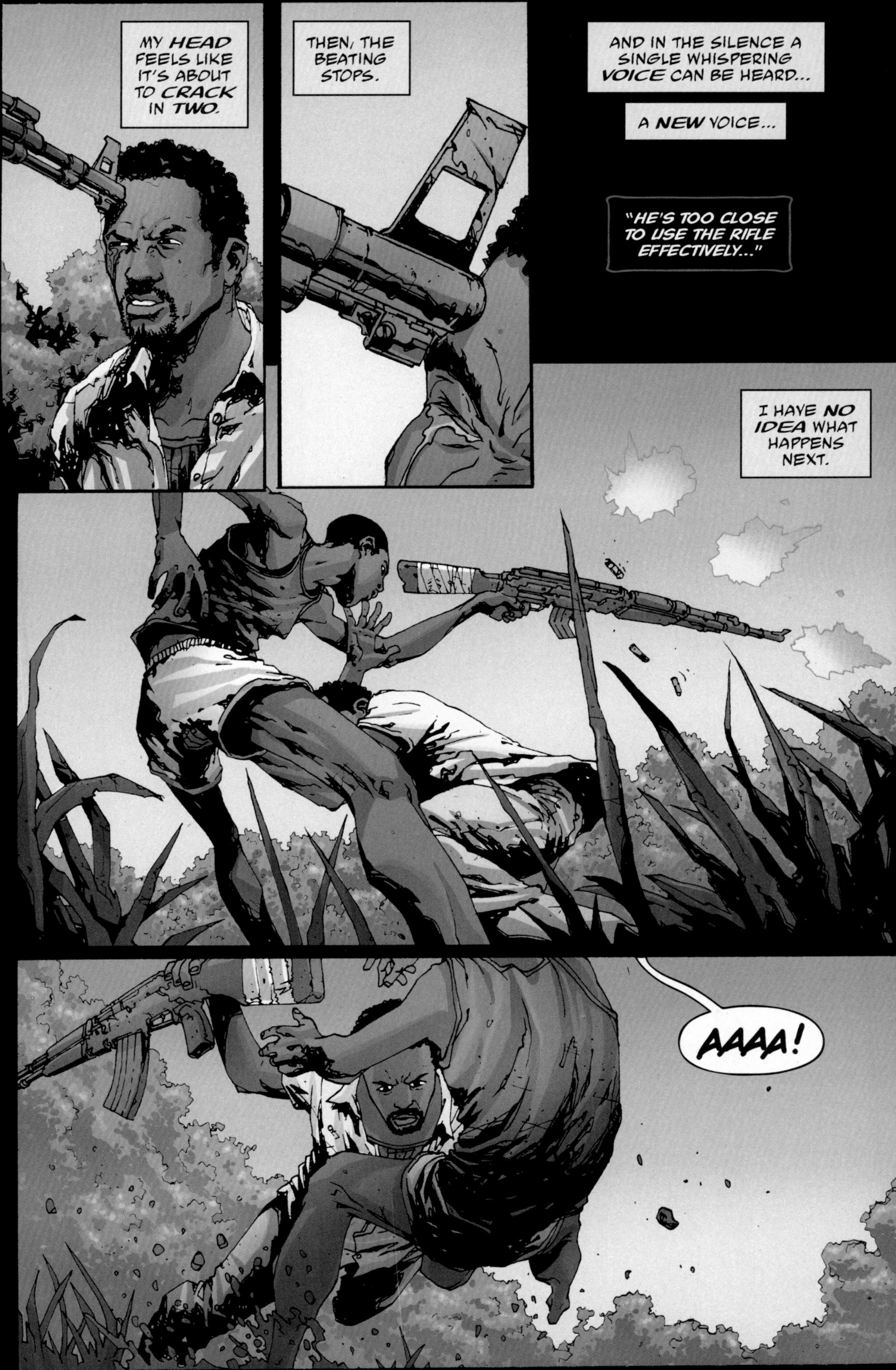

MY HEAD FEELS LIKE IT'S ABOUT TO CRACK IN TWO.
THEN, THE BEATING STOPS.
AND IN THE SILENCE A SINGLE WHISPERING VOICE CAN BE HEARD...
A NEW VOICE...
"HE'S TOO CLOSE TO USE THE RIFLE EFFECTIVELY..."
I HAVE NO IDEA WHAT HAPPENS NEXT.
AAAA!

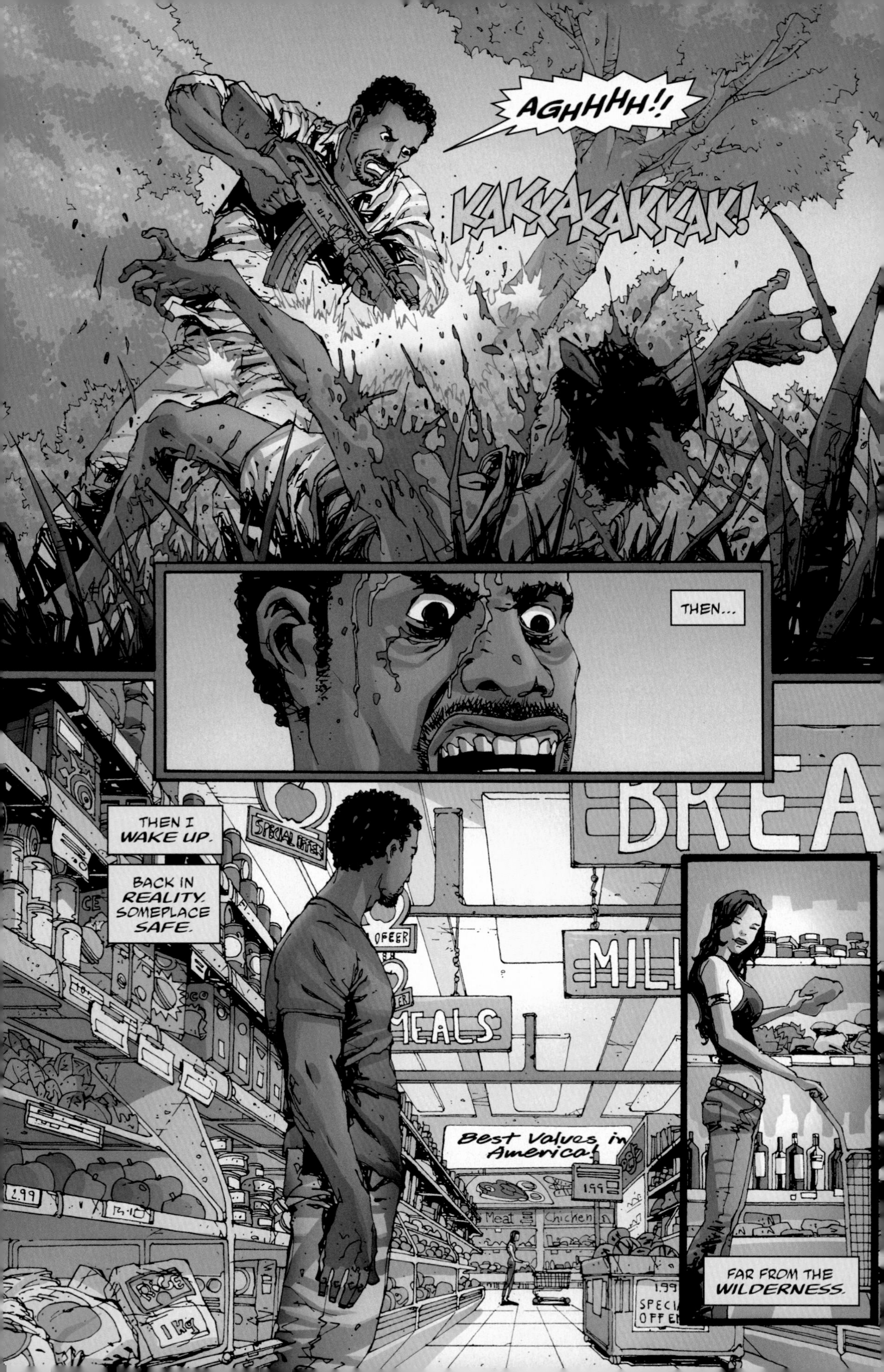
AGHHHH!!
KAKKAKAKKAK!
THEN...
THEN I WAKE UP.
BACK IN REALITY. SOMEPLACE SAFE.
FAR FROM THE WILDERNESS.
SPECIAL OFFER
BREA
MILI
MEALS
Best Values in America!
Meat
Chicken
1.99
2.99
RICE
1 kg

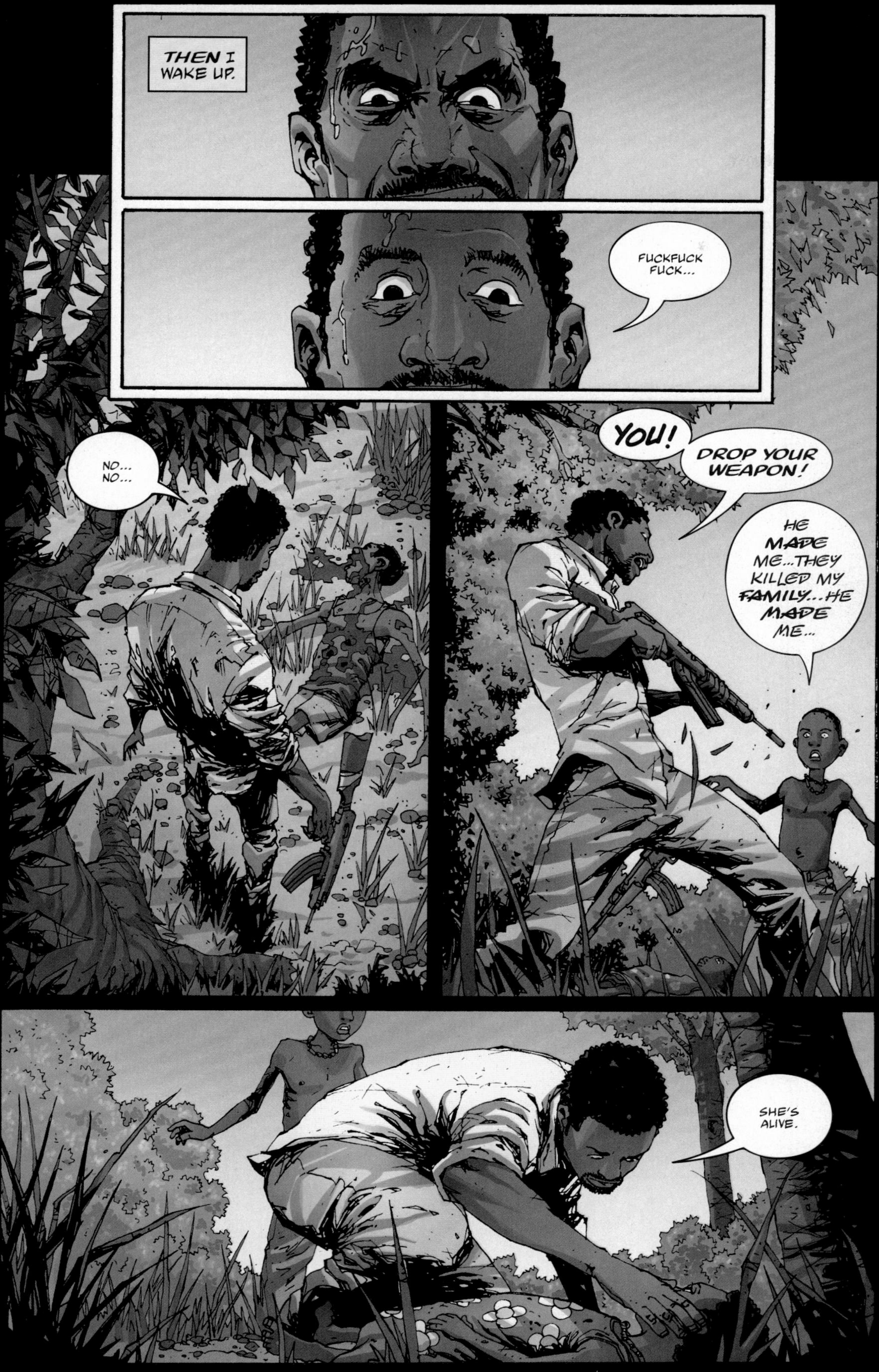
THEN I WAKE UP.
FUCKFUCK FUCK...
NO... NO...
YOU!
DROP YOUR WEAPON!
HE MADE ME...THEY KILLED MY FAMILY...HE MADE ME...
SHE'S ALIVE.

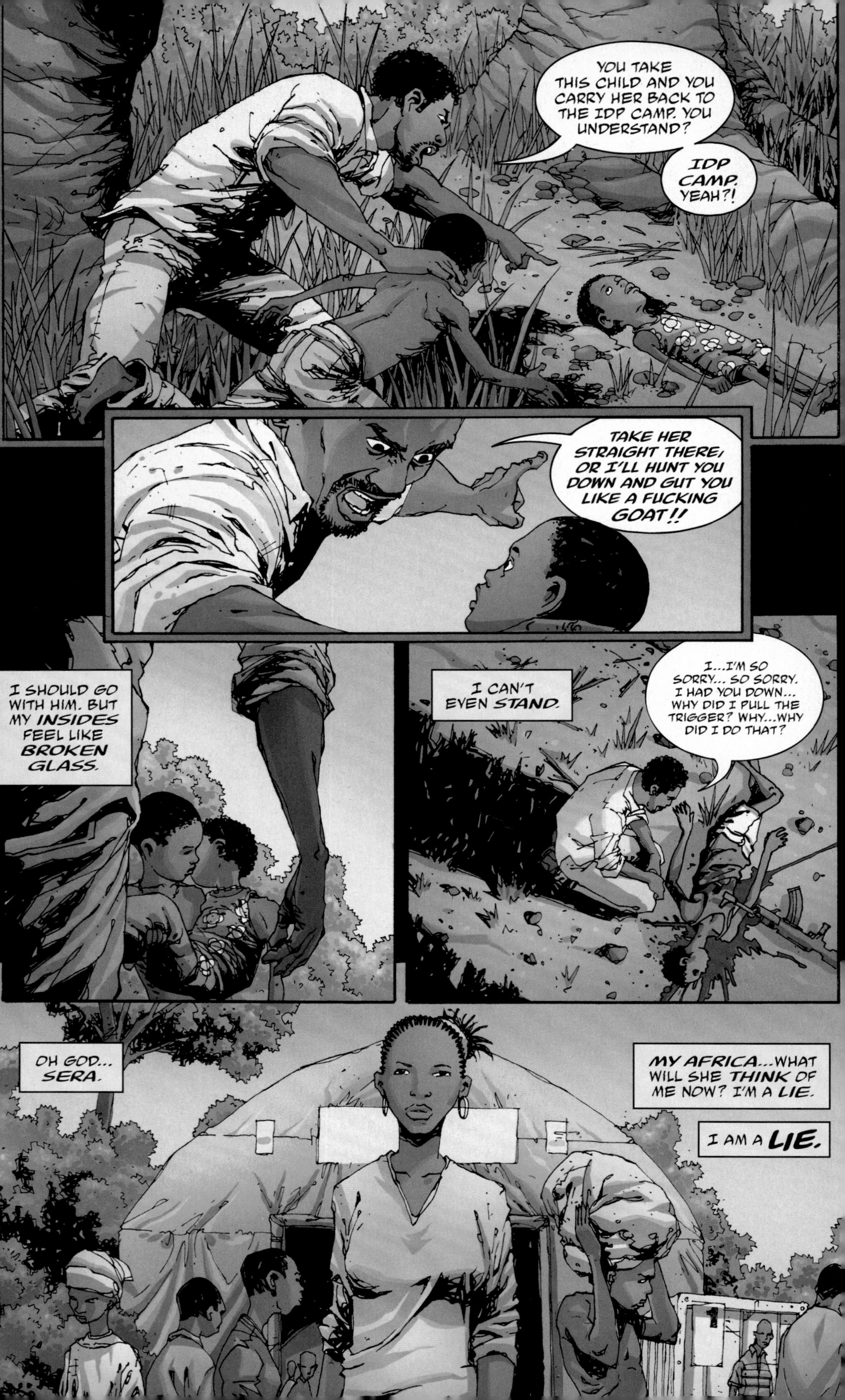
YOU TAKE THIS CHILD AND YOU CARRY HER BACK TO THE IDP CAMP. YOU UNDERSTAND?
IDP CAMP. YEAH?!
TAKE HER STRAIGHT THERE, OR I'LL HUNT YOU DOWN AND GUT YOU LIKE A FUCKING GOAT!!
I SHOULD GO WITH HIM. BUT MY INSIDES FEEL LIKE BROKEN GLASS.
I CAN'T EVEN STAND.
I...I'M SO SORRY... SO SORRY. I HAD YOU DOWN... WHY DID I PULL THE TRIGGER? WHY...WHY DID I DO THAT?
OH GOD... SERA.
MY AFRICA...WHAT WILL SHE THINK OF ME NOW? I'M A LIE.
I AM A LIE.

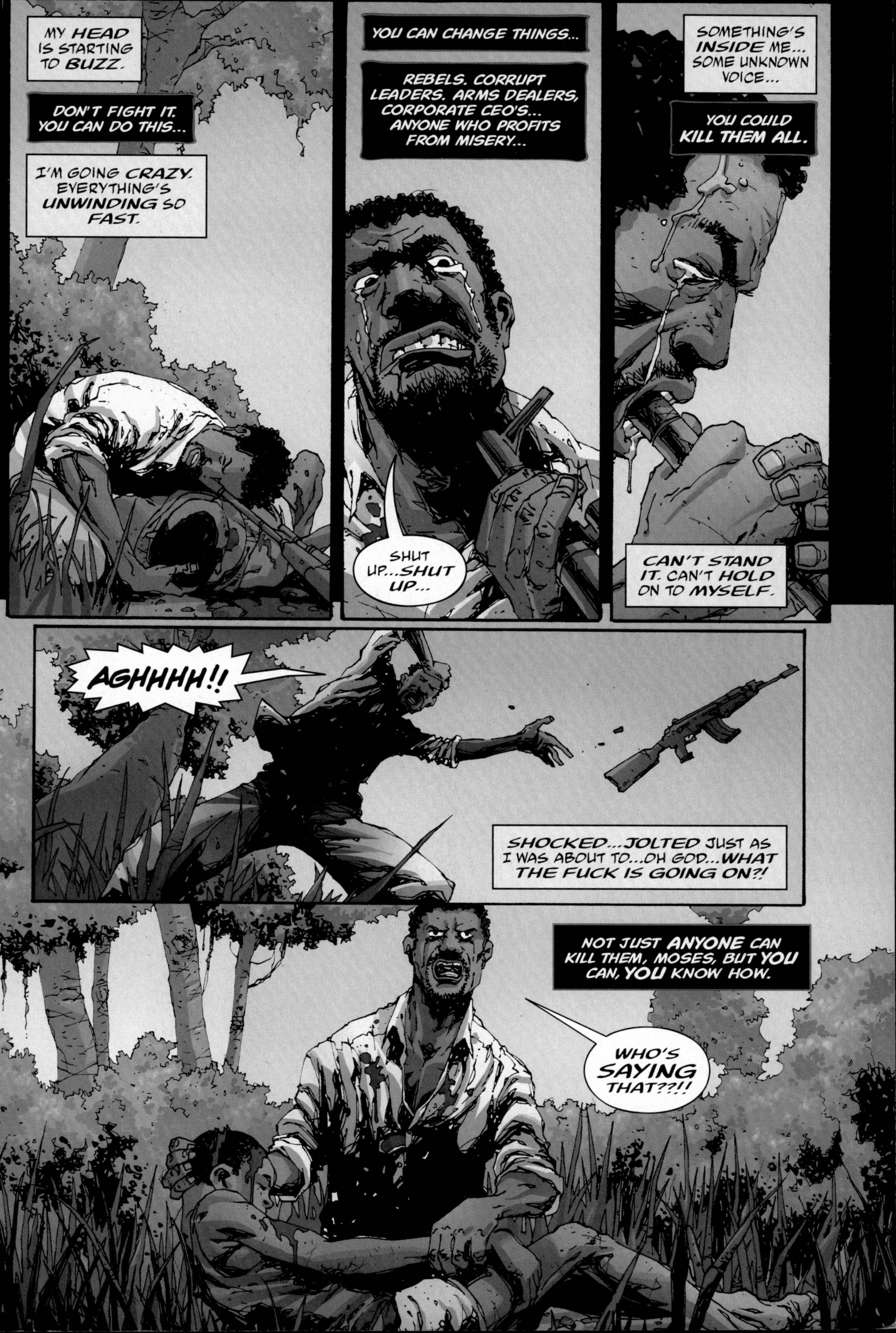

MY HEAD IS STARTING TO BUZZ.
DON'T FIGHT IT. YOU CAN DO THIS...
I'M GOING CRAZY. EVERYTHING'S UNWINDING SO FAST.
YOU CAN CHANGE THINGS...
REBELS. CORRUPT LEADERS. ARMS DEALERS, CORPORATE CEO'S... ANYONE WHO PROFITS FROM MISERY...
SHUT UP...SHUT UP...
SOMETHING'S INSIDE ME... SOME UNKNOWN VOICE...
YOU COULD KILL THEM ALL.
CAN'T STAND IT. CAN'T HOLD ON TO MYSELF.
AGHHHH!!
SHOCKED...JOLTED JUST AS I WAS ABOUT TO...OH GOD...WHAT THE FUCK IS GOING ON?!
NOT JUST ANYONE CAN KILL THEM, MOSES, BUT YOU CAN, YOU KNOW HOW.
WHO'S SAYING THAT??!!

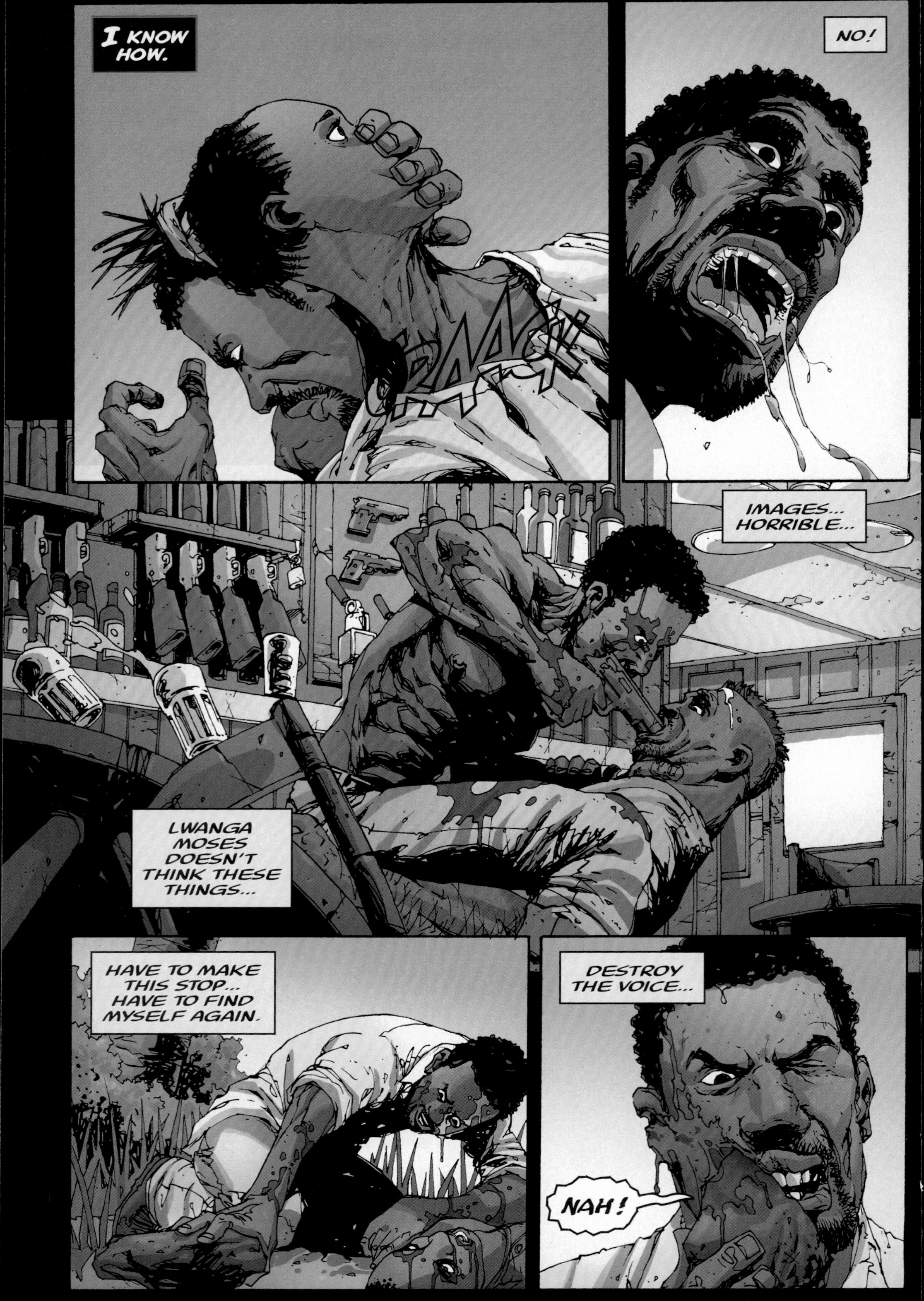
I KNOW HOW.
NO!
IMAGES... HORRIBLE...
LWANGA MOSES DOESN'T THINK THESE THINGS...
HAVE TO MAKE THIS STOP... HAVE TO FIND MYSELF AGAIN.
DESTROY THE VOICE...
NAH!

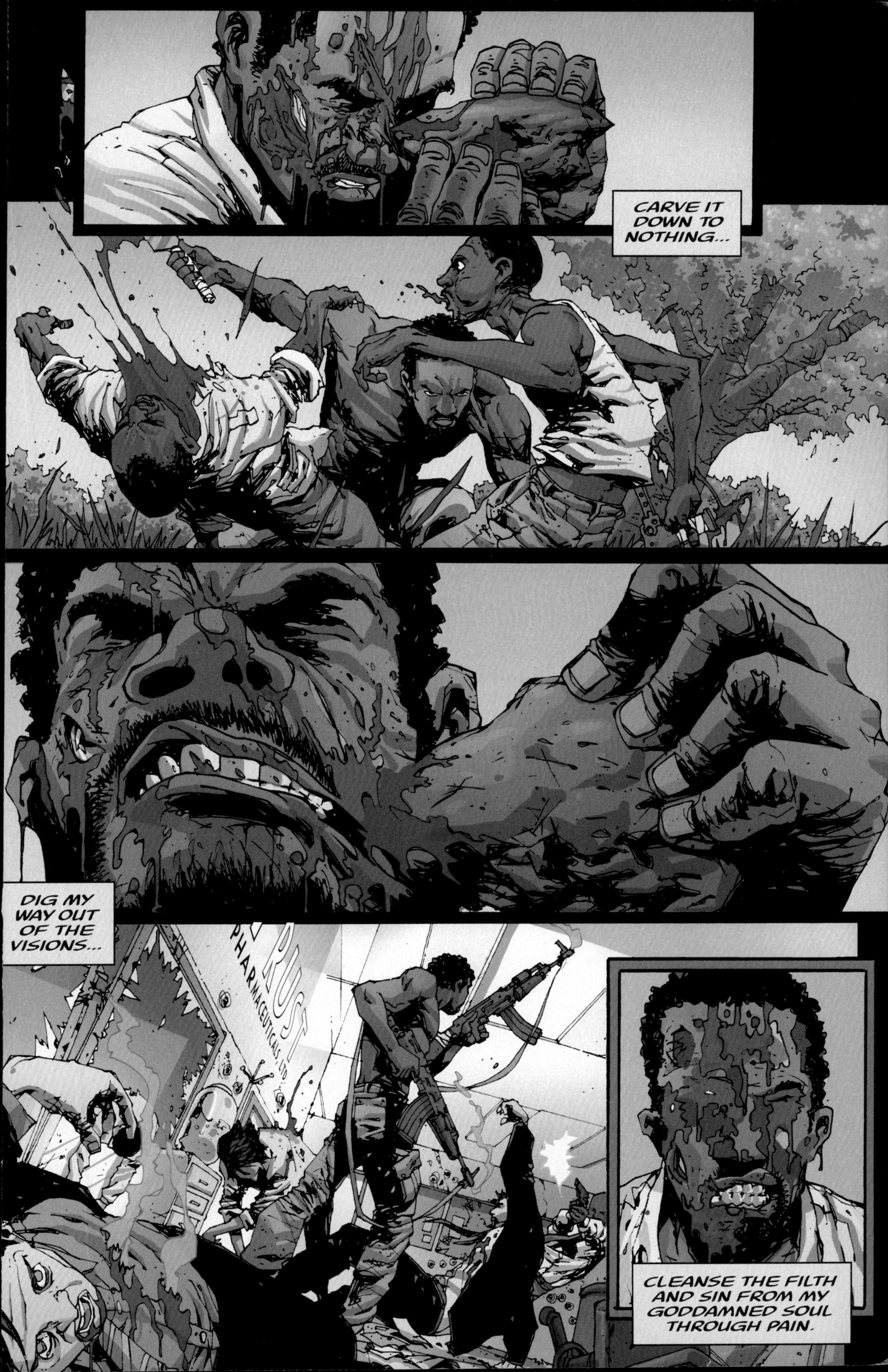
CARVE IT DOWN TO NOTHING...
DIG MY WAY OUT OF THE VISIONS...
RUST PHARMACEUTICALS LTD
CLEANSE THE FILTH AND SIN FROM MY GODDAMNED SOUL THROUGH PAIN.

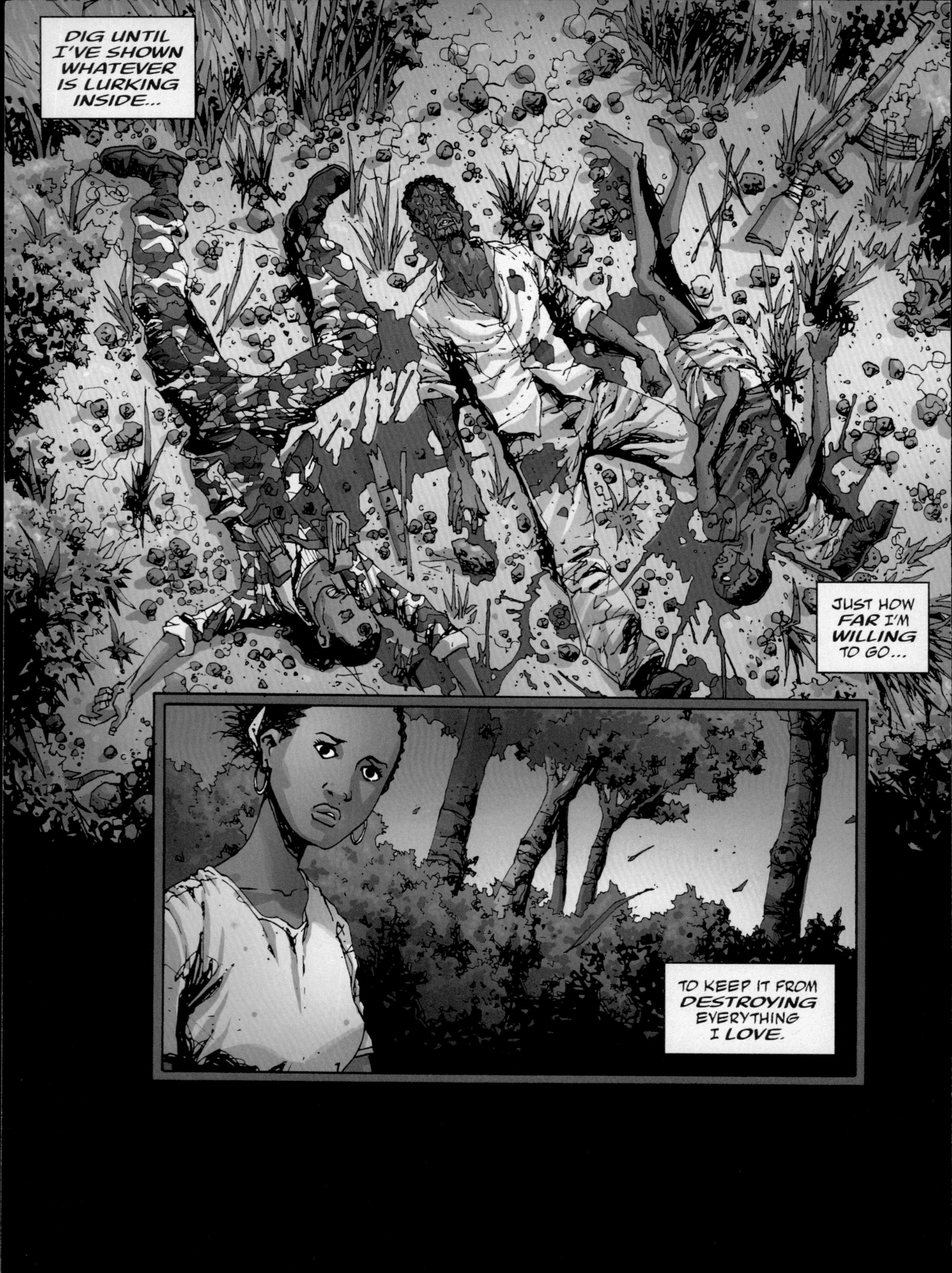
DIG UNTIL I'VE SHOWN WHATEVER IS LURKING INSIDE...
JUST HOW FAR I'M WILLING TO GO...
TO KEEP IT FROM DESTROYING EVERYTHING I LOVE.

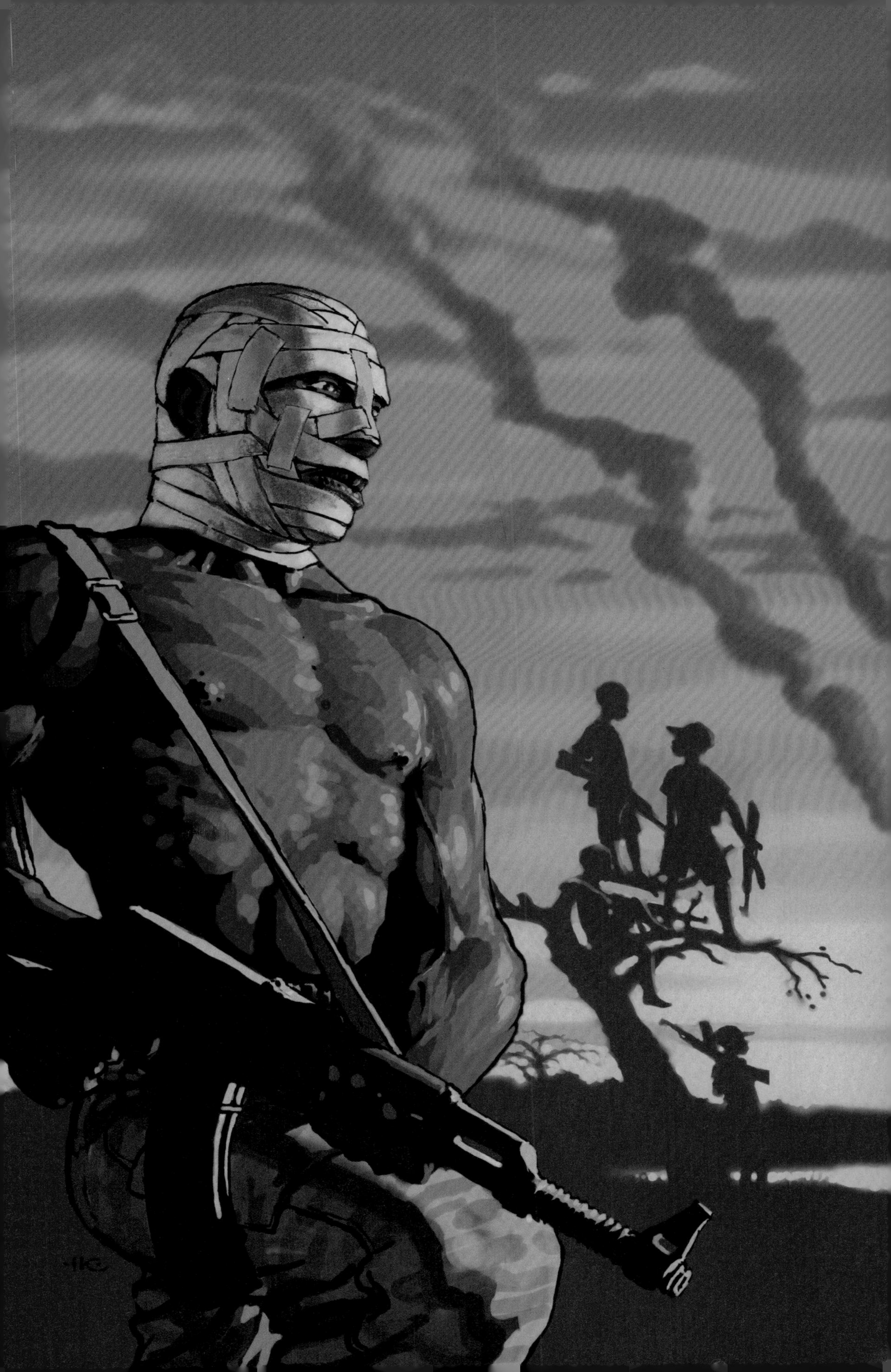

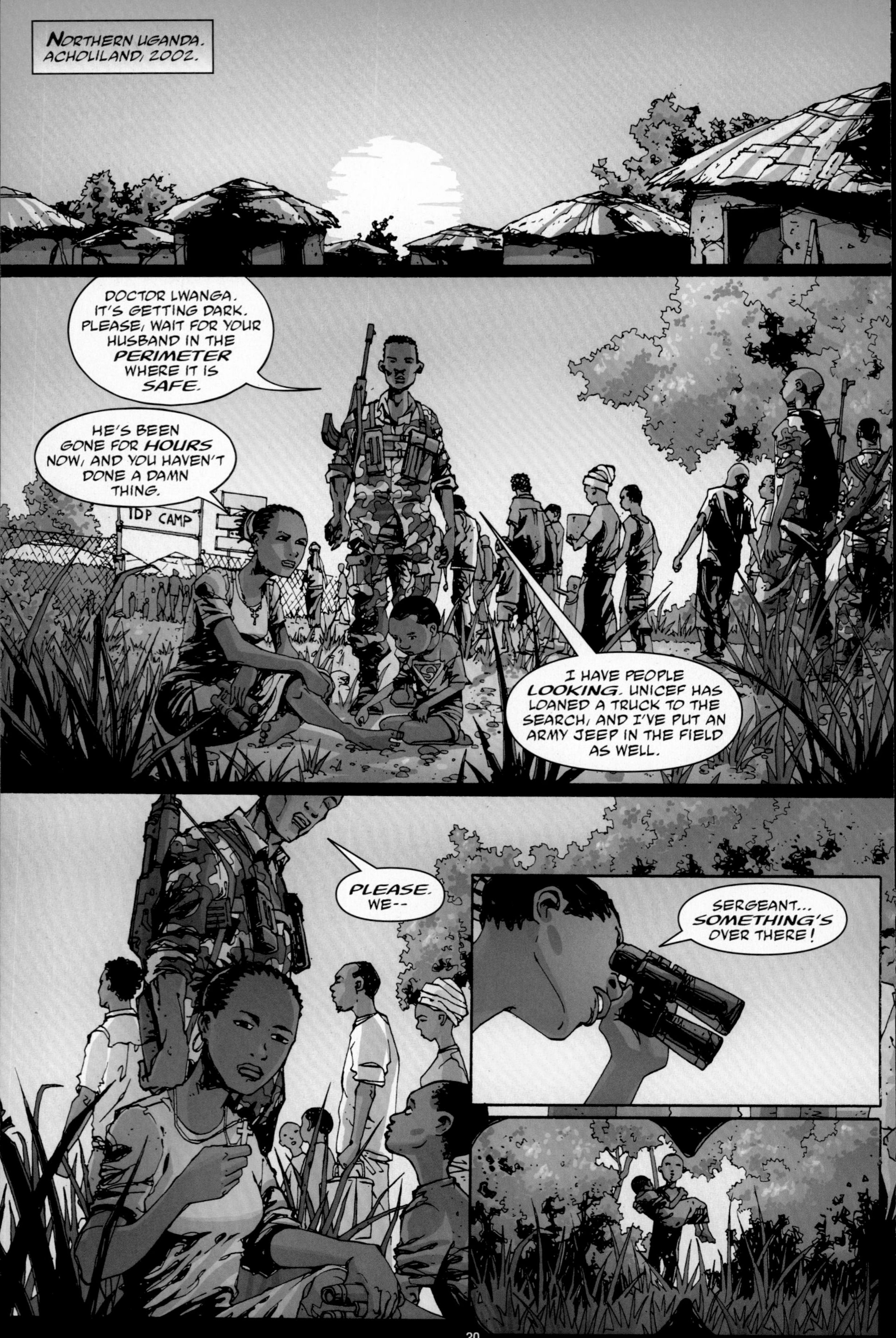

NORTHERN UGANDA. ACHOLILAND, 2002.
DOCTOR LWANGA. IT'S GETTING DARK. PLEASE, WAIT FOR YOUR HUSBAND IN THE PERIMETER WHERE IT IS SAFE.
HE'S BEEN GONE FOR HOURS NOW, AND YOU HAVEN'T DONE A DAMN THING.
IDP CAMP
I HAVE PEOPLE LOOKING. UNICEF HAS LOANED A TRUCK TO THE SEARCH, AND I'VE PUT AN ARMY JEEP IN THE FIELD AS WELL.
PLEASE. WE--
SERGEANT... SOMETHING'S OVER THERE!

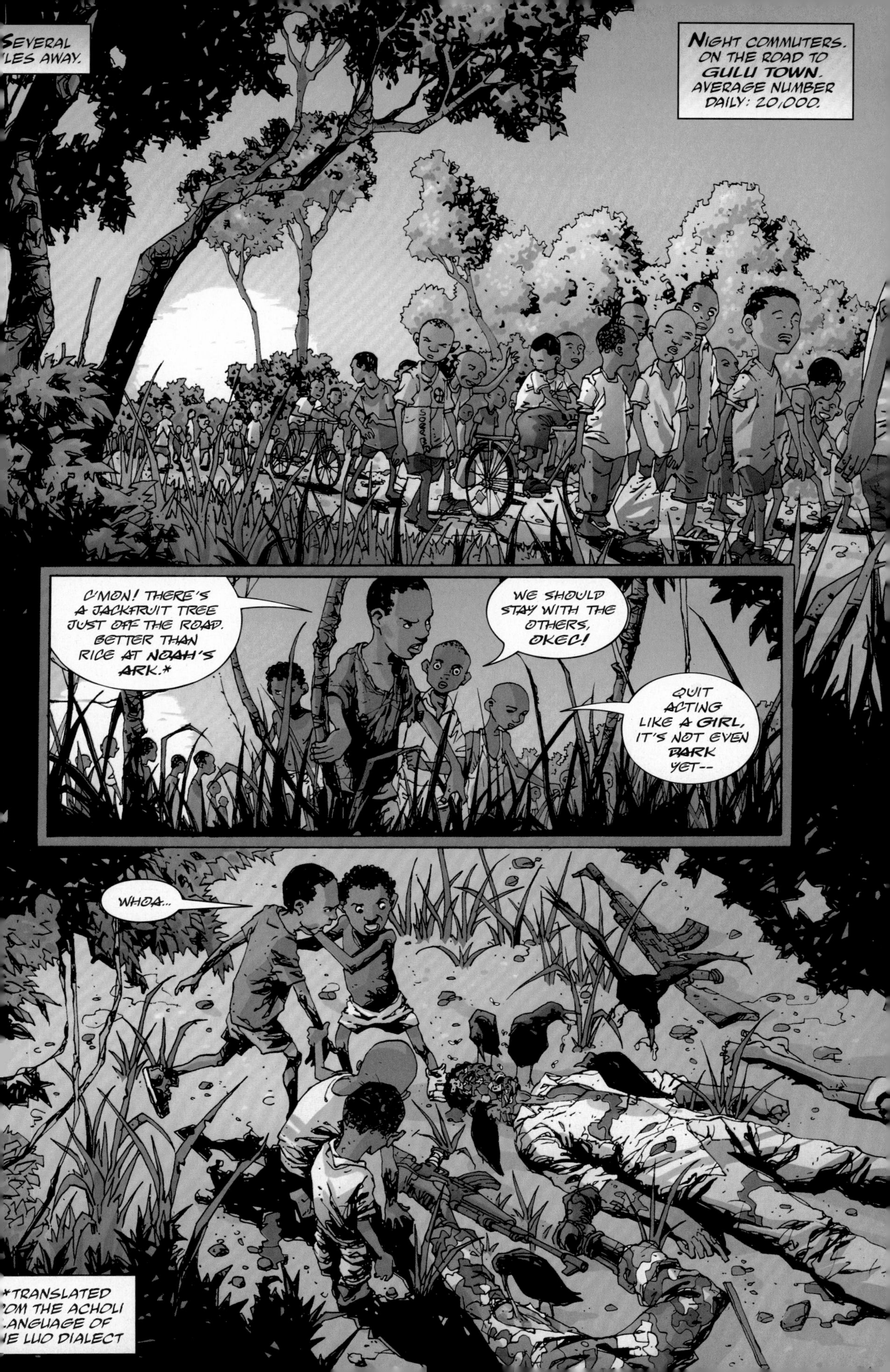
SEVERAL
[M]ILES AWAY.
NIGHT COMMUTERS. ON THE ROAD TO GULU TOWN. AVERAGE NUMBER DAILY: 20,000.
C'MON! THERE'S A JACKFRUIT TREE JUST OFF THE ROAD. BETTER THAN RICE AT NOAH'S ARK.*
WE SHOULD STAY WITH THE OTHERS, OKEC!
QUIT ACTING LIKE A GIRL, IT'S NOT EVEN DARK YET--
WHOA...
*TRANSLATED [FR]OM THE ACHOLI LANGUAGE OF [TH]E LUO DIALECT

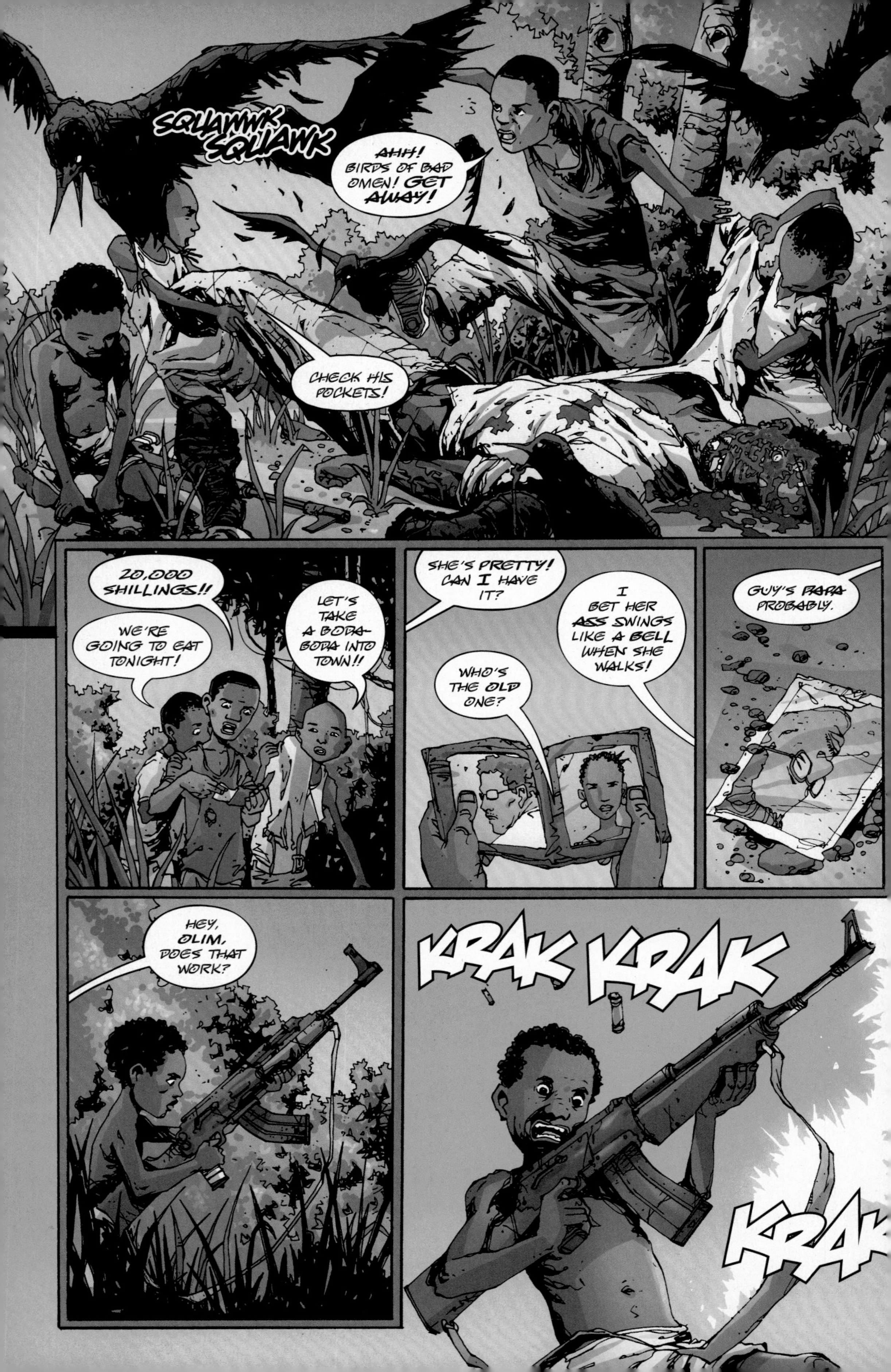
SQUAWWK SQUAWK
AHH! BIRDS OF BAD OMEN! GET AWAY!
CHECK HIS POCKETS!
20,000 SHILLINGS!!
WE'RE GOING TO EAT TONIGHT!
LET'S TAKE A BODA-BODA INTO TOWN!!
SHE'S PRETTY! CAN I HAVE IT?
I BET HER ASS SWINGS LIKE A BELL WHEN SHE WALKS!
WHO'S THE OLD ONE?
GUY'S PAPA PROBABLY.
HEY, OLIM, DOES THAT WORK?
KRAK KRAK
KRAK

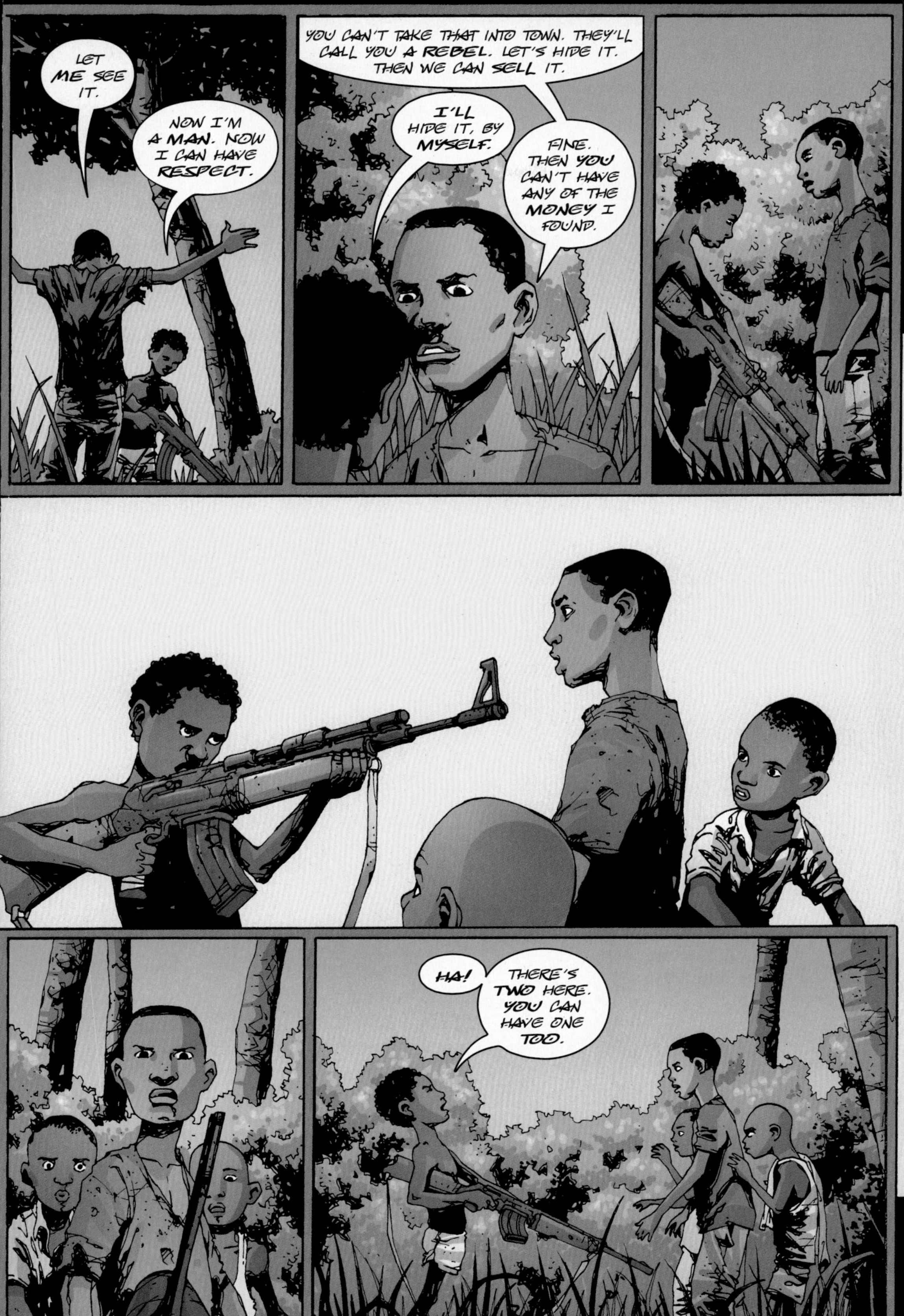
LET ME SEE IT.
NOW I'M A MAN. NOW I CAN HAVE RESPECT.
YOU CAN'T TAKE THAT INTO TOWN. THEY'LL CALL YOU A REBEL. LET'S HIDE IT. THEN WE CAN SELL IT.
I'LL HIDE IT, BY MYSELF.
FINE. THEN YOU CAN'T HAVE ANY OF THE MONEY I FOUND.
HA!
THERE'S TWO HERE. YOU CAN HAVE ONE TOO.

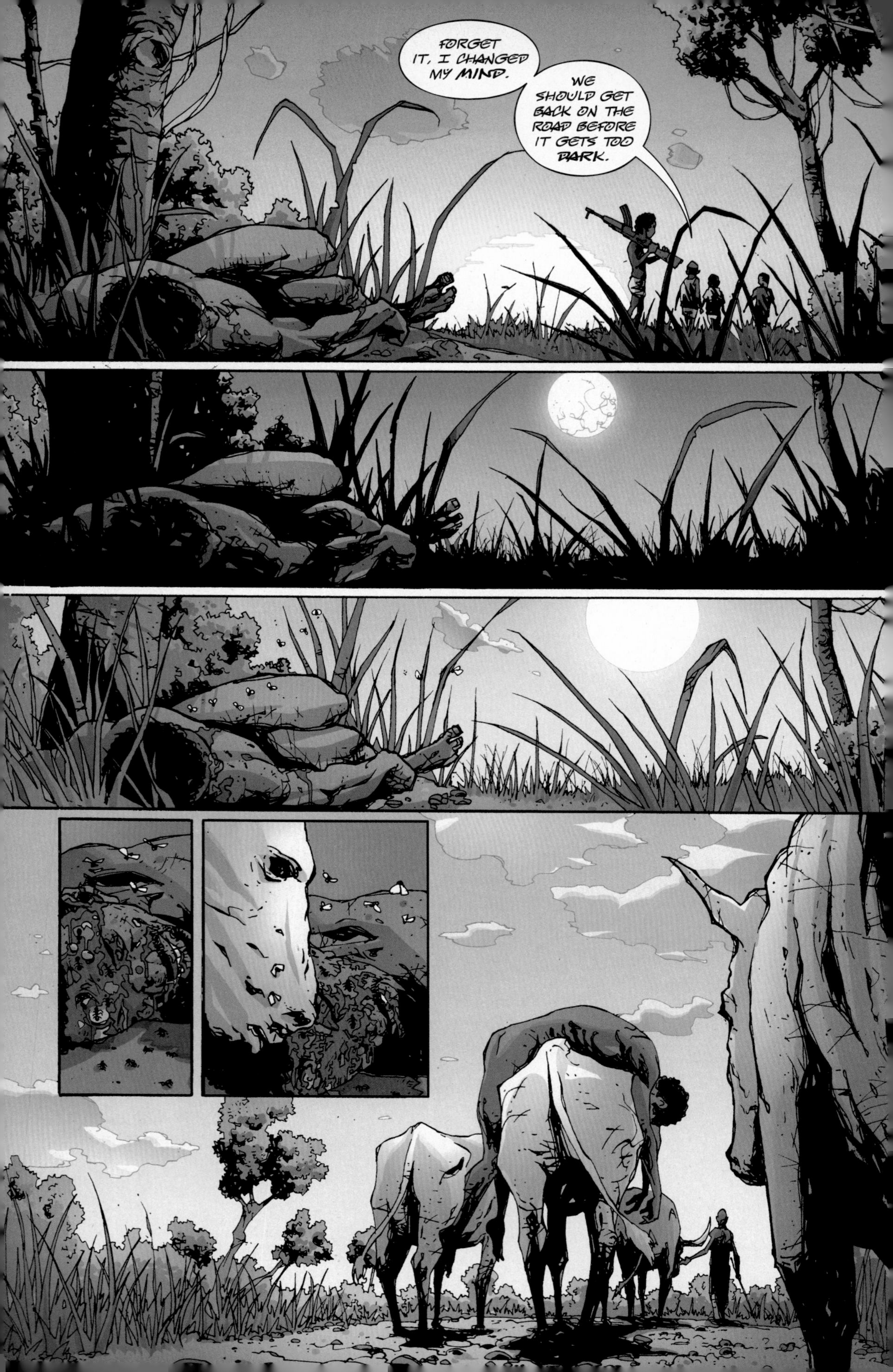
FORGET IT, I CHANGED MY MIND.
WE SHOULD GET BACK ON THE ROAD BEFORE IT GETS TOO DARK.

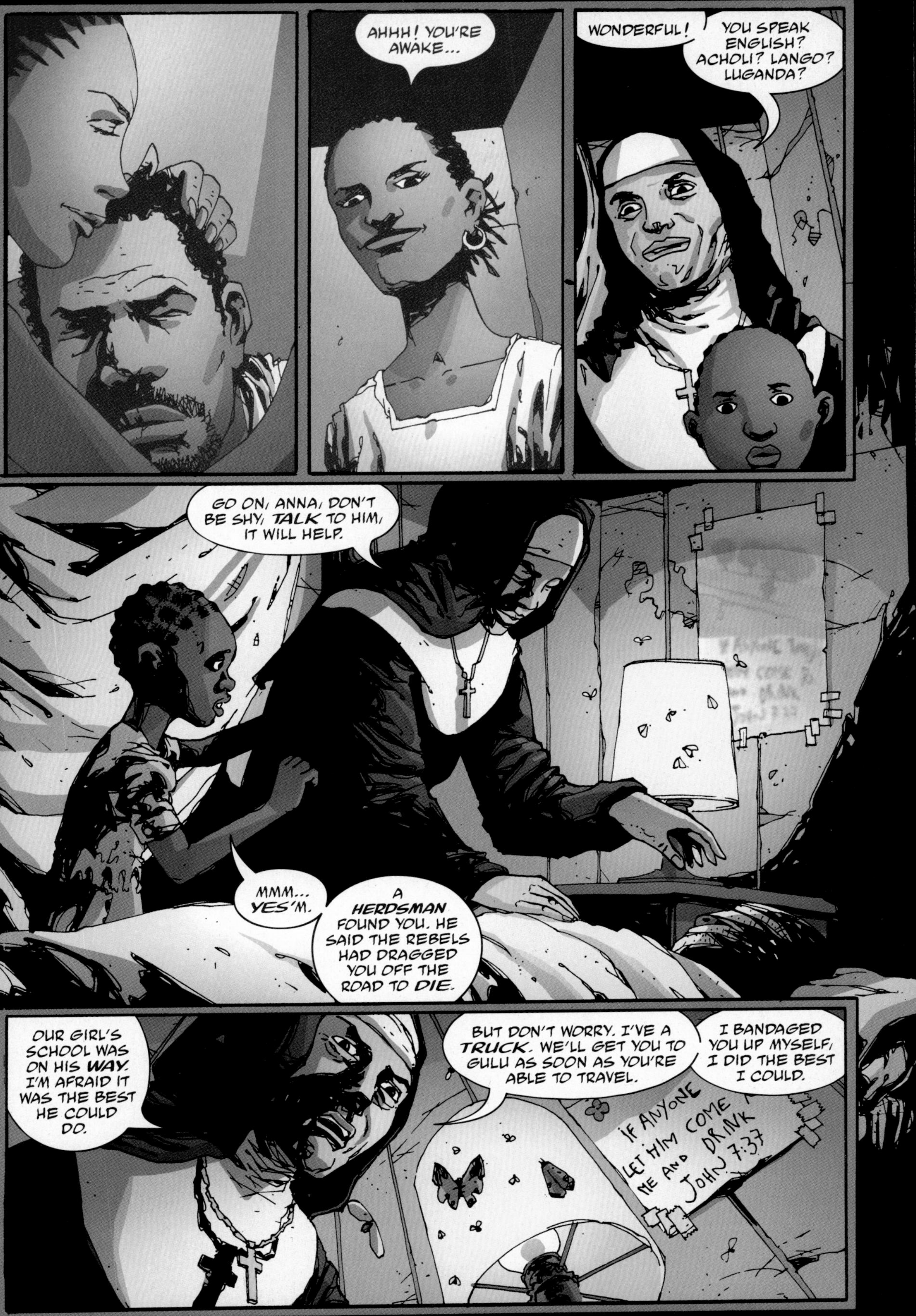

AHHH! YOU'RE AWAKE...
WONDERFUL!
YOU SPEAK ENGLISH? ACHOLI? LANGO? LUGANDA?
GO ON, ANNA, DON'T BE SHY, TALK TO HIM, IT WILL HELP.
MMM... YES'M.
A HERDSMAN FOUND YOU. HE SAID THE REBELS HAD DRAGGED YOU OFF THE ROAD TO DIE.
OUR GIRL'S SCHOOL WAS ON HIS WAY. I'M AFRAID IT WAS THE BEST HE COULD DO.
BUT DON'T WORRY. I'VE A TRUCK. WE'LL GET YOU TO GULU AS SOON AS YOU'RE ABLE TO TRAVEL.
I BANDAGED YOU UP MYSELF, I DID THE BEST I COULD.
IF ANYONE LET HIM COME ME AND DRINK JOHN 7:37

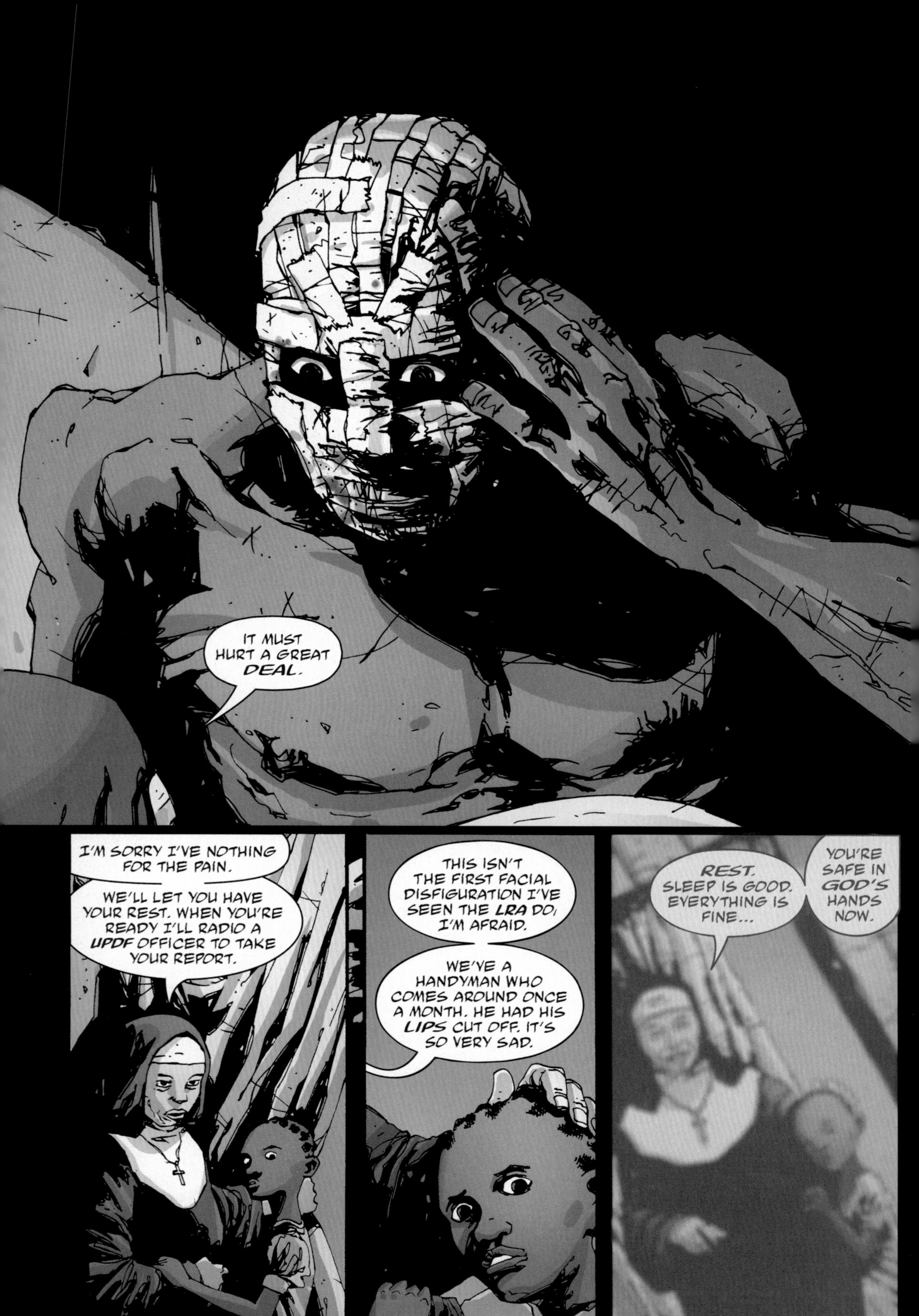
IT MUST HURT A GREAT DEAL.
I'M SORRY I'VE NOTHING FOR THE PAIN.
WE'LL LET YOU HAVE YOUR REST. WHEN YOU'RE READY I'LL RADIO A UPDF OFFICER TO TAKE YOUR REPORT.
THIS ISN'T THE FIRST FACIAL DISFIGURATION I'VE SEEN THE LRA DO, I'M AFRAID.
WE'VE A HANDYMAN WHO COMES AROUND ONCE A MONTH. HE HAD HIS LIPS CUT OFF. IT'S SO VERY SAD.
REST. SLEEP IS GOOD. EVERYTHING IS FINE...
YOU'RE SAFE IN GOD'S HANDS NOW.

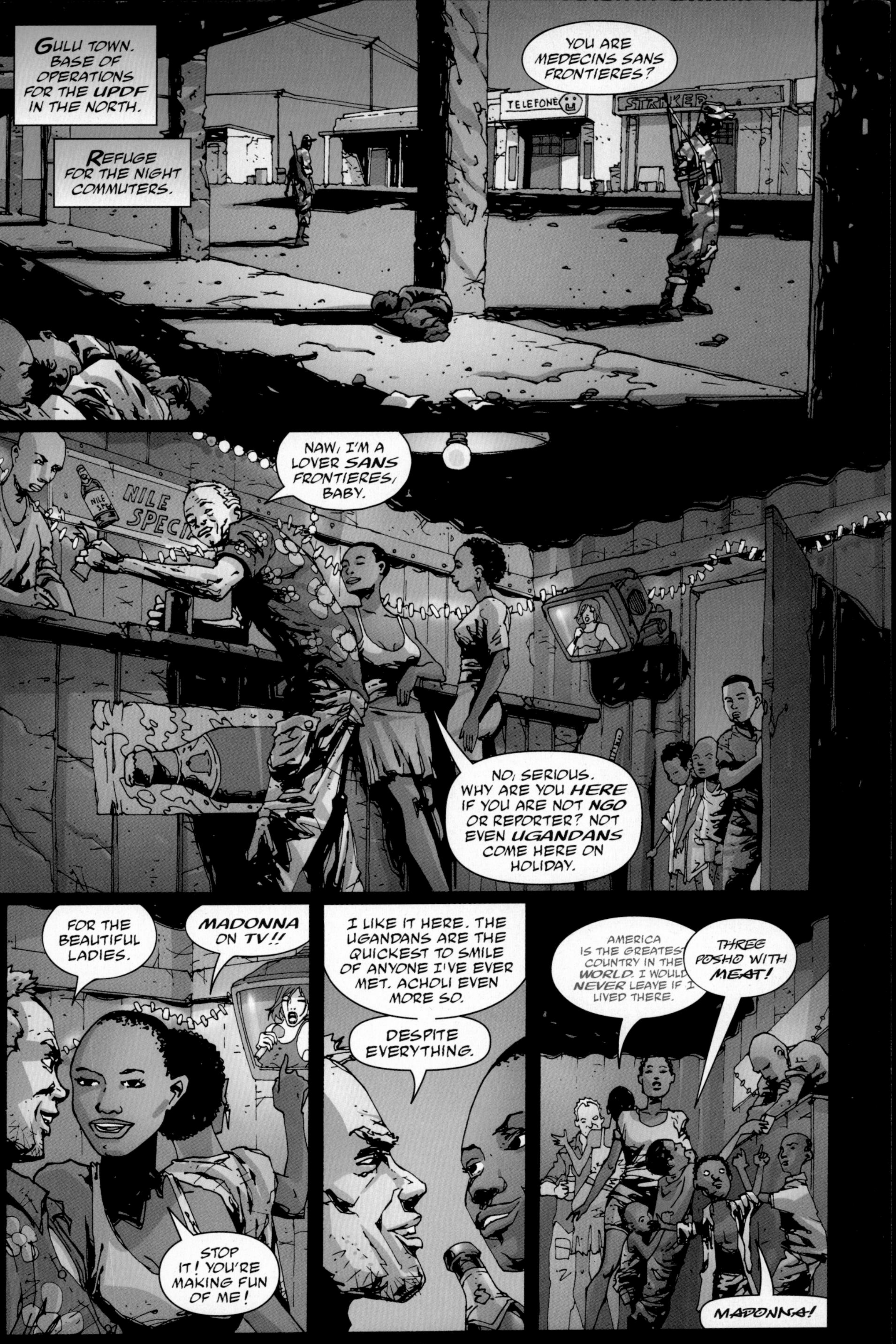
GULU TOWN. BASE OF OPERATIONS FOR THE UPDF IN THE NORTH.
REFUGE FOR THE NIGHT COMMUTERS.
YOU ARE MEDECINS SANS FRONTIERES?
TELEFONE
NAW, I'M A LOVER SANS FRONTIERES, BABY.
NILE SPECI
NO, SERIOUS. WHY ARE YOU HERE IF YOU ARE NOT NGO OR REPORTER? NOT EVEN UGANDANS COME HERE ON HOLIDAY.
FOR THE BEAUTIFUL LADIES.
MADONNA ON TV!!
STOP IT! YOU'RE MAKING FUN OF ME!
I LIKE IT HERE. THE UGANDANS ARE THE QUICKEST TO SMILE OF ANYONE I'VE EVER MET. ACHOLI EVEN MORE SO.
DESPITE EVERYTHING.
AMERICA IS THE GREATEST COUNTRY IN THE WORLD. I WOULD NEVER LEAVE IF I LIVED THERE.
THREE POSHO WITH MEAT!
MADONNA!

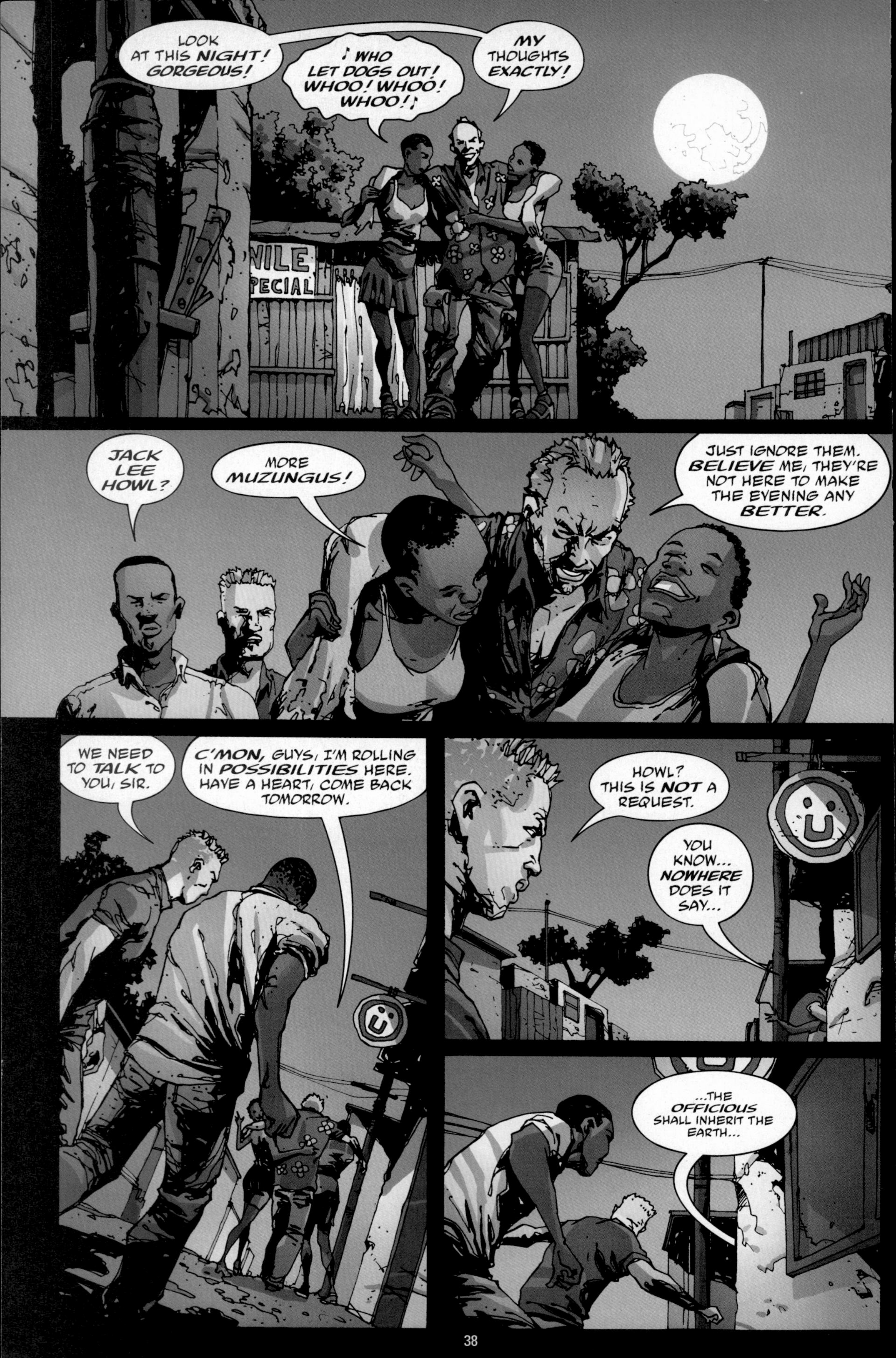

LOOK AT THIS NIGHT! GORGEOUS!
♪ WHO LET DOGS OUT! WHOO! WHOO! WHOO! ♪
MY THOUGHTS EXACTLY!
NILE
PECIAL
JACK LEE HOWL?
MORE MUZUNGUS!
JUST IGNORE THEM. BELIEVE ME, THEY'RE NOT HERE TO MAKE THE EVENING ANY BETTER.
WE NEED TO TALK TO YOU, SIR.
C'MON, GUYS, I'M ROLLING IN POSSIBILITIES HERE. HAVE A HEART, COME BACK TOMORROW.
HOWL? THIS IS NOT A REQUEST.
YOU KNOW... NOWHERE DOES IT SAY...
...THE OFFICIOUS SHALL INHERIT THE EARTH...

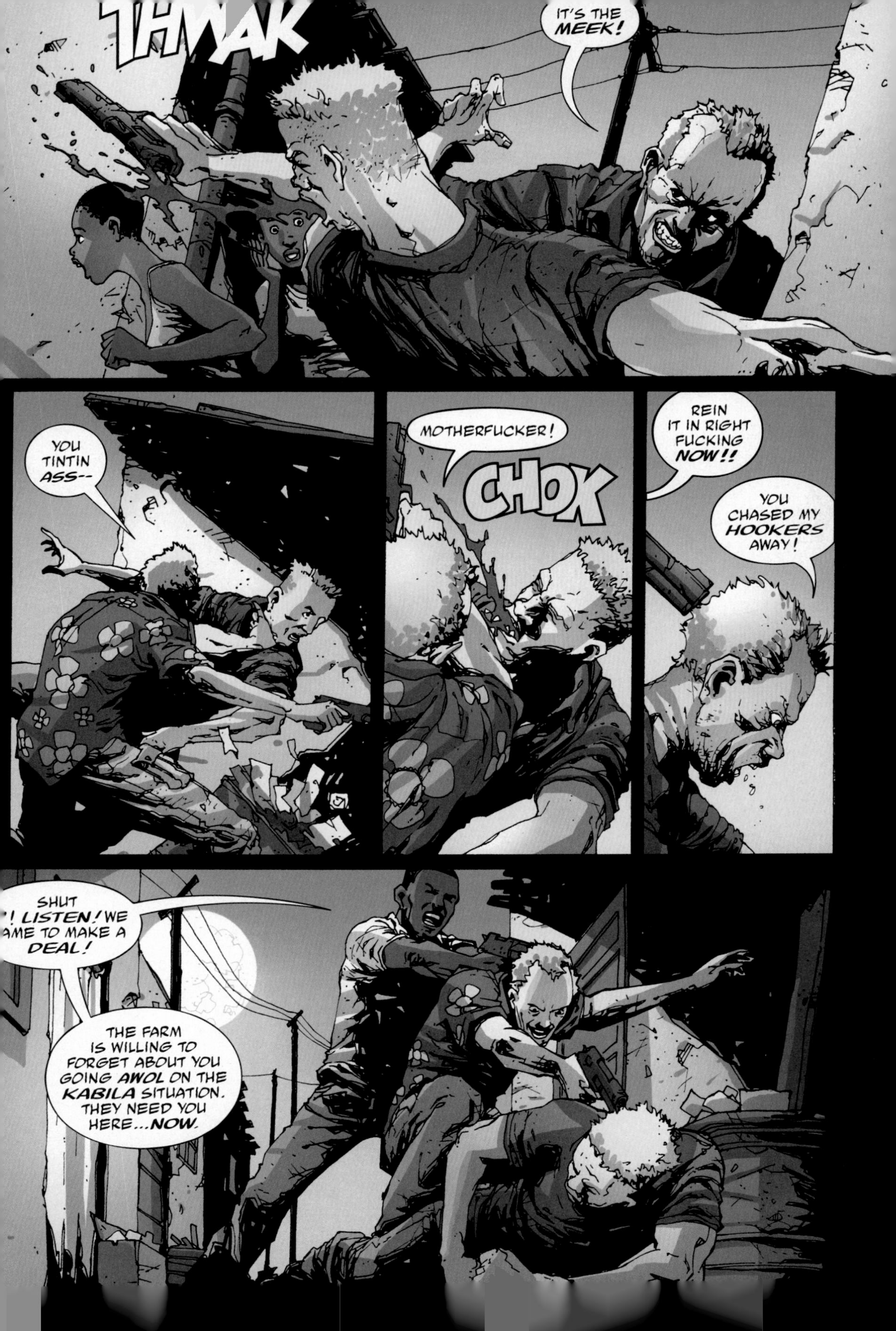
THWAK
IT'S THE MEEK!
YOU TINTIN ASS--
MOTHERFUCKER!
CHOK
REIN IT IN RIGHT FUCKING NOW!!
YOU CHASED MY HOOKERS AWAY!
SHUT
! LISTEN! WE
AME TO MAKE A DEAL!
THE FARM IS WILLING TO FORGET ABOUT YOU GOING AWOL ON THE KABILA SITUATION. THEY NEED YOU HERE...NOW.

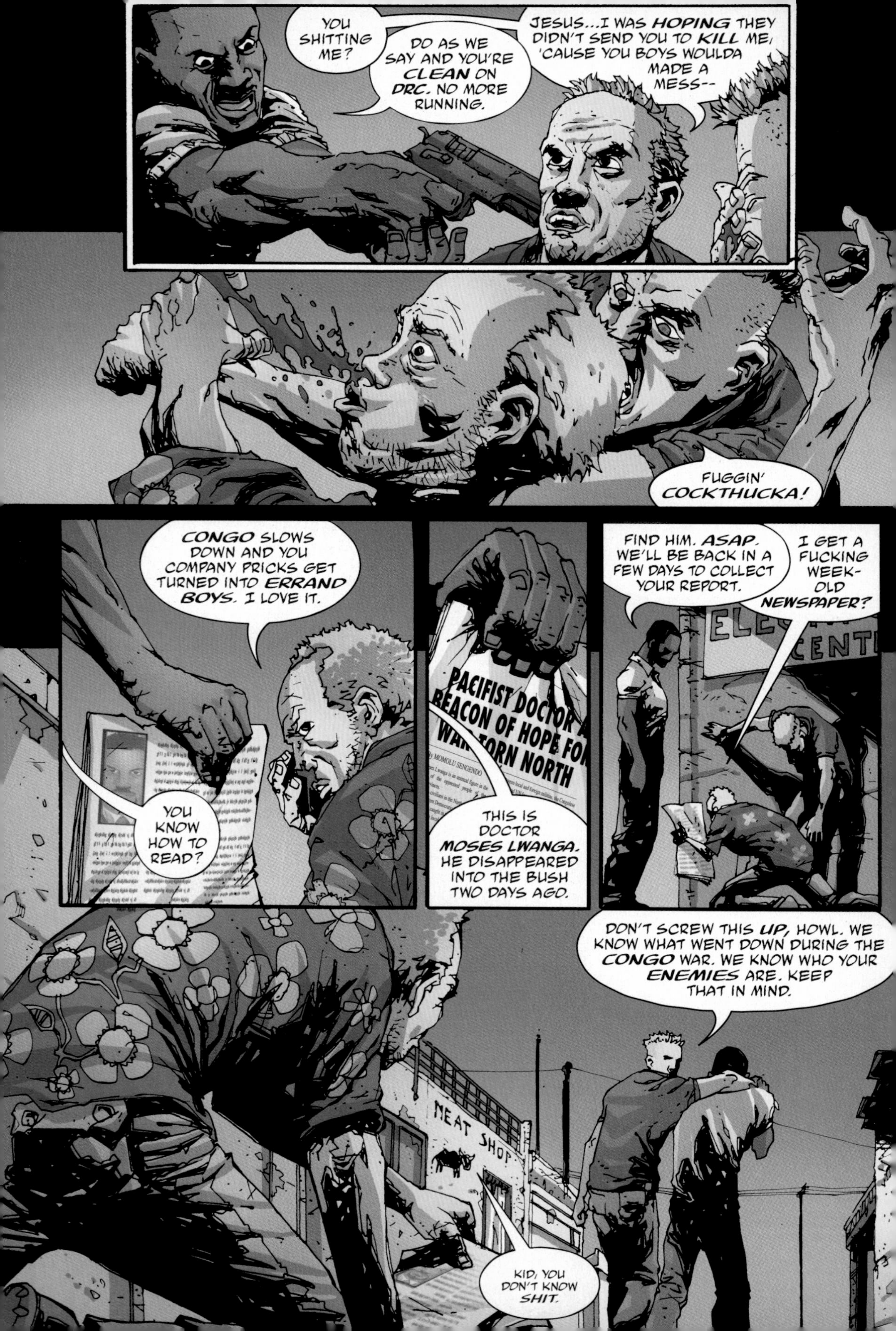
YOU SHITTING ME?
DO AS WE SAY AND YOU'RE CLEAN ON DRC. NO MORE RUNNING.
JESUS...I WAS HOPING THEY DIDN'T SEND YOU TO KILL ME, 'CAUSE YOU BOYS WOULDA MADE A MESS--
FUGGIN' COCKTHUCKA!
CONGO SLOWS DOWN AND YOU COMPANY PRICKS GET TURNED INTO ERRAND BOYS. I LOVE IT.
YOU KNOW HOW TO READ?
PACIFIST DOCTOR A
EACON OF HOPE FO
TORN NORTH
THIS IS DOCTOR MOSES LWANGA. HE DISAPPEARED INTO THE BUSH TWO DAYS AGO.
FIND HIM. ASAP. WE'LL BE BACK IN A FEW DAYS TO COLLECT YOUR REPORT.
I GET A FUCKING WEEK-OLD NEWSPAPER?
DON'T SCREW THIS UP, HOWL. WE KNOW WHAT WENT DOWN DURING THE CONGO WAR. WE KNOW WHO YOUR ENEMIES ARE. KEEP THAT IN MIND.
MEAT SHOP
KID, YOU DON'T KNOW SHIT.

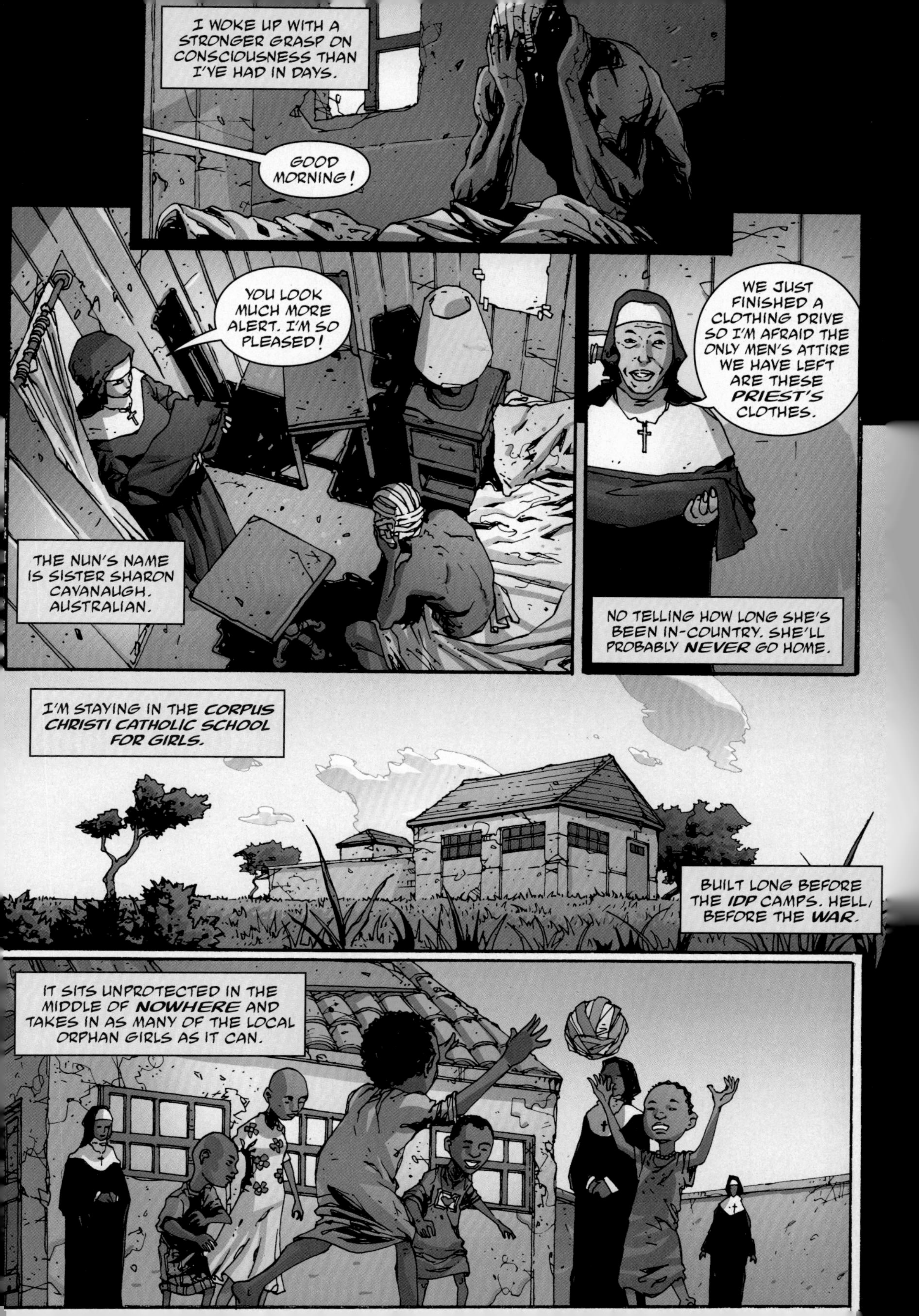
I WOKE UP WITH A STRONGER GRASP ON CONSCIOUSNESS THAN I'VE HAD IN DAYS.
GOOD MORNING!
YOU LOOK MUCH MORE ALERT. I'M SO PLEASED!
THE NUN'S NAME IS SISTER SHARON CAVANAUGH. AUSTRALIAN.
WE JUST FINISHED A CLOTHING DRIVE SO I'M AFRAID THE ONLY MEN'S ATTIRE WE HAVE LEFT ARE THESE *PRIEST'S* CLOTHES.
NO TELLING HOW LONG SHE'S BEEN IN-COUNTRY. SHE'LL PROBABLY ***NEVER*** GO HOME.
I'M STAYING IN THE *CORPUS CHRISTI CATHOLIC SCHOOL FOR GIRLS.*
BUILT LONG BEFORE THE *IDP* CAMPS. HELL, BEFORE THE *WAR*.
IT SITS UNPROTECTED IN THE MIDDLE OF ***NOWHERE*** AND TAKES IN AS MANY OF THE LOCAL ORPHAN GIRLS AS IT CAN.

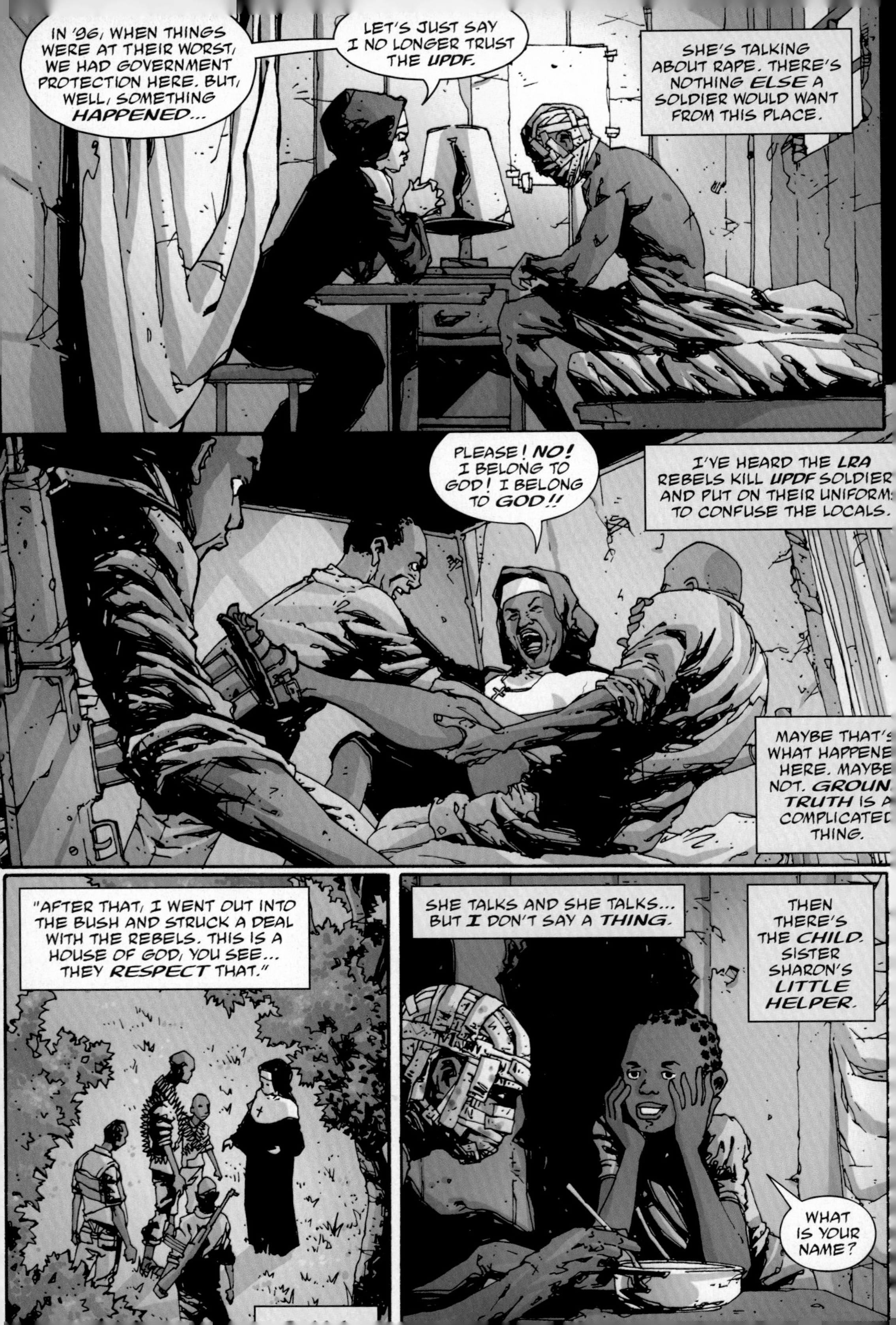
IN '96, WHEN THINGS WERE AT THEIR WORST, WE HAD GOVERNMENT PROTECTION HERE. BUT, WELL, SOMETHING HAPPENED...
LET'S JUST SAY I NO LONGER TRUST THE UPDF.
SHE'S TALKING ABOUT RAPE. THERE'S NOTHING ELSE A SOLDIER WOULD WANT FROM THIS PLACE.
PLEASE! NO! I BELONG TO GOD! I BELONG TO GOD!!
I'VE HEARD THE LRA REBELS KILL UPDF SOLDIER AND PUT ON THEIR UNIFORM TO CONFUSE THE LOCALS.
MAYBE THAT'S WHAT HAPPENE HERE. MAYBE NOT. GROUN TRUTH IS A COMPLICATED THING.
"AFTER THAT, I WENT OUT INTO THE BUSH AND STRUCK A DEAL WITH THE REBELS. THIS IS A HOUSE OF GOD, YOU SEE... THEY RESPECT THAT."
SHE TALKS AND SHE TALKS... BUT I DON'T SAY A THING.
THEN THERE'S THE CHILD. SISTER SHARON'S LITTLE HELPER.
WHAT IS YOUR NAME?

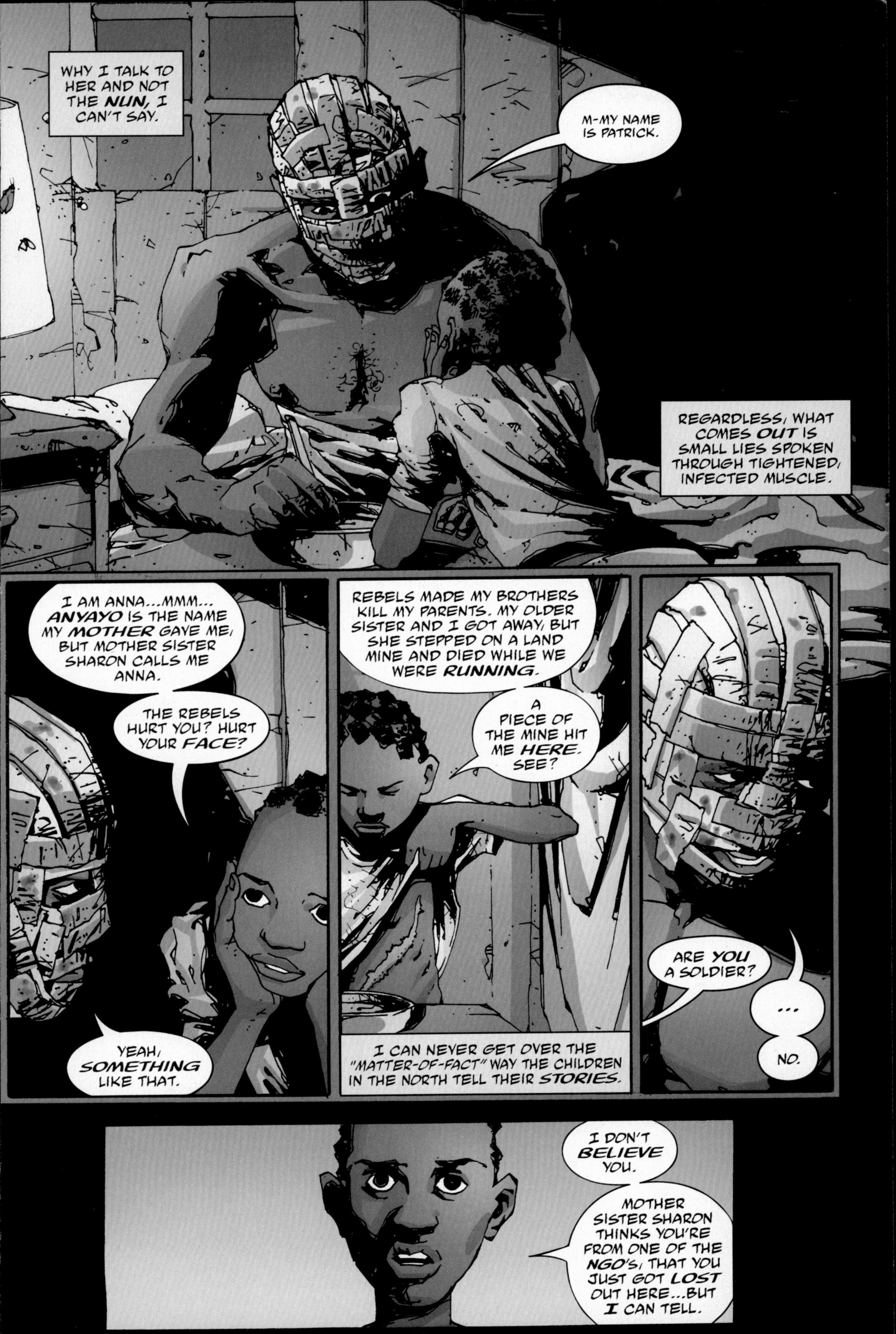
WHY I TALK TO HER AND NOT THE NUN, I CAN'T SAY.
M-MY NAME IS PATRICK.
REGARDLESS, WHAT COMES OUT IS SMALL LIES SPOKEN THROUGH TIGHTENED, INFECTED MUSCLE.
I AM ANNA...MMM... ANYAYO IS THE NAME MY MOTHER GAVE ME, BUT MOTHER SISTER SHARON CALLS ME ANNA.
THE REBELS HURT YOU? HURT YOUR FACE?
YEAH, SOMETHING LIKE THAT.
REBELS MADE MY BROTHERS KILL MY PARENTS. MY OLDER SISTER AND I GOT AWAY, BUT SHE STEPPED ON A LAND MINE AND DIED WHILE WE WERE RUNNING.
A PIECE OF THE MINE HIT ME HERE. SEE?
I CAN NEVER GET OVER THE "MATTER-OF-FACT" WAY THE CHILDREN IN THE NORTH TELL THEIR STORIES.
ARE YOU A SOLDIER?
...
NO.
I DON'T BELIEVE YOU.
MOTHER SISTER SHARON THINKS YOU'RE FROM ONE OF THE NGO'S, THAT YOU JUST GOT LOST OUT HERE...BUT I CAN TELL.

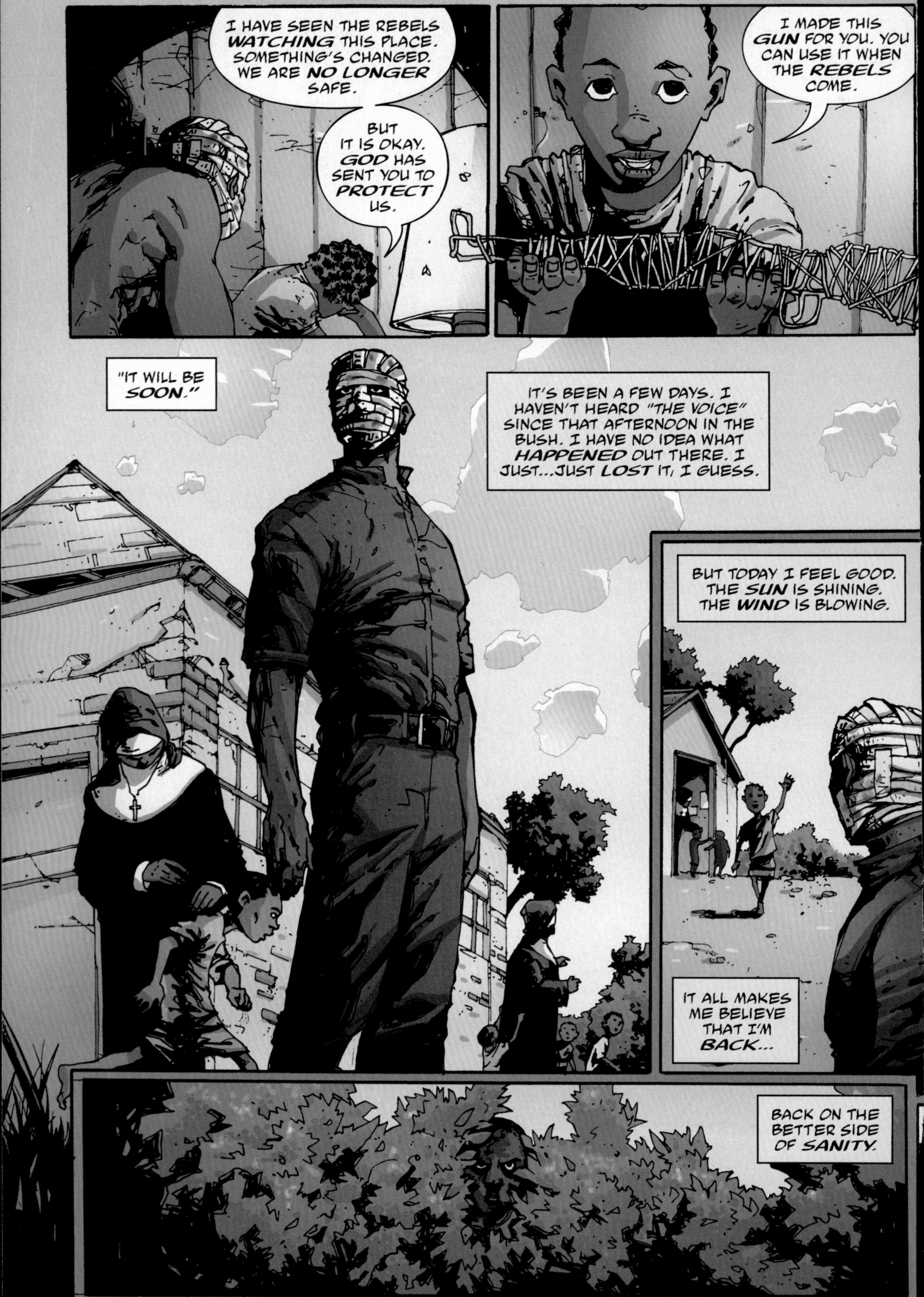

I HAVE SEEN THE REBELS WATCHING THIS PLACE. SOMETHING'S CHANGED. WE ARE NO LONGER SAFE.
BUT IT IS OKAY. GOD HAS SENT YOU TO PROTECT US.
I MADE THIS GUN FOR YOU. YOU CAN USE IT WHEN THE REBELS COME.
"IT WILL BE SOON."
IT'S BEEN A FEW DAYS. I HAVEN'T HEARD "THE VOICE" SINCE THAT AFTERNOON IN THE BUSH. I HAVE NO IDEA WHAT HAPPENED OUT THERE. I JUST...JUST LOST IT, I GUESS.
BUT TODAY I FEEL GOOD. THE SUN IS SHINING. THE WIND IS BLOWING.
IT ALL MAKES ME BELIEVE THAT I'M BACK...
BACK ON THE BETTER SIDE OF SANITY.

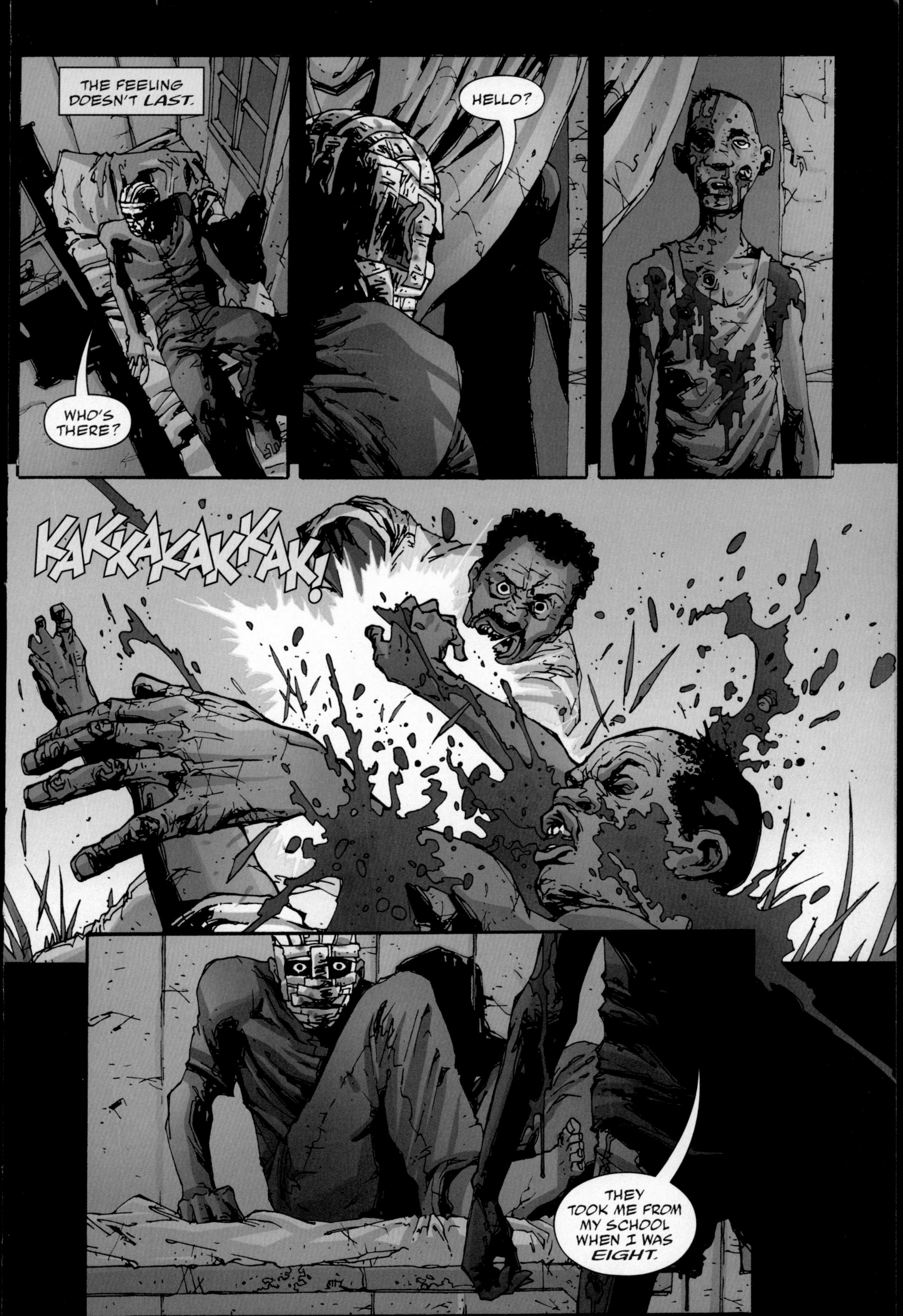
THE FEELING DOESN'T LAST.
WHO'S THERE?
HELLO?
KAKKAKAKKAK!
THEY TOOK ME FROM MY SCHOOL WHEN I WAS EIGHT.

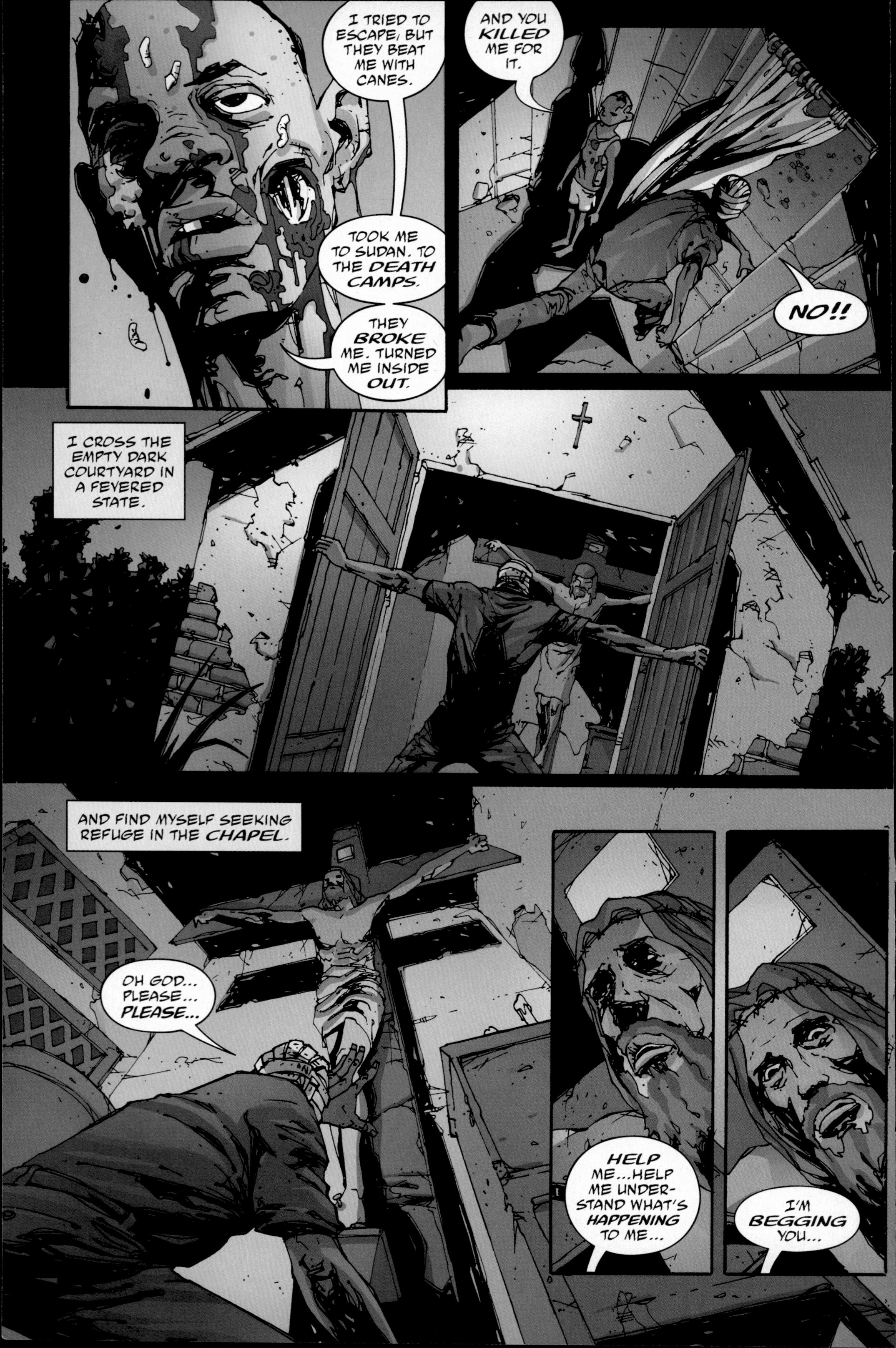
I TRIED TO ESCAPE, BUT THEY BEAT ME WITH CANES.
TOOK ME TO SUDAN. TO THE DEATH CAMPS.
THEY BROKE ME. TURNED ME INSIDE OUT.
AND YOU KILLED ME FOR IT.
NO!!
I CROSS THE EMPTY DARK COURTYARD IN A FEVERED STATE.
AND FIND MYSELF SEEKING REFUGE IN THE CHAPEL.
OH GOD... PLEASE... PLEASE...
HELP ME...HELP ME UNDERSTAND WHAT'S HAPPENING TO ME...
I'M BEGGING YOU...

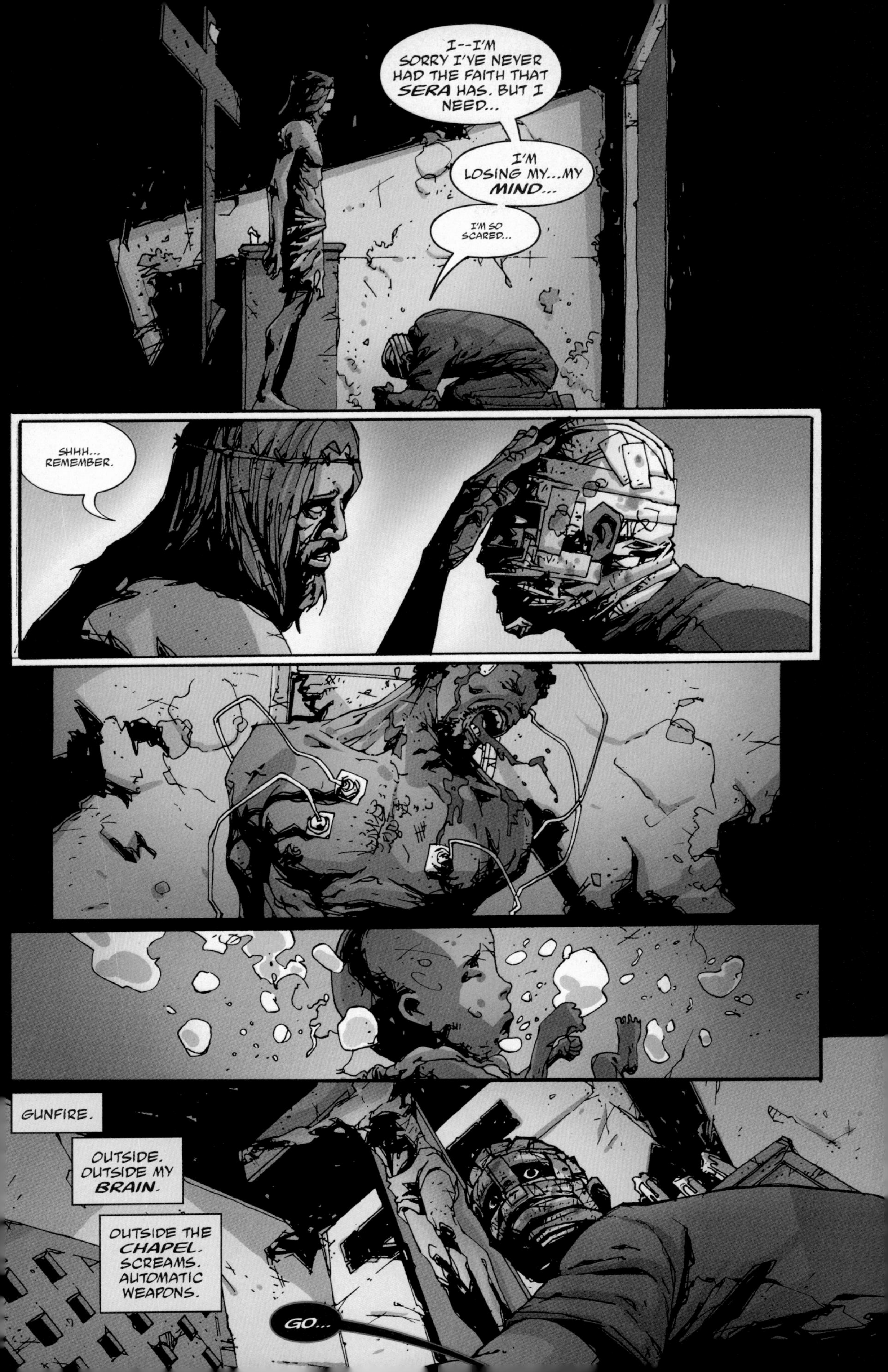
I--I'M SORRY I'VE NEVER HAD THE FAITH THAT SERA HAS. BUT I NEED...
I'M LOSING MY...MY MIND...
I'M SO SCARED...
SHHH... REMEMBER.
GUNFIRE.
OUTSIDE. OUTSIDE MY BRAIN.
OUTSIDE THE CHAPEL. SCREAMS. AUTOMATIC WEAPONS.
GO...

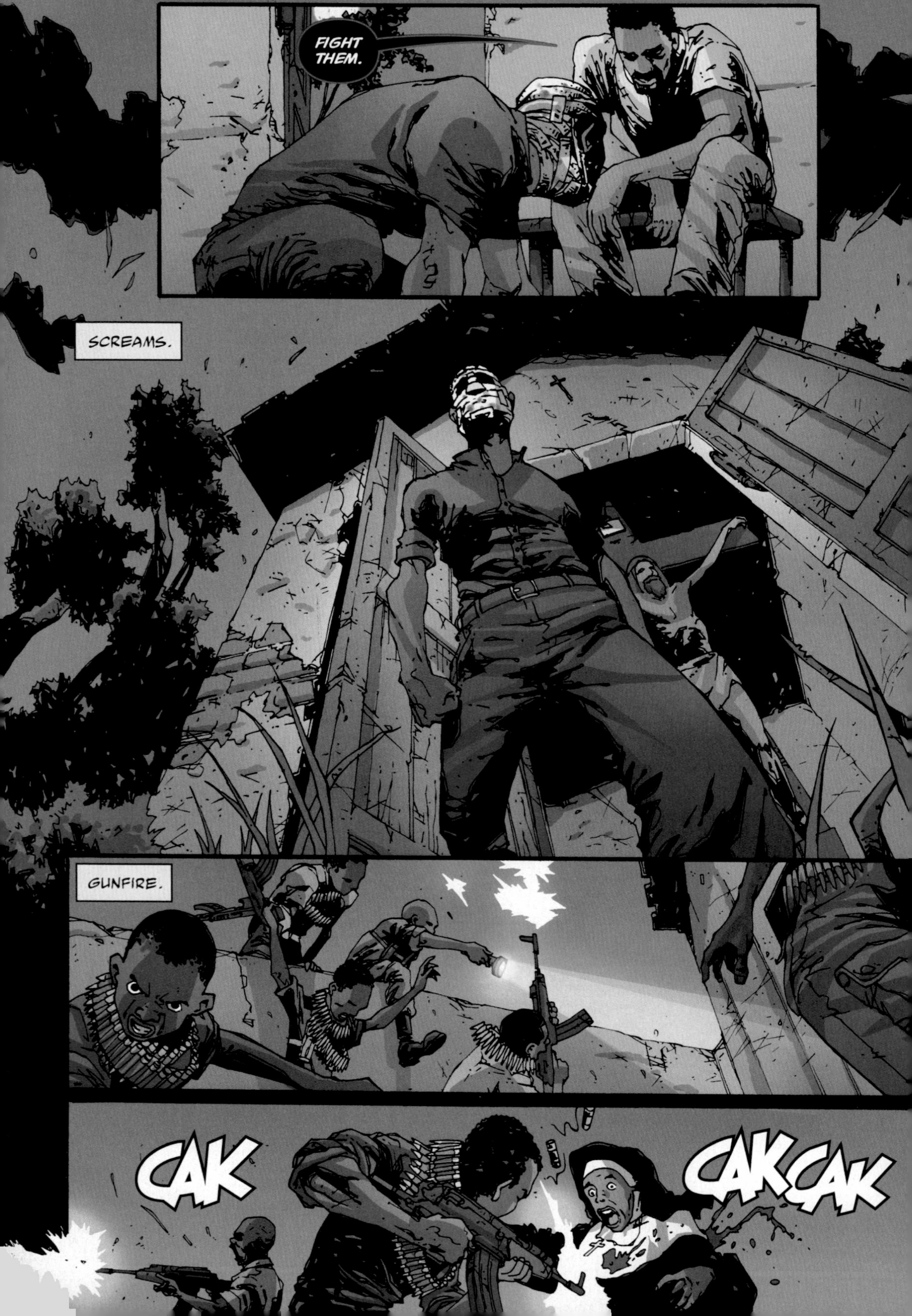
FIGHT THEM.
SCREAMS.
GUNFIRE.
CAK
CAK CAK

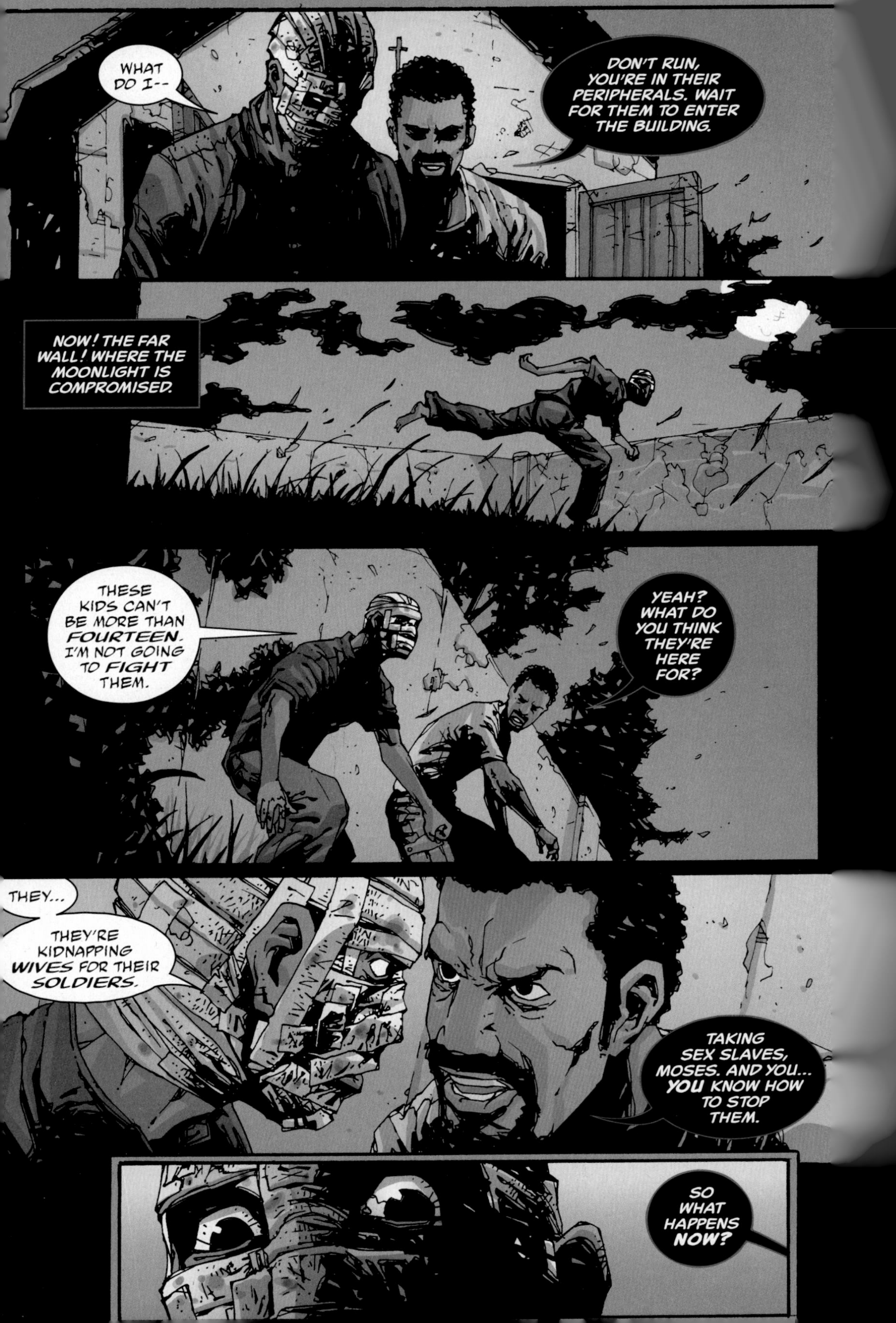
WHAT DO I--
DON'T RUN, YOU'RE IN THEIR PERIPHERALS. WAIT FOR THEM TO ENTER THE BUILDING.
NOW! THE FAR WALL! WHERE THE MOONLIGHT IS COMPROMISED.
THESE KIDS CAN'T BE MORE THAN FOURTEEN. I'M NOT GOING TO FIGHT THEM.
YEAH? WHAT DO YOU THINK THEY'RE HERE FOR?
THEY...
THEY'RE KIDNAPPING WIVES FOR THEIR SOLDIERS.
TAKING SEX SLAVES, MOSES. AND YOU... YOU KNOW HOW TO STOP THEM.
SO WHAT HAPPENS NOW?

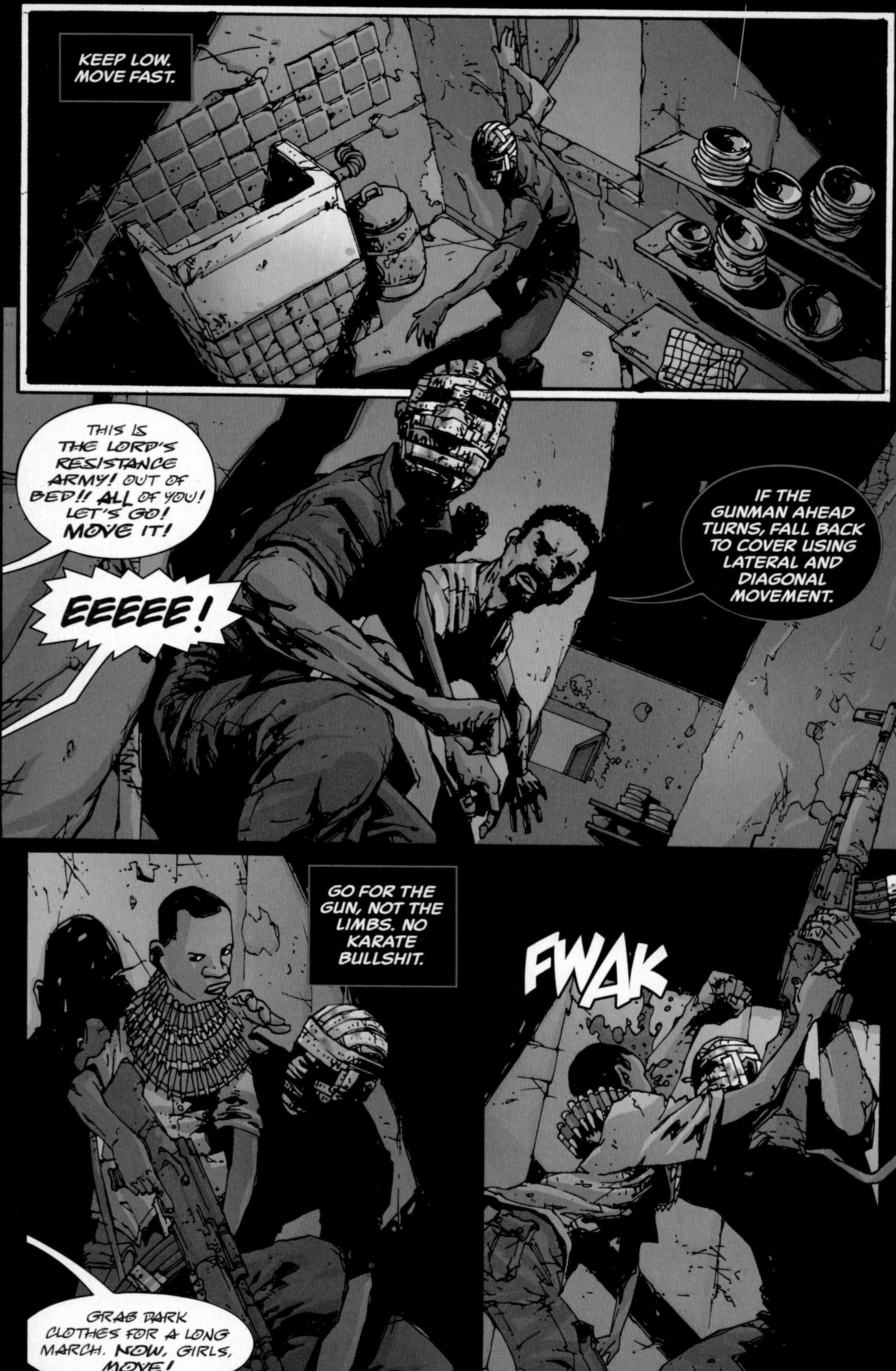
KEEP LOW. MOVE FAST.
THIS IS THE LORD'S RESISTANCE ARMY! OUT OF BED!! ALL OF YOU! LET'S GO! MOVE IT!
EEEEE!
IF THE GUNMAN AHEAD TURNS, FALL BACK TO COVER USING LATERAL AND DIAGONAL MOVEMENT.
GO FOR THE GUN, NOT THE LIMBS. NO KARATE BULLSHIT.
GRAB DARK CLOTHES FOR A LONG MARCH. NOW, GIRLS, MOVE!
FWAK

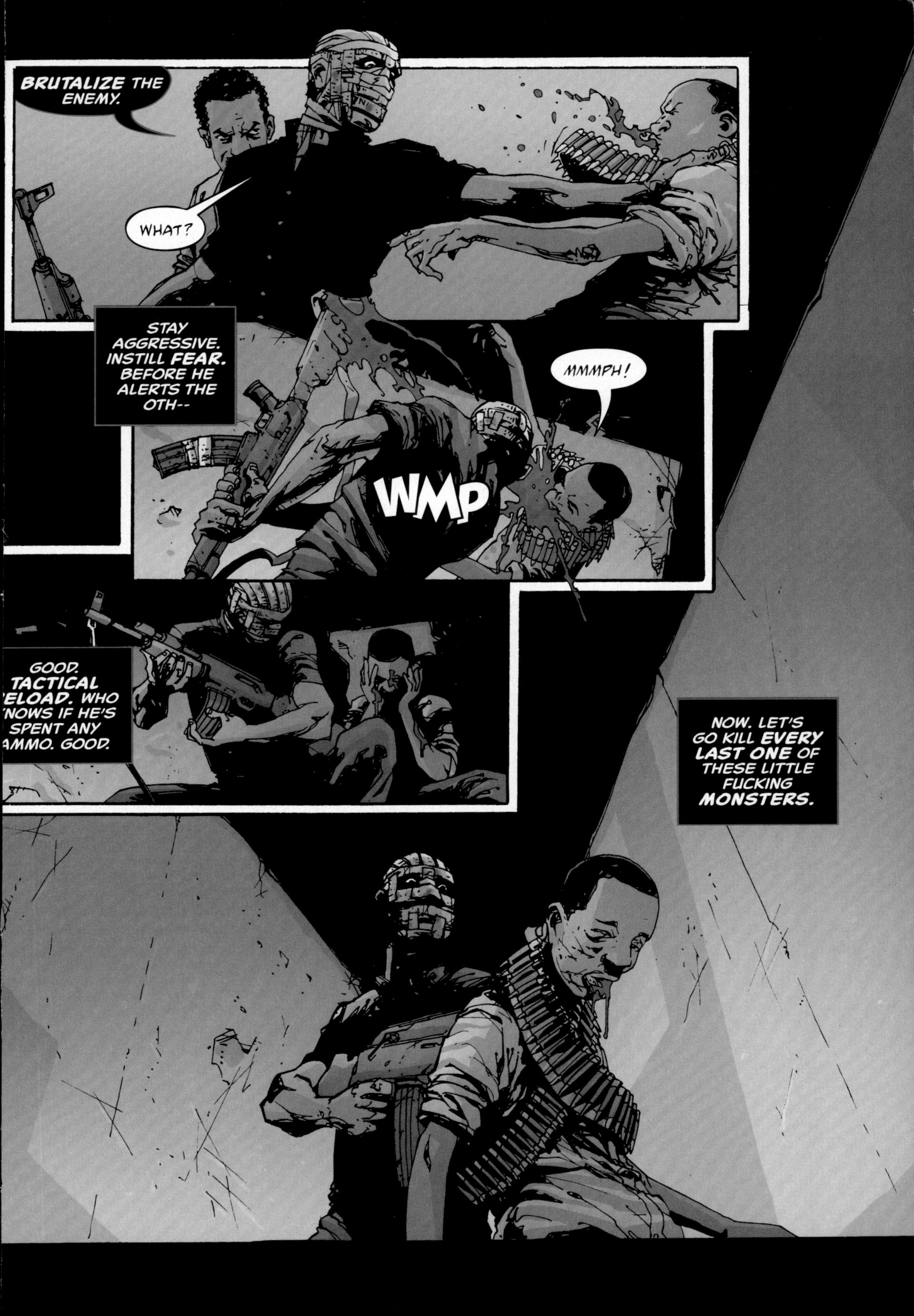
BRUTALIZE THE ENEMY.
WHAT?
STAY AGGRESSIVE. INSTILL FEAR. BEFORE HE ALERTS THE OTH--
MMMPH!
WMP
GOOD. TACTICAL RELOAD. WHO KNOWS IF HE'S SPENT ANY AMMO. GOOD.
NOW. LET'S GO KILL EVERY LAST ONE OF THESE LITTLE FUCKING MONSTERS.

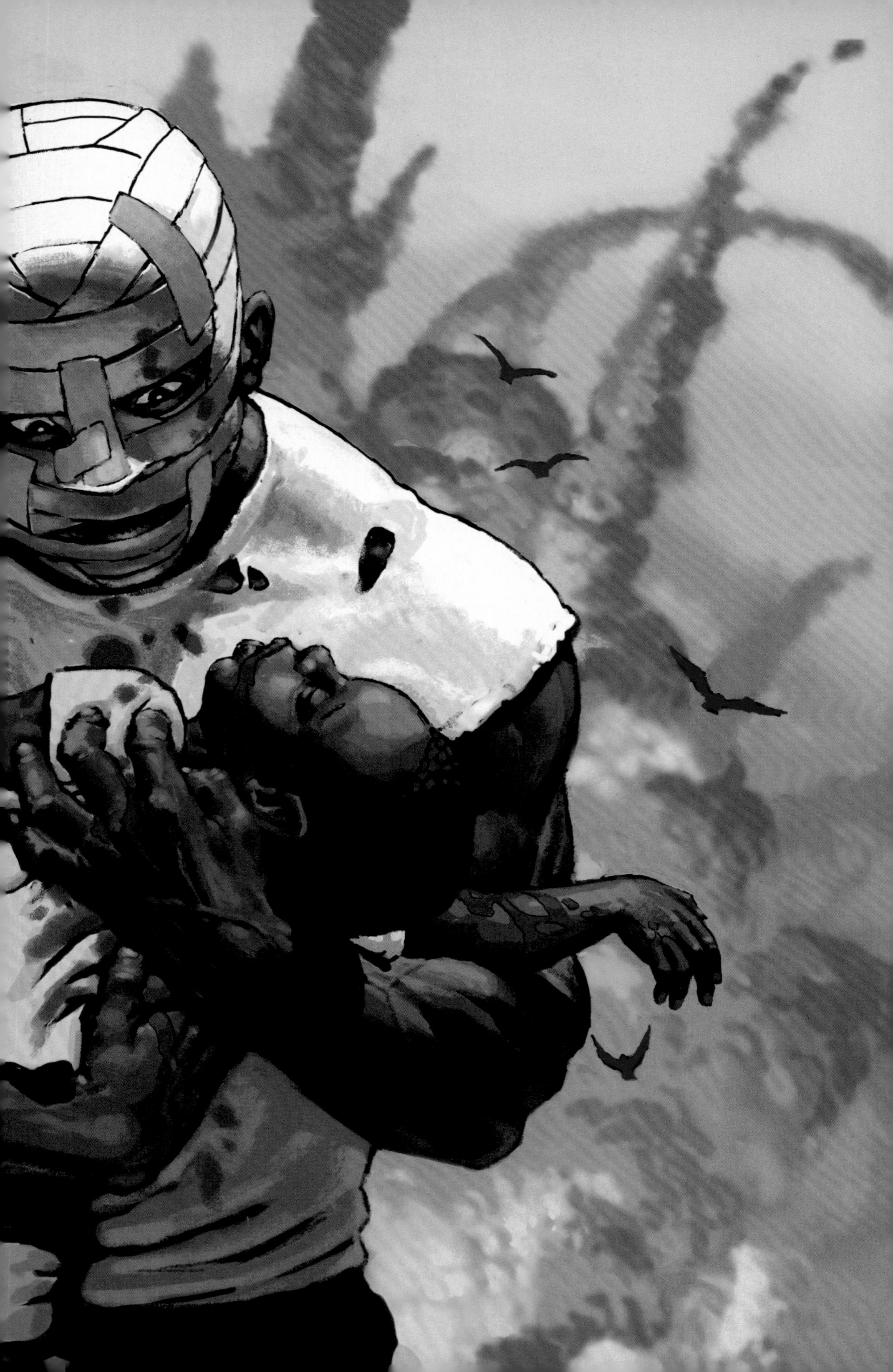

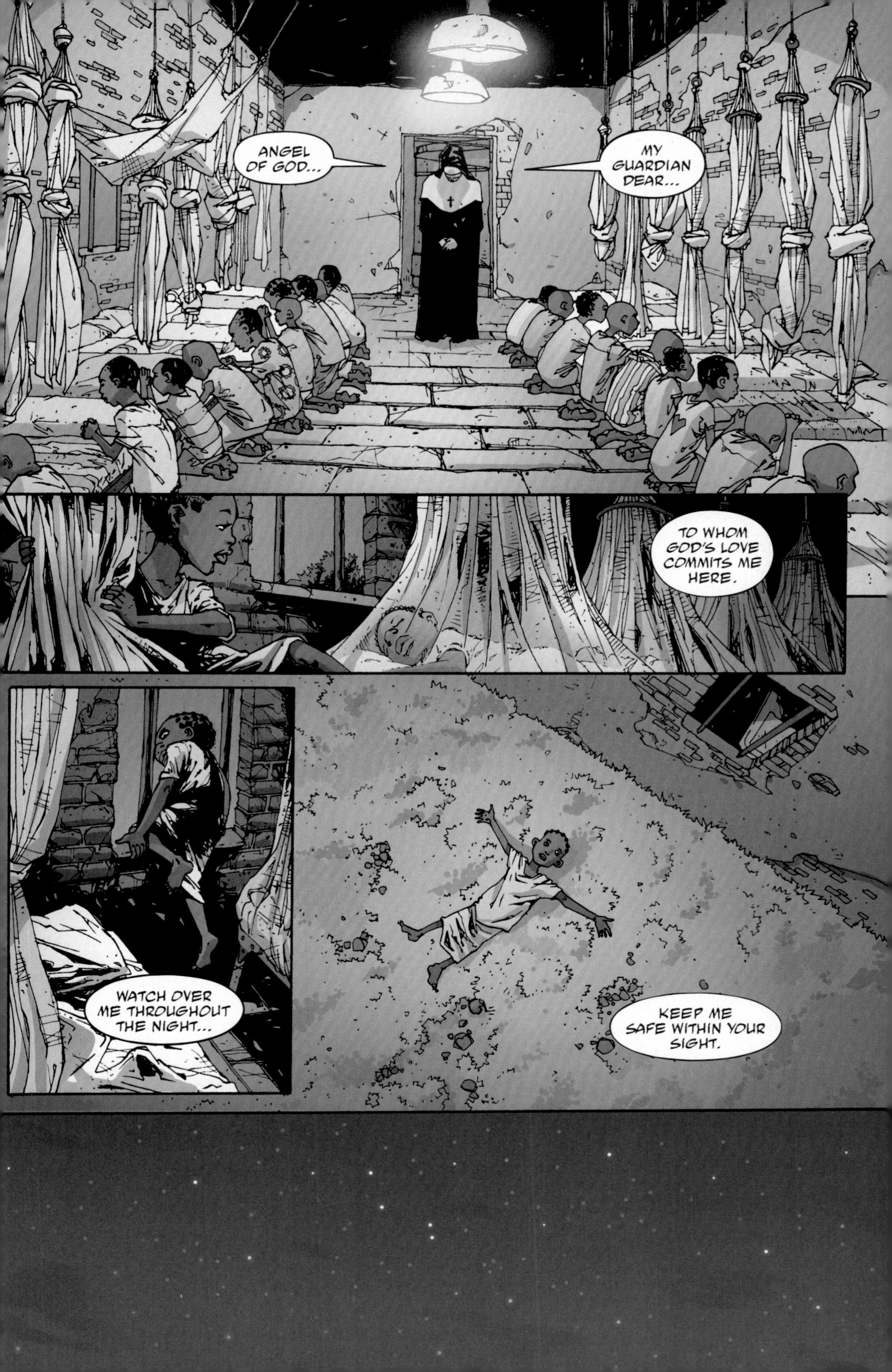
ANGEL OF GOD...
MY GUARDIAN DEAR...
TO WHOM GOD'S LOVE COMMITS ME HERE.
WATCH OVER ME THROUGHOUT THE NIGHT...
KEEP ME SAFE WITHIN YOUR SIGHT.

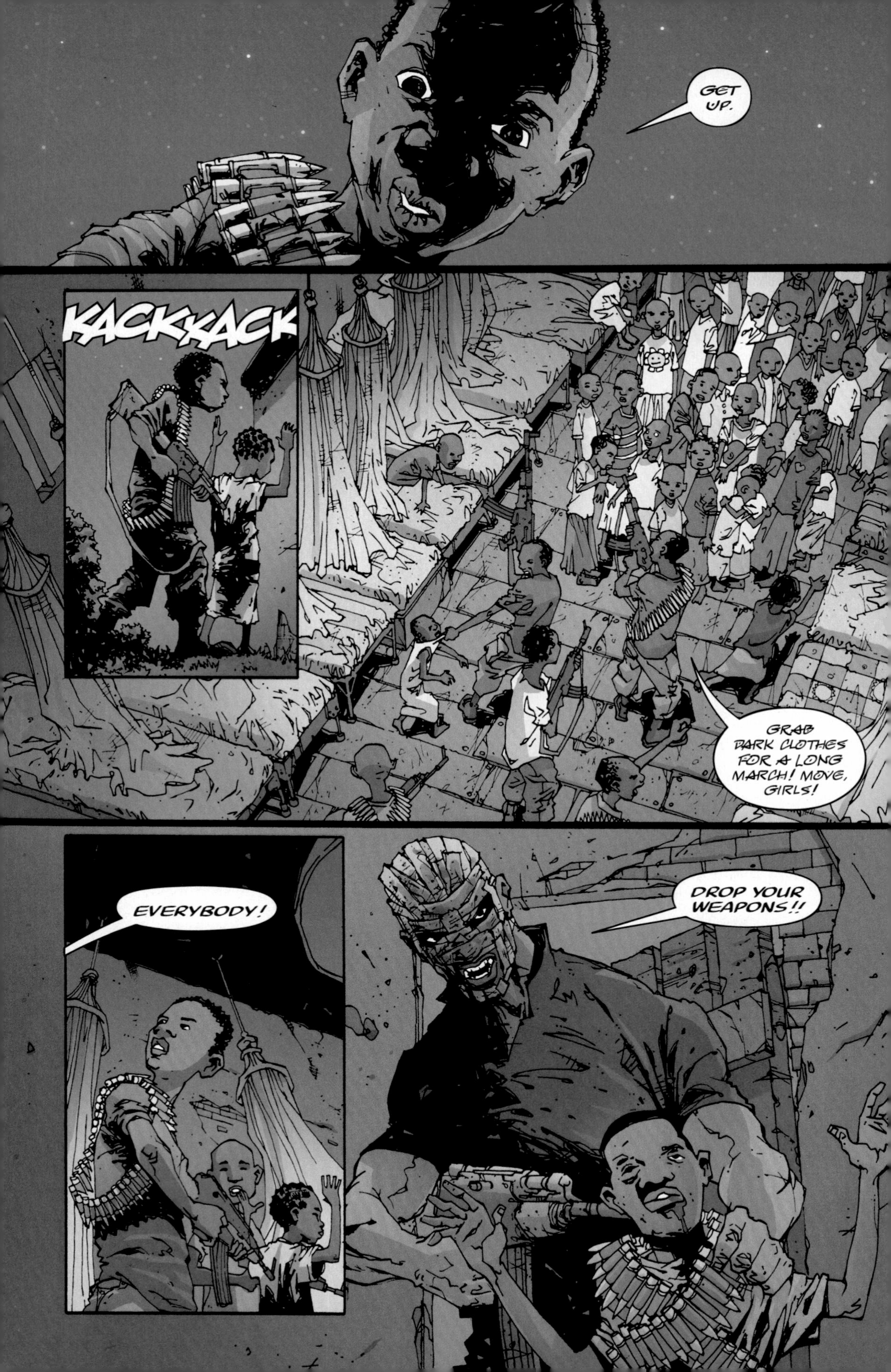
GET UP.
KACKKACK
GRAB DARK CLOTHES FOR A LONG MARCH! MOVE, GIRLS!
EVERYBODY!
DROP YOUR WEAPONS!!

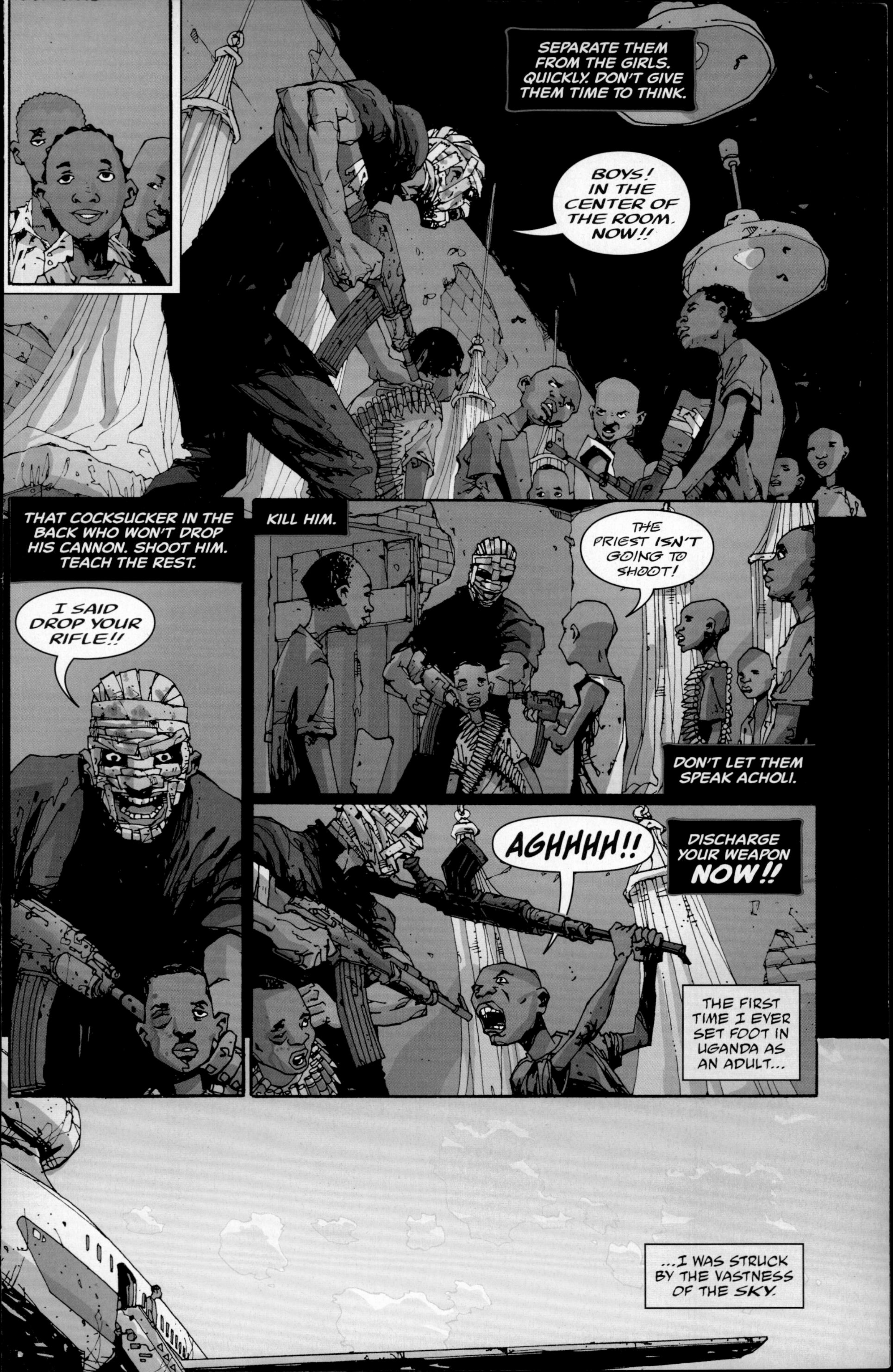
SEPARATE THEM FROM THE GIRLS. QUICKLY. DON'T GIVE THEM TIME TO THINK.
BOYS! IN THE CENTER OF THE ROOM. NOW!!
THAT COCKSUCKER IN THE BACK WHO WON'T DROP HIS CANNON. SHOOT HIM. TEACH THE REST.
I SAID DROP YOUR RIFLE!!
KILL HIM.
THE PRIEST ISN'T GOING TO SHOOT!
DON'T LET THEM SPEAK ACHOLI.
AGHHHH!!
DISCHARGE YOUR WEAPON NOW!!
THE FIRST TIME I EVER SET FOOT IN UGANDA AS AN ADULT...
...I WAS STRUCK BY THE VASTNESS OF THE SKY.

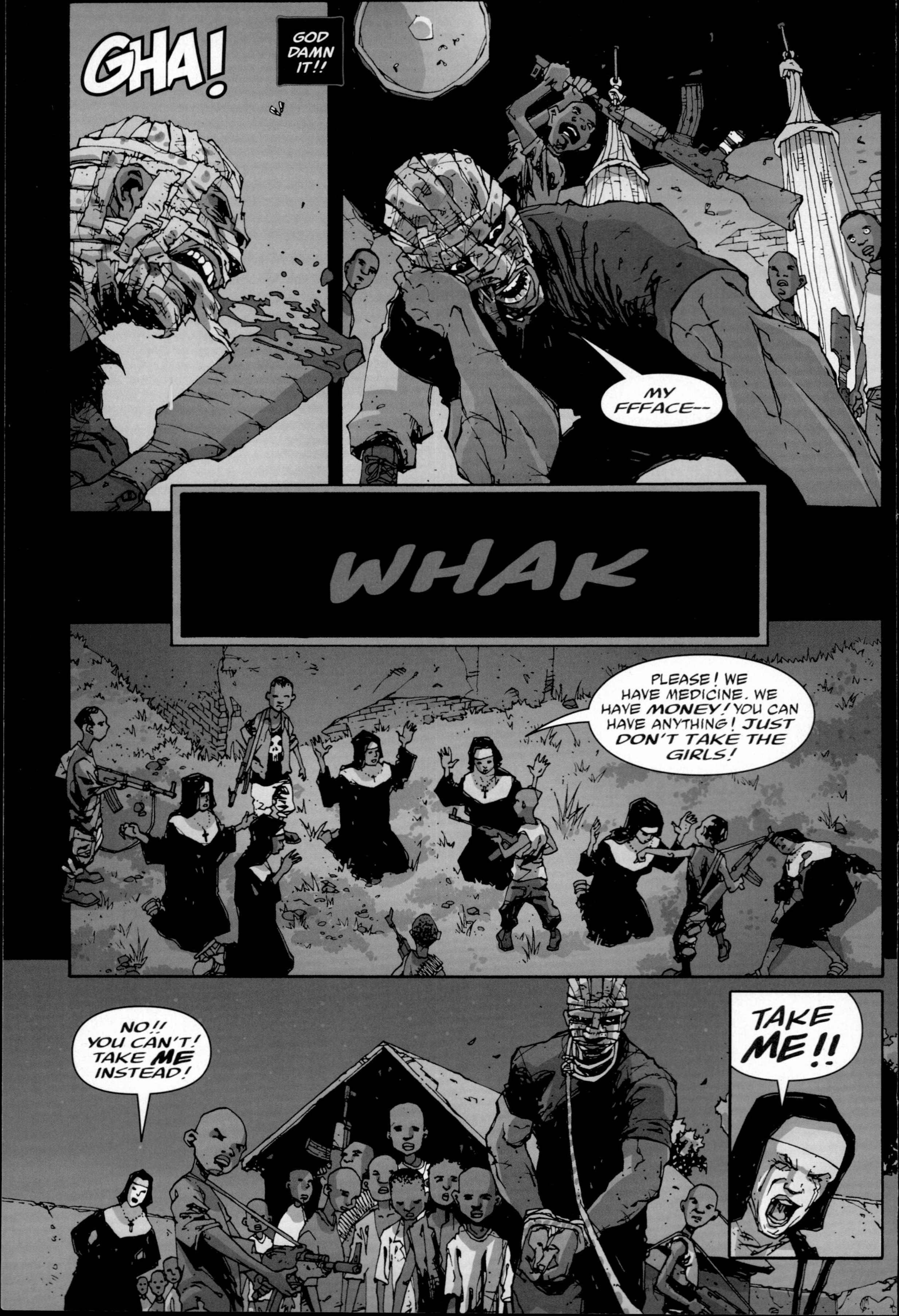
GHA!
GOD DAMN IT!!
MY FFFACE--
WHAK
PLEASE! WE HAVE MEDICINE. WE HAVE MONEY! YOU CAN HAVE ANYTHING! JUST DON'T TAKE THE GIRLS!
NO!! YOU CAN'T! TAKE ME INSTEAD!
TAKE ME!!

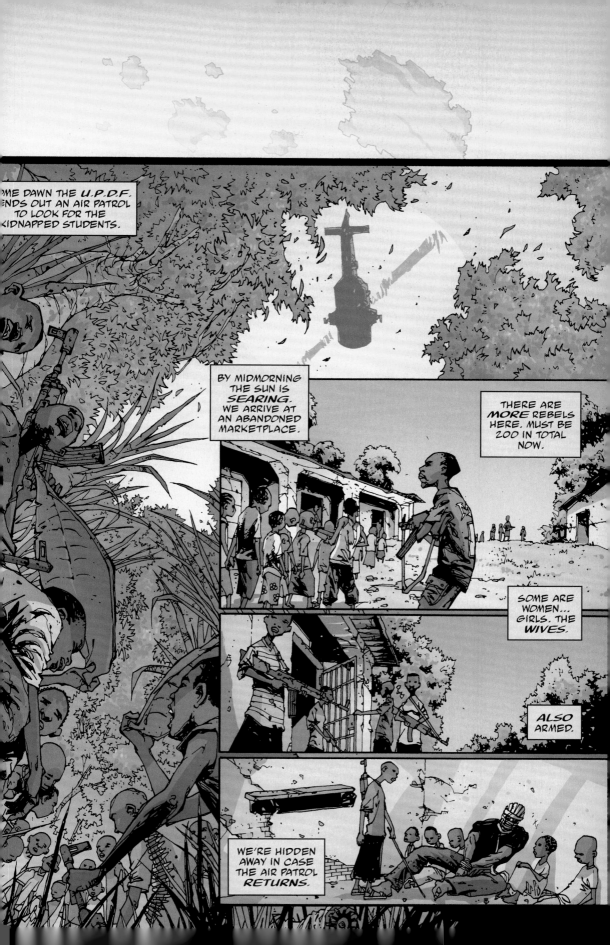

[CO]ME DAWN THE *U.P.D.F.* [SE]NDS OUT AN AIR PATROL TO LOOK FOR THE [K]IDNAPPED STUDENTS.

BY MIDMORNING THE SUN IS *SEARING*. WE ARRIVE AT AN ABANDONED MARKETPLACE.

THERE ARE *MORE* REBELS HERE. MUST BE 200 IN TOTAL NOW.

SOME ARE WOMEN... GIRLS. THE *WIVES*.

ALSO ARMED.

WE'RE HIDDEN AWAY IN CASE THE AIR PATROL *RETURNS*.

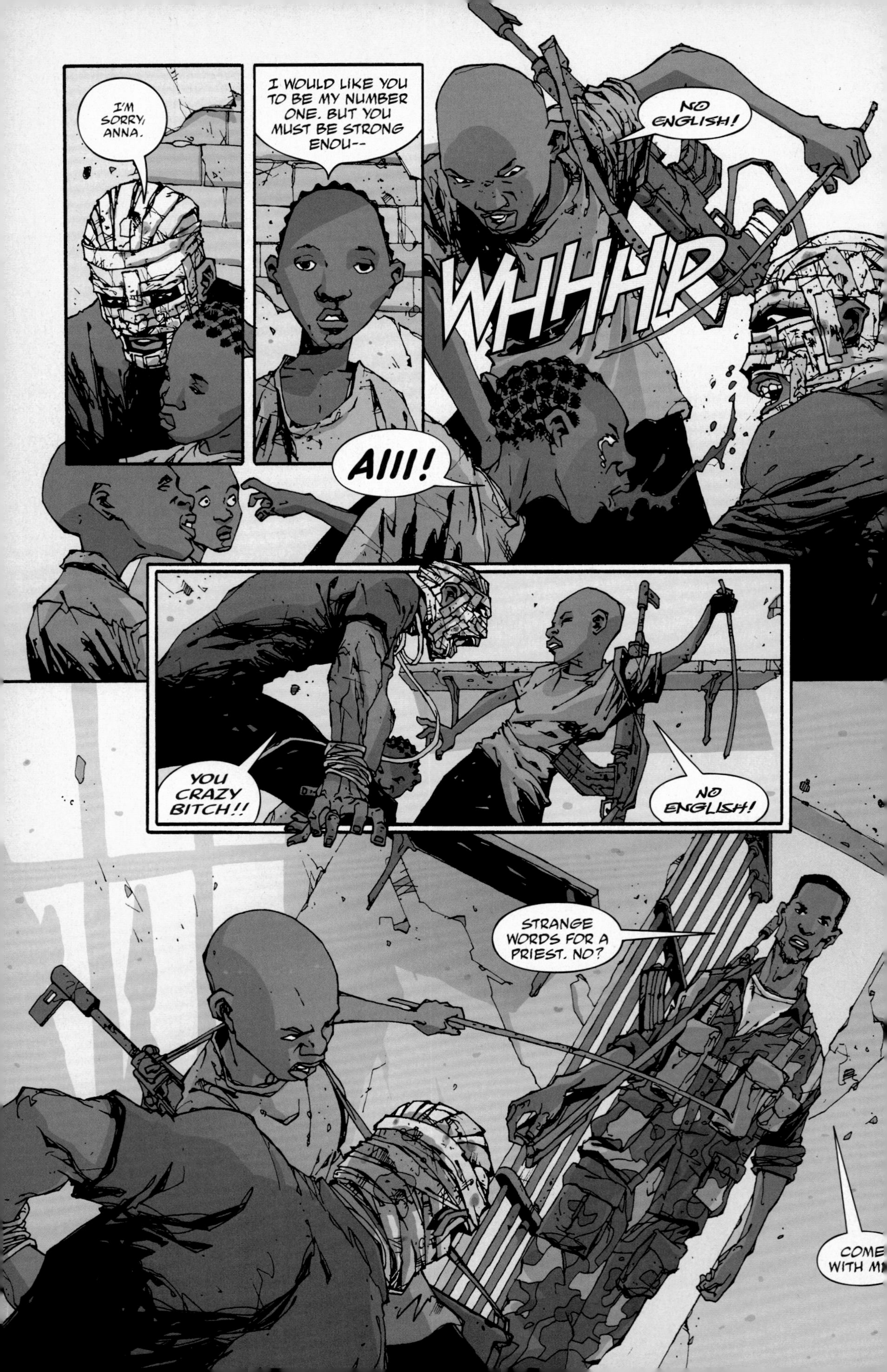
I'M SORRY, ANNA.
I WOULD LIKE YOU TO BE MY NUMBER ONE. BUT YOU MUST BE STRONG ENOU--
NO ENGLISH!
WHHHP
AIII!
YOU CRAZY BITCH!!
NO ENGLISH!
STRANGE WORDS FOR A PRIEST. NO?
COME WITH M

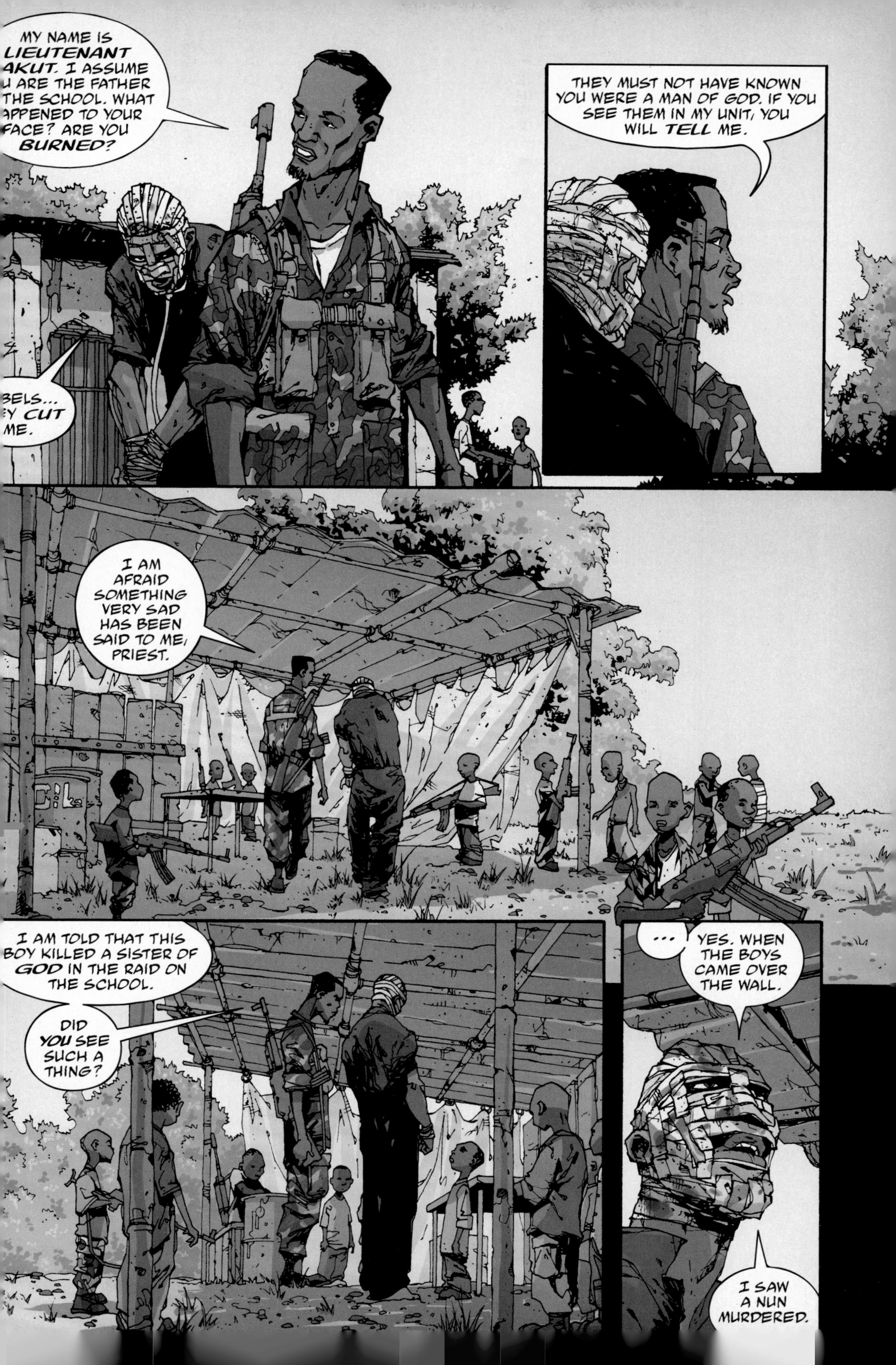
MY NAME IS LIEUTENANT AKUT. I ASSUME U ARE THE FATHER THE SCHOOL. WHAT APPENED TO YOUR FACE? ARE YOU BURNED?
BELS... EY CUT ME.
THEY MUST NOT HAVE KNOWN YOU WERE A MAN OF GOD. IF YOU SEE THEM IN MY UNIT, YOU WILL TELL ME.
I AM AFRAID SOMETHING VERY SAD HAS BEEN SAID TO ME, PRIEST.
I AM TOLD THAT THIS BOY KILLED A SISTER OF GOD IN THE RAID ON THE SCHOOL.
DID YOU SEE SUCH A THING?
...
YES. WHEN THE BOYS CAME OVER THE WALL.
I SAW A NUN MURDERED.

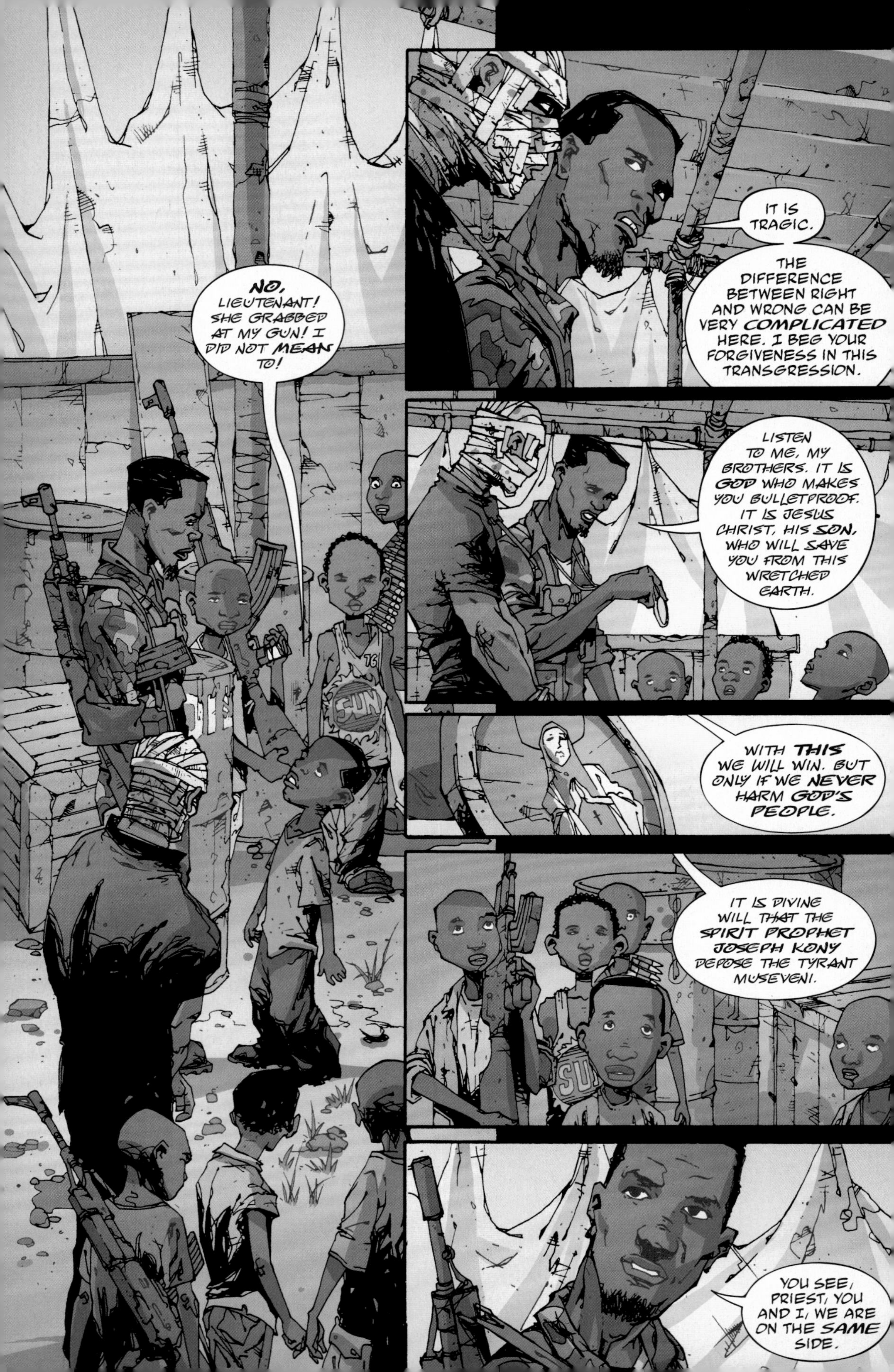
NO, LIEUTENANT! SHE GRABBED AT MY GUN! I DID NOT MEAN TO!
IT IS TRAGIC.
THE DIFFERENCE BETWEEN RIGHT AND WRONG CAN BE VERY COMPLICATED HERE. I BEG YOUR FORGIVENESS IN THIS TRANSGRESSION.
LISTEN TO ME, MY BROTHERS. IT IS GOD WHO MAKES YOU BULLETPROOF. IT IS JESUS CHRIST, HIS SON, WHO WILL SAVE YOU FROM THIS WRETCHED EARTH.
WITH THIS WE WILL WIN. BUT ONLY IF WE NEVER HARM GOD'S PEOPLE.
IT IS DIVINE WILL THAT THE SPIRIT PROPHET JOSEPH KONY DEPOSE THE TYRANT MUSEVENI.
YOU SEE, PRIEST, YOU AND I, WE ARE ON THE SAME SIDE.

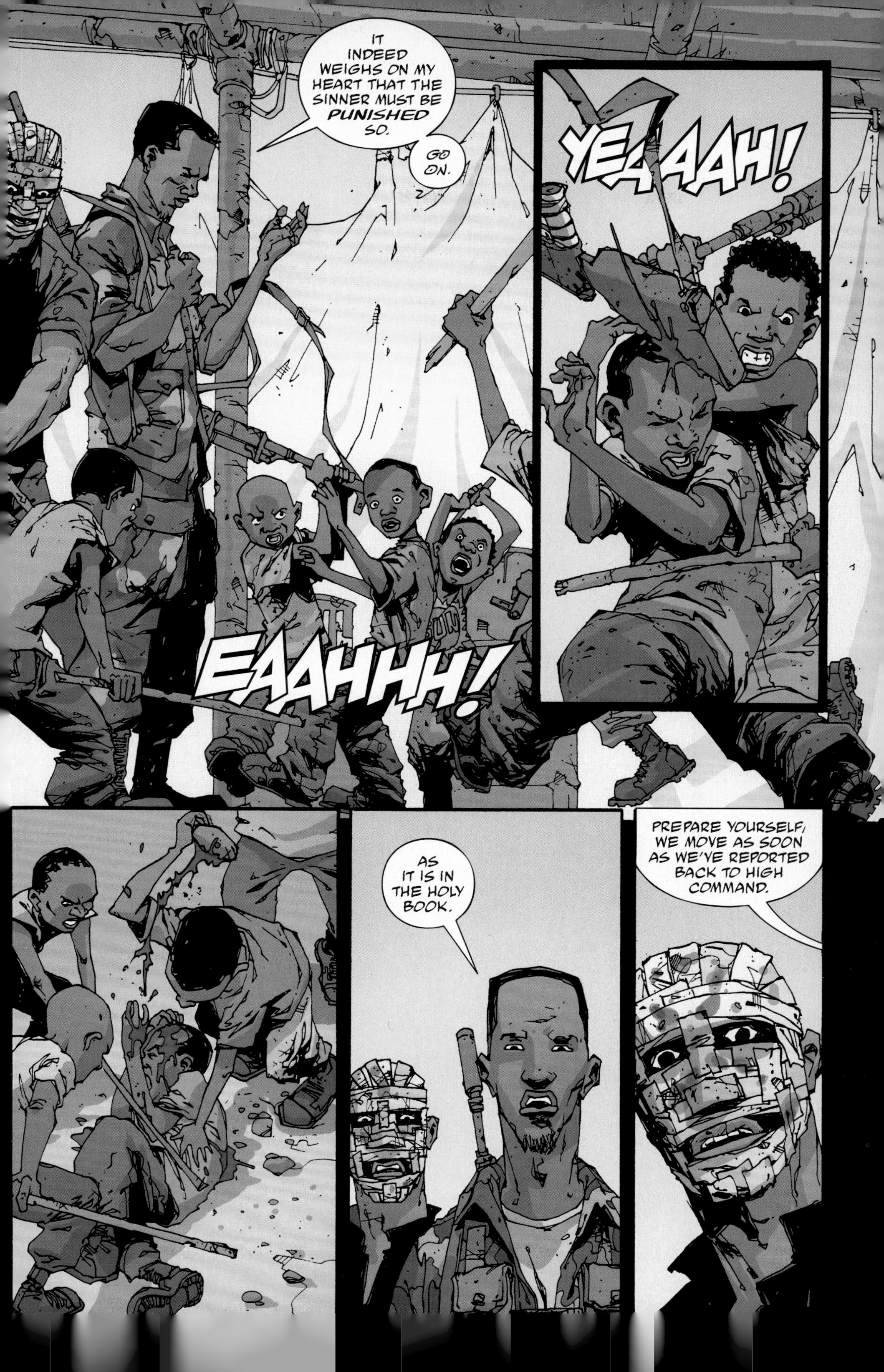
IT INDEED WEIGHS ON MY HEART THAT THE SINNER MUST BE PUNISHED SO.
GO ON.
YEAAAH!
EAAHHH!
AS IT IS IN THE HOLY BOOK.
PREPARE YOURSELF, WE MOVE AS SOON AS WE'VE REPORTED BACK TO HIGH COMMAND.

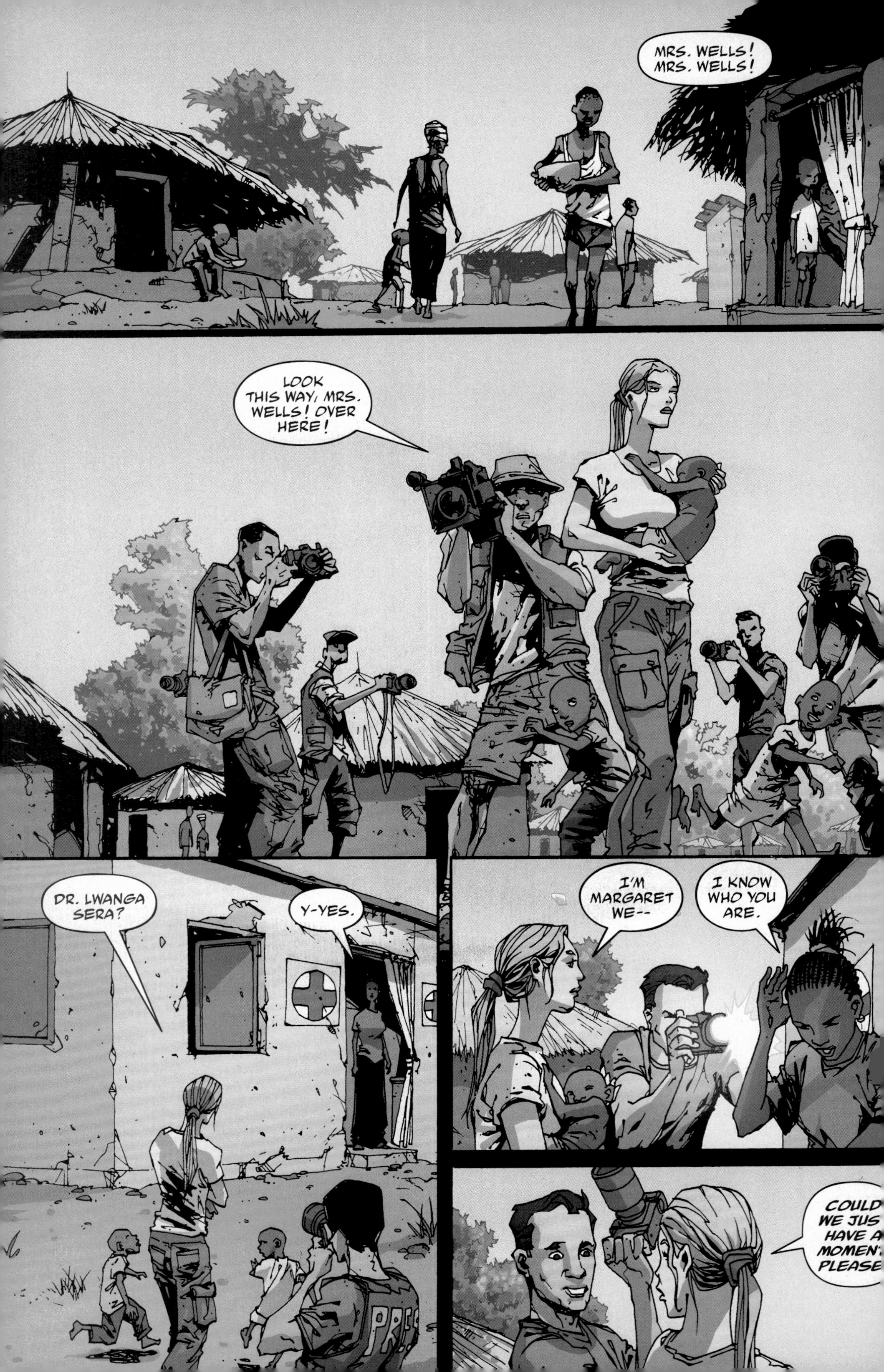
MRS. WELLS! MRS. WELLS!
LOOK THIS WAY, MRS. WELLS! OVER HERE!
DR. LWANGA SERA?
Y-YES.
I'M MARGARET WE--
I KNOW WHO YOU ARE.
COULD WE JUS HAVE A MOMEN PLEASE
PRES

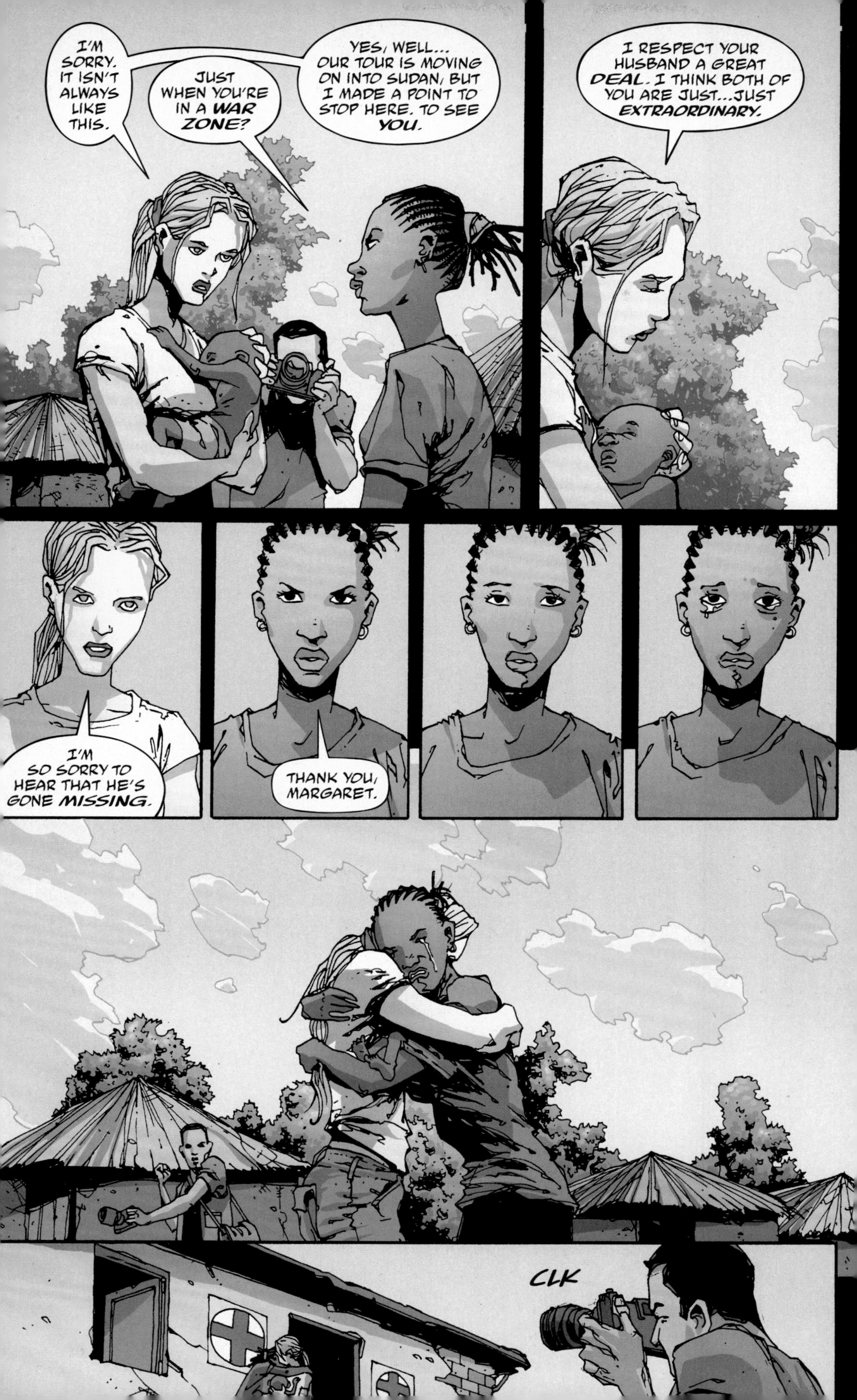
I'M SORRY. IT ISN'T ALWAYS LIKE THIS.
JUST WHEN YOU'RE IN A WAR ZONE?
YES, WELL... OUR TOUR IS MOVING ON INTO SUDAN, BUT I MADE A POINT TO STOP HERE. TO SEE YOU.
I RESPECT YOUR HUSBAND A GREAT DEAL. I THINK BOTH OF YOU ARE JUST...JUST EXTRAORDINARY.
I'M SO SORRY TO HEAR THAT HE'S GONE MISSING.
THANK YOU, MARGARET.
CLK

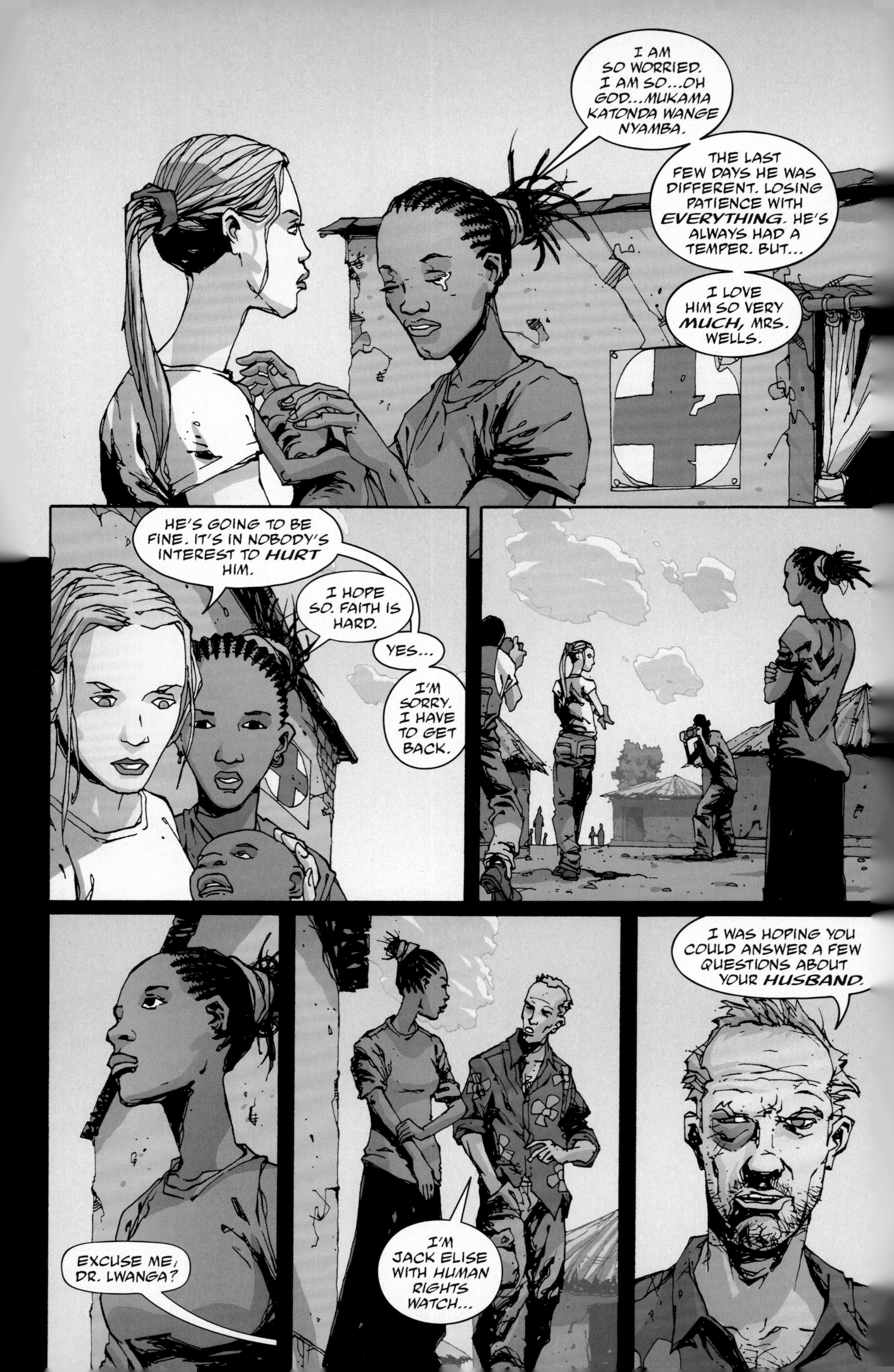
I AM SO WORRIED. I AM SO...OH GOD...MUKAMA KATONDA WANGE NYAMBA.
THE LAST FEW DAYS HE WAS DIFFERENT. LOSING PATIENCE WITH EVERYTHING. HE'S ALWAYS HAD A TEMPER. BUT...
I LOVE HIM SO VERY MUCH, MRS. WELLS.
HE'S GOING TO BE FINE. IT'S IN NOBODY'S INTEREST TO HURT HIM.
I HOPE SO. FAITH IS HARD.
YES...
I'M SORRY. I HAVE TO GET BACK.
EXCUSE ME, DR. LWANGA?
I'M JACK ELISE WITH HUMAN RIGHTS WATCH...
I WAS HOPING YOU COULD ANSWER A FEW QUESTIONS ABOUT YOUR HUSBAND.

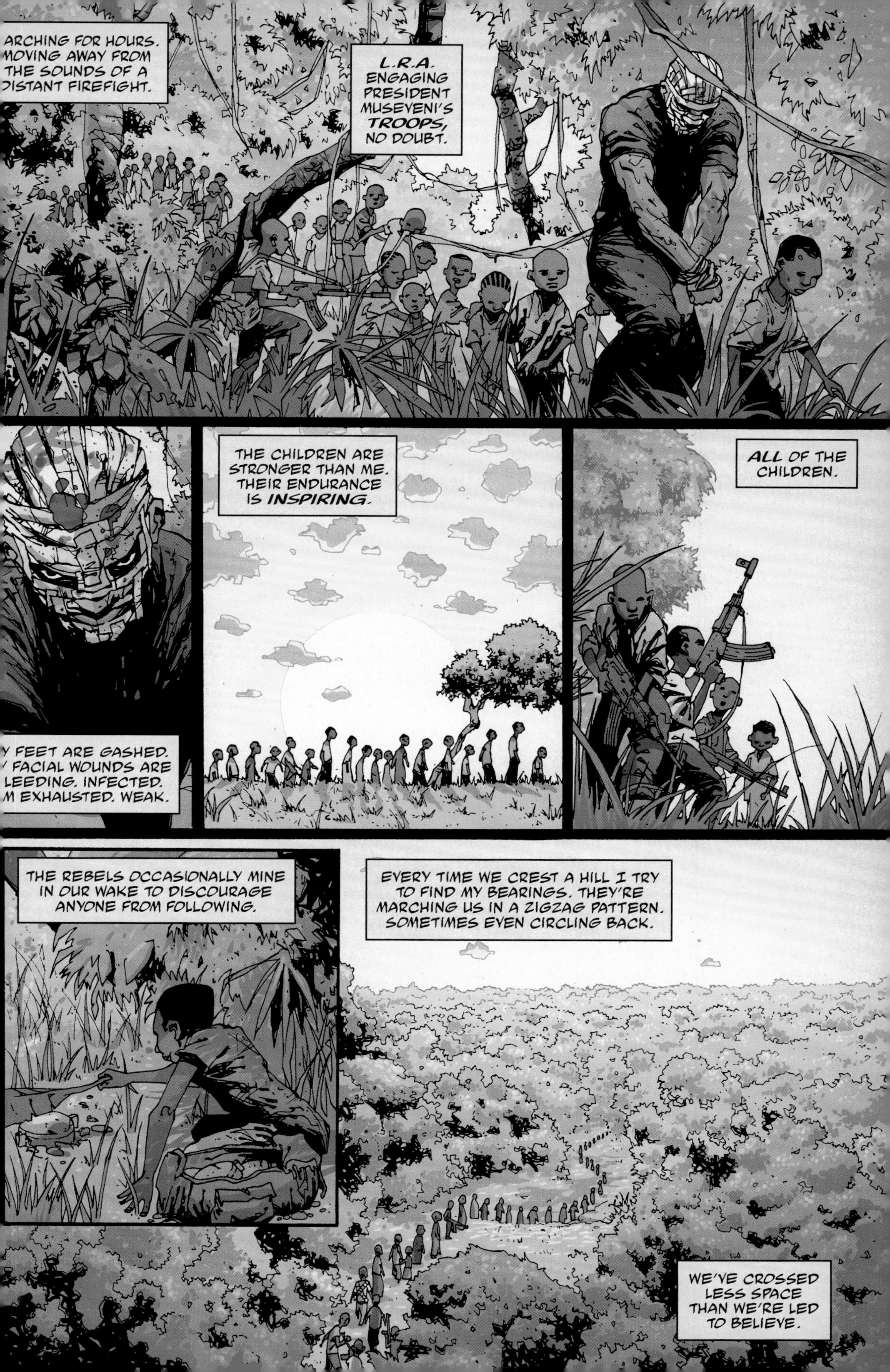

ARCHING FOR HOURS. MOVING AWAY FROM THE SOUNDS OF A DISTANT FIREFIGHT.
L.R.A. ENGAGING PRESIDENT MUSEVENI'S TROOPS, NO DOUBT.
Y FEET ARE GASHED. Y FACIAL WOUNDS ARE LEEDING. INFECTED. M EXHAUSTED. WEAK.
THE CHILDREN ARE STRONGER THAN ME. THEIR ENDURANCE IS INSPIRING.
ALL OF THE CHILDREN.
THE REBELS OCCASIONALLY MINE IN OUR WAKE TO DISCOURAGE ANYONE FROM FOLLOWING.
EVERY TIME WE CREST A HILL I TRY TO FIND MY BEARINGS. THEY'RE MARCHING US IN A ZIGZAG PATTERN. SOMETIMES EVEN CIRCLING BACK.
WE'VE CROSSED LESS SPACE THAN WE'RE LED TO BELIEVE.

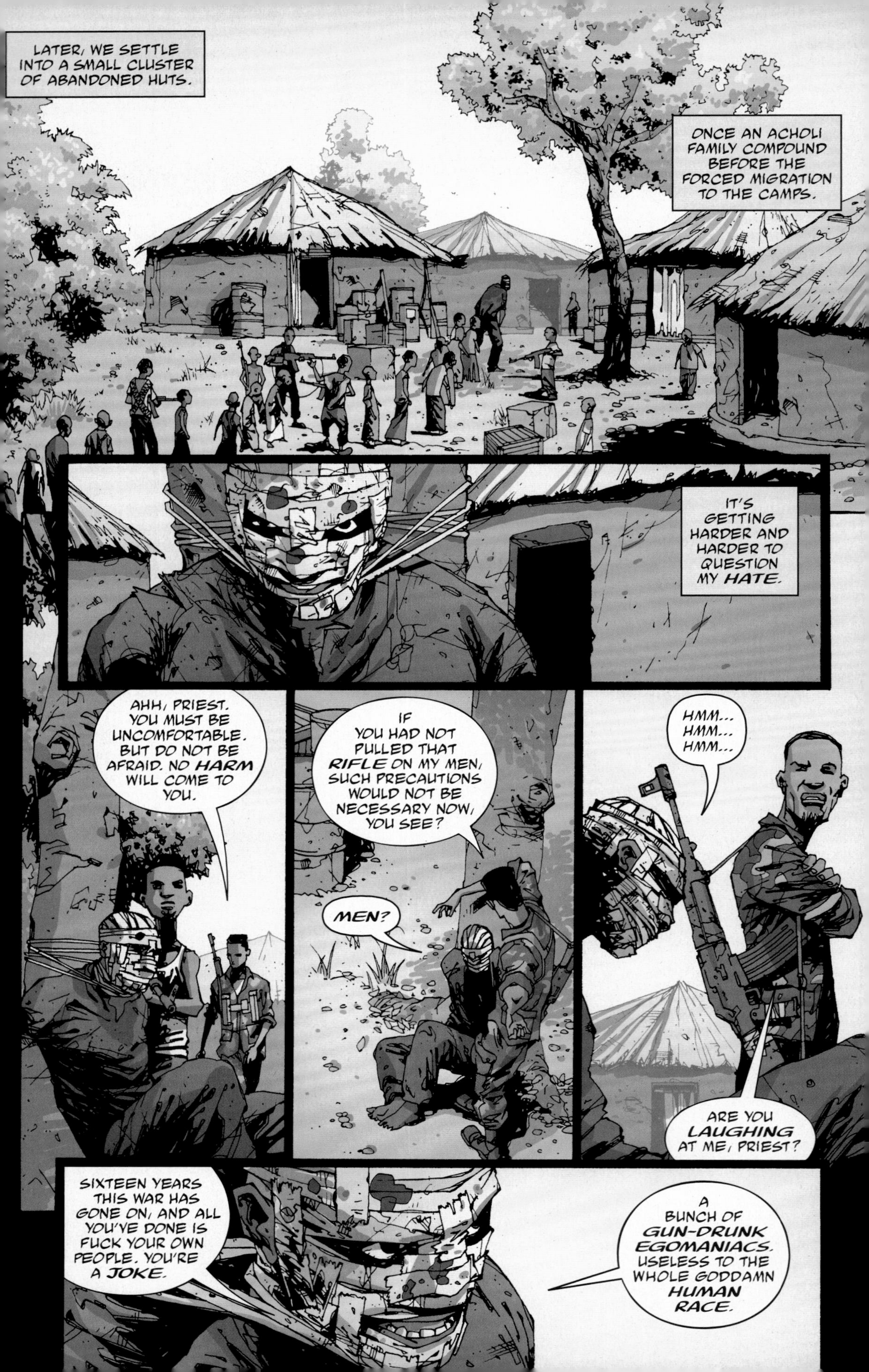
LATER, WE SETTLE INTO A SMALL CLUSTER OF ABANDONED HUTS.
ONCE AN ACHOLI FAMILY COMPOUND BEFORE THE FORCED MIGRATION TO THE CAMPS.
IT'S GETTING HARDER AND HARDER TO QUESTION MY *HATE*.
AHH, PRIEST. YOU MUST BE UNCOMFORTABLE. BUT DO NOT BE AFRAID. NO *HARM* WILL COME TO YOU.
IF YOU HAD NOT PULLED THAT *RIFLE* ON MY MEN, SUCH PRECAUTIONS WOULD NOT BE NECESSARY NOW, YOU SEE?
MEN?
HMM... HMM... HMM...
ARE YOU *LAUGHING* AT ME, PRIEST?
SIXTEEN YEARS THIS WAR HAS GONE ON, AND ALL YOU'VE DONE IS FUCK YOUR OWN PEOPLE. YOU'RE A *JOKE*.
A BUNCH OF *GUN-DRUNK EGOMANIACS*. USELESS TO THE WHOLE GODDAMN *HUMAN RACE*.

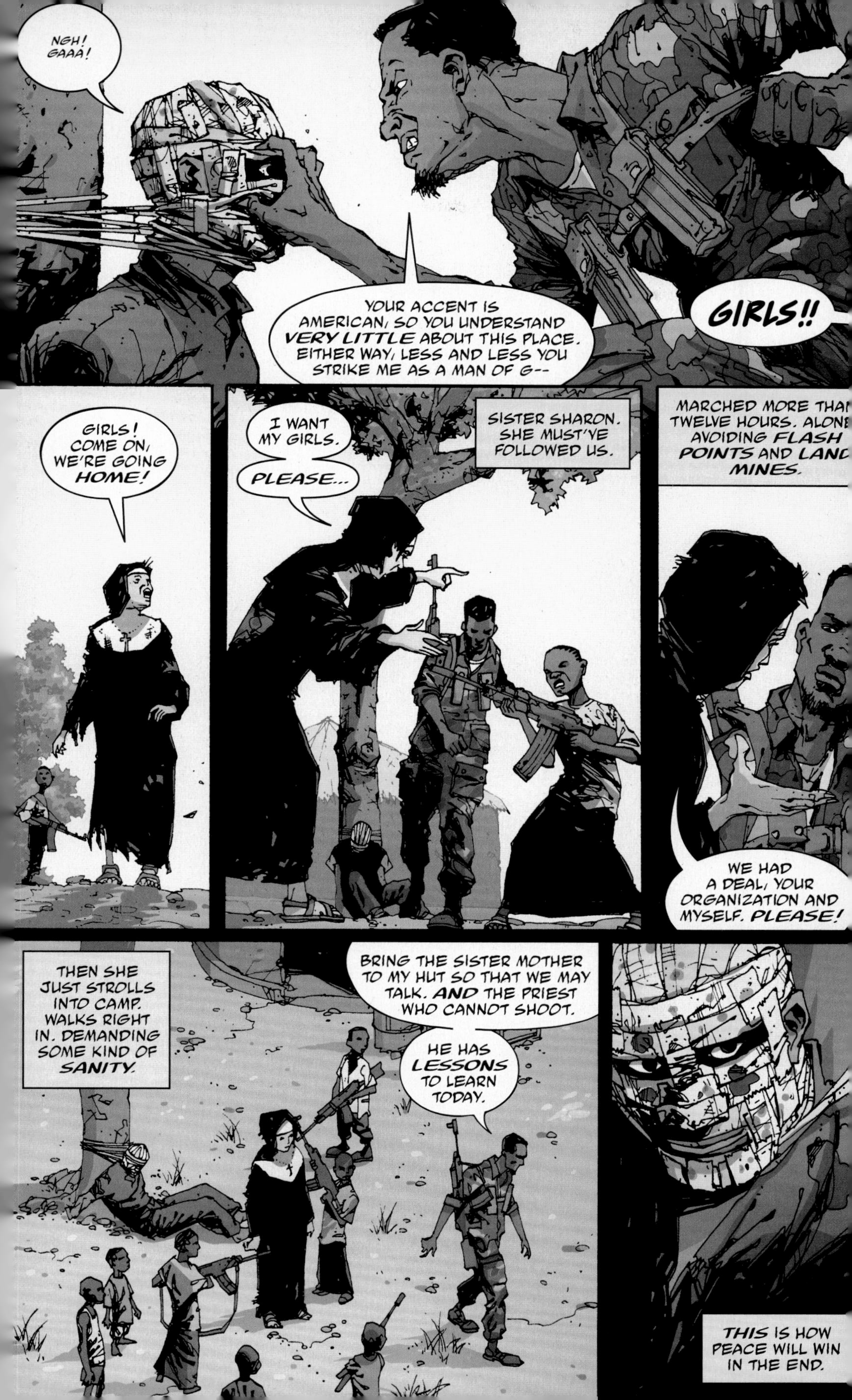
NGH! GAAA!
YOUR ACCENT IS AMERICAN, SO YOU UNDERSTAND VERY LITTLE ABOUT THIS PLACE. EITHER WAY, LESS AND LESS YOU STRIKE ME AS A MAN OF G--
GIRLS!!
GIRLS! COME ON, WE'RE GOING HOME!
I WANT MY GIRLS.
PLEASE...
SISTER SHARON. SHE MUST'VE FOLLOWED US.
MARCHED MORE THAN TWELVE HOURS. ALONE AVOIDING FLASH POINTS AND LAND MINES.
WE HAD A DEAL, YOUR ORGANIZATION AND MYSELF. PLEASE!
THEN SHE JUST STROLLS INTO CAMP. WALKS RIGHT IN. DEMANDING SOME KIND OF SANITY.
BRING THE SISTER MOTHER TO MY HUT SO THAT WE MAY TALK. AND THE PRIEST WHO CANNOT SHOOT.
HE HAS LESSONS TO LEARN TODAY.
THIS IS HOW PEACE WILL WIN IN THE END.

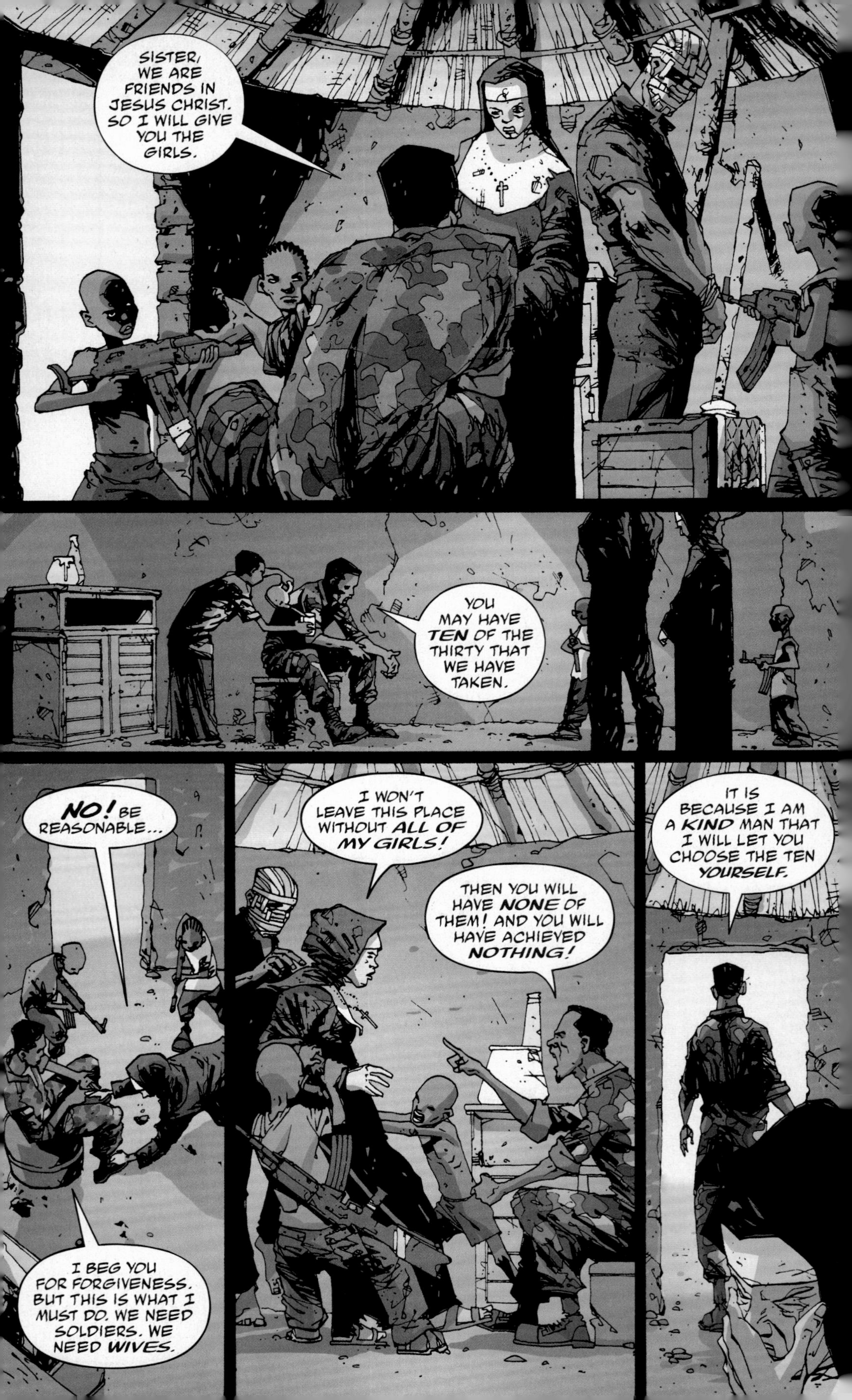
SISTER, WE ARE FRIENDS IN JESUS CHRIST. SO I WILL GIVE YOU THE GIRLS.
YOU MAY HAVE TEN OF THE THIRTY THAT WE HAVE TAKEN.
NO! BE REASONABLE...
I BEG YOU FOR FORGIVENESS. BUT THIS IS WHAT I MUST DO. WE NEED SOLDIERS. WE NEED WIVES.
I WON'T LEAVE THIS PLACE WITHOUT ALL OF MY GIRLS!
THEN YOU WILL HAVE NONE OF THEM! AND YOU WILL HAVE ACHIEVED NOTHING!
IT IS BECAUSE I AM A KIND MAN THAT I WILL LET YOU CHOOSE THE TEN YOURSELF.

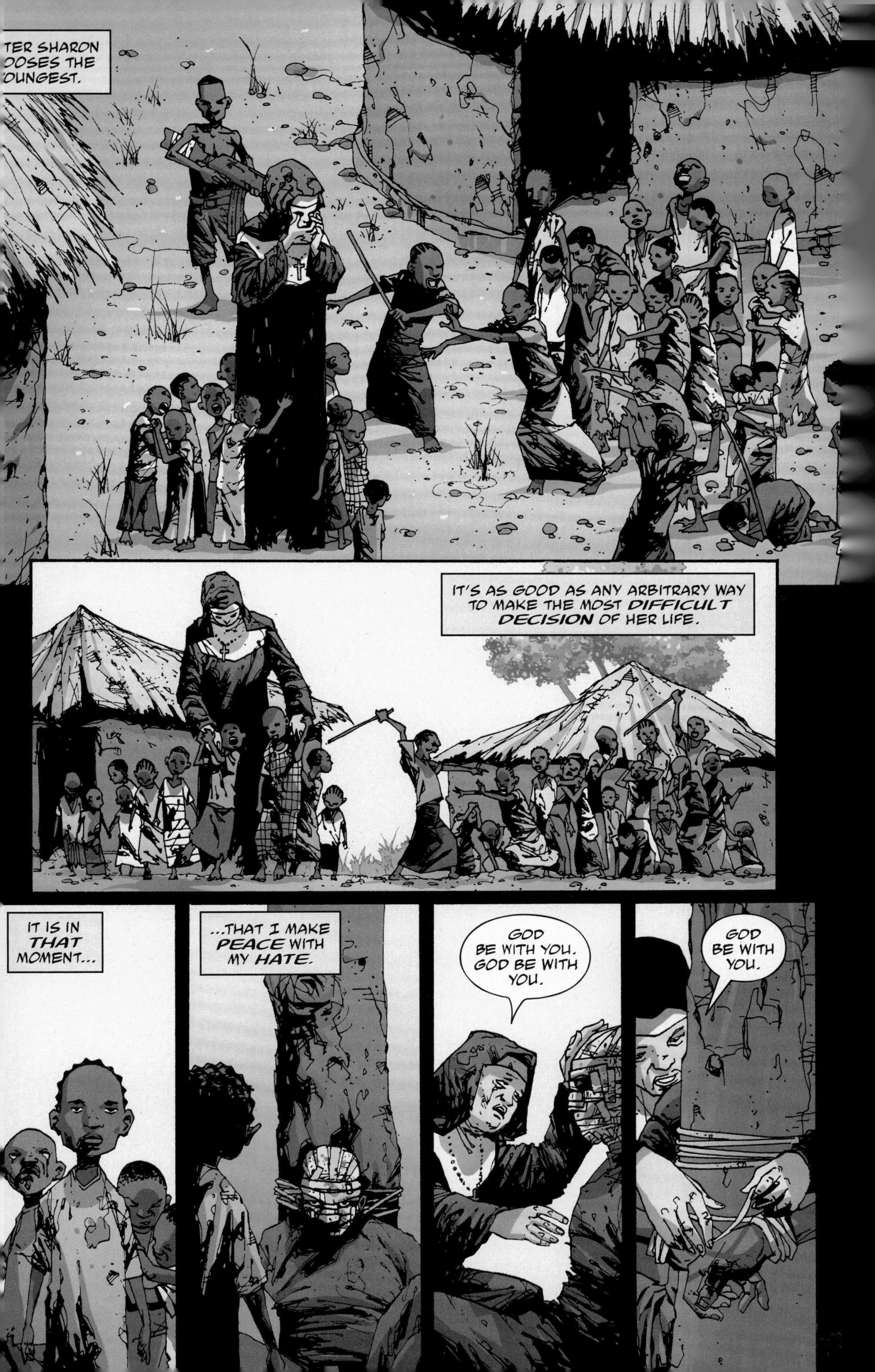
TER SHARON
OOSES THE
OUNGEST.
IT'S AS GOOD AS ANY ARBITRARY WAY TO MAKE THE MOST DIFFICULT DECISION OF HER LIFE.
IT IS IN THAT MOMENT...
...THAT I MAKE PEACE WITH MY HATE.
GOD BE WITH YOU. GOD BE WITH YOU.
GOD BE WITH YOU.

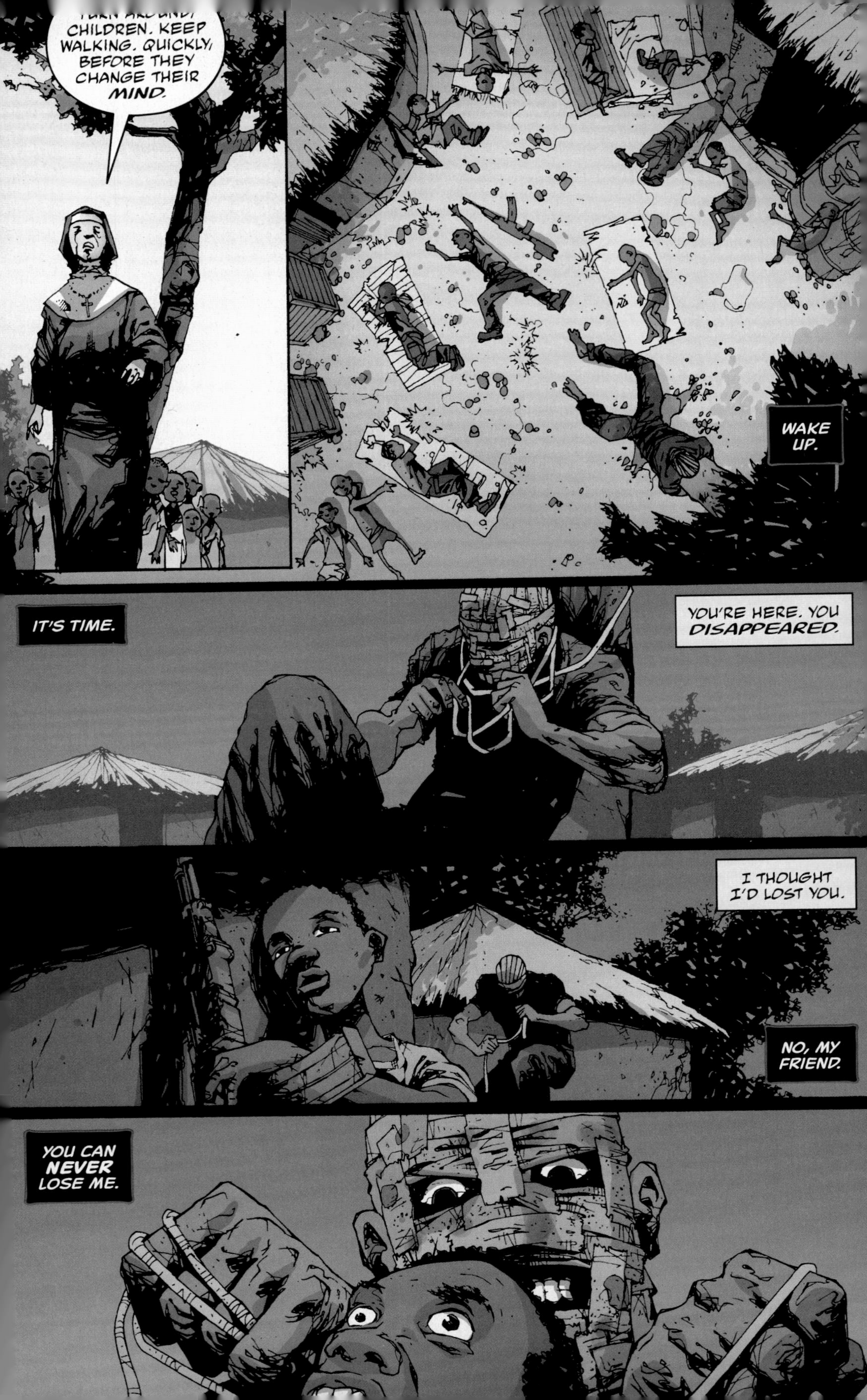
CHILDREN. KEEP WALKING. QUICKLY, BEFORE THEY CHANGE THEIR MIND.
WAKE UP.
IT'S TIME.
YOU'RE HERE. YOU DISAPPEARED.
I THOUGHT I'D LOST YOU.
NO, MY FRIEND.
YOU CAN NEVER LOSE ME.

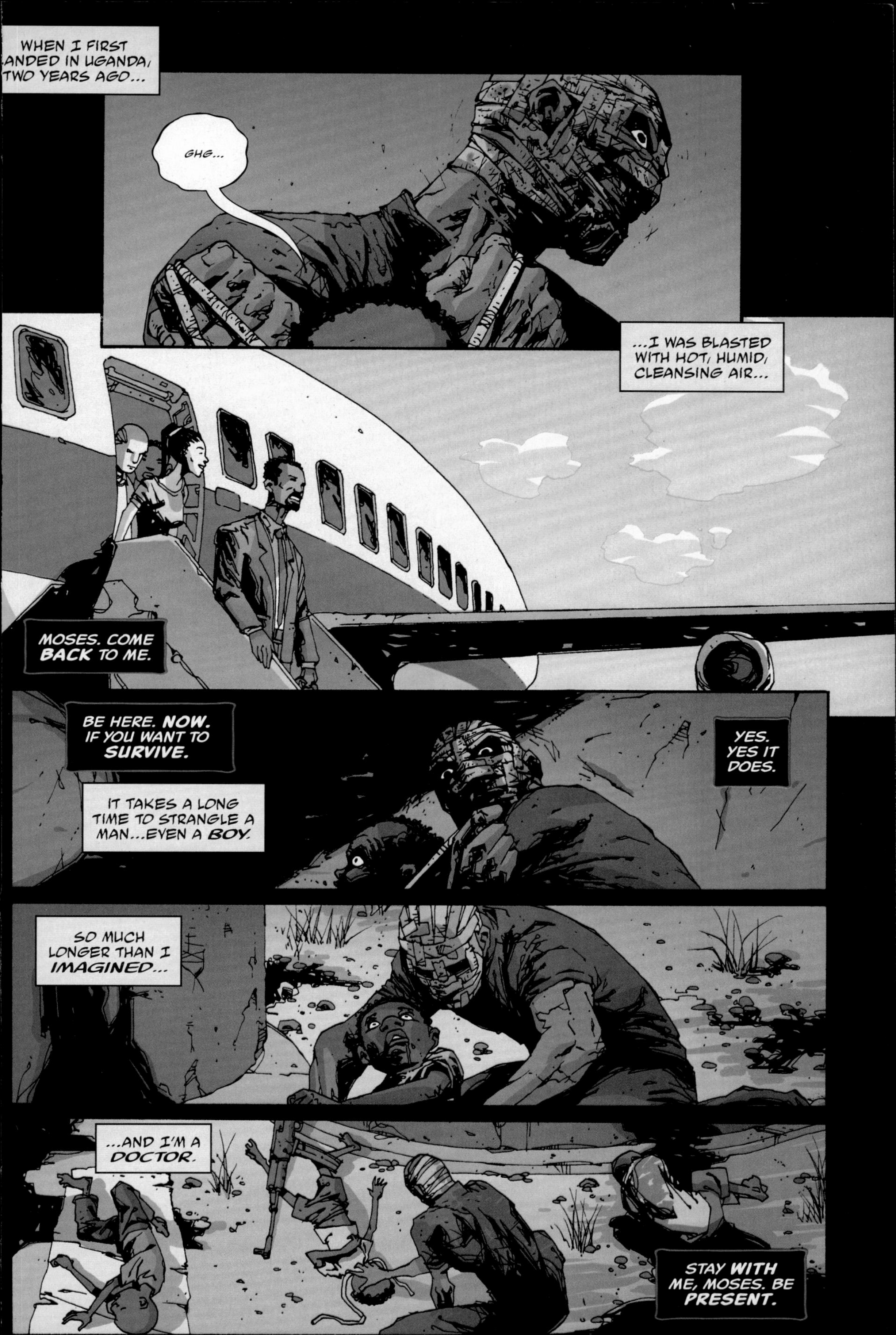
WHEN I FIRST LANDED IN UGANDA, TWO YEARS AGO...
GHG...
...I WAS BLASTED WITH HOT, HUMID, CLEANSING AIR...
MOSES. COME BACK TO ME.
BE HERE. NOW. IF YOU WANT TO SURVIVE.
IT TAKES A LONG TIME TO STRANGLE A MAN...EVEN A BOY.
YES. YES IT DOES.
SO MUCH LONGER THAN I IMAGINED...
...AND I'M A DOCTOR.
STAY WITH ME, MOSES. BE PRESENT.

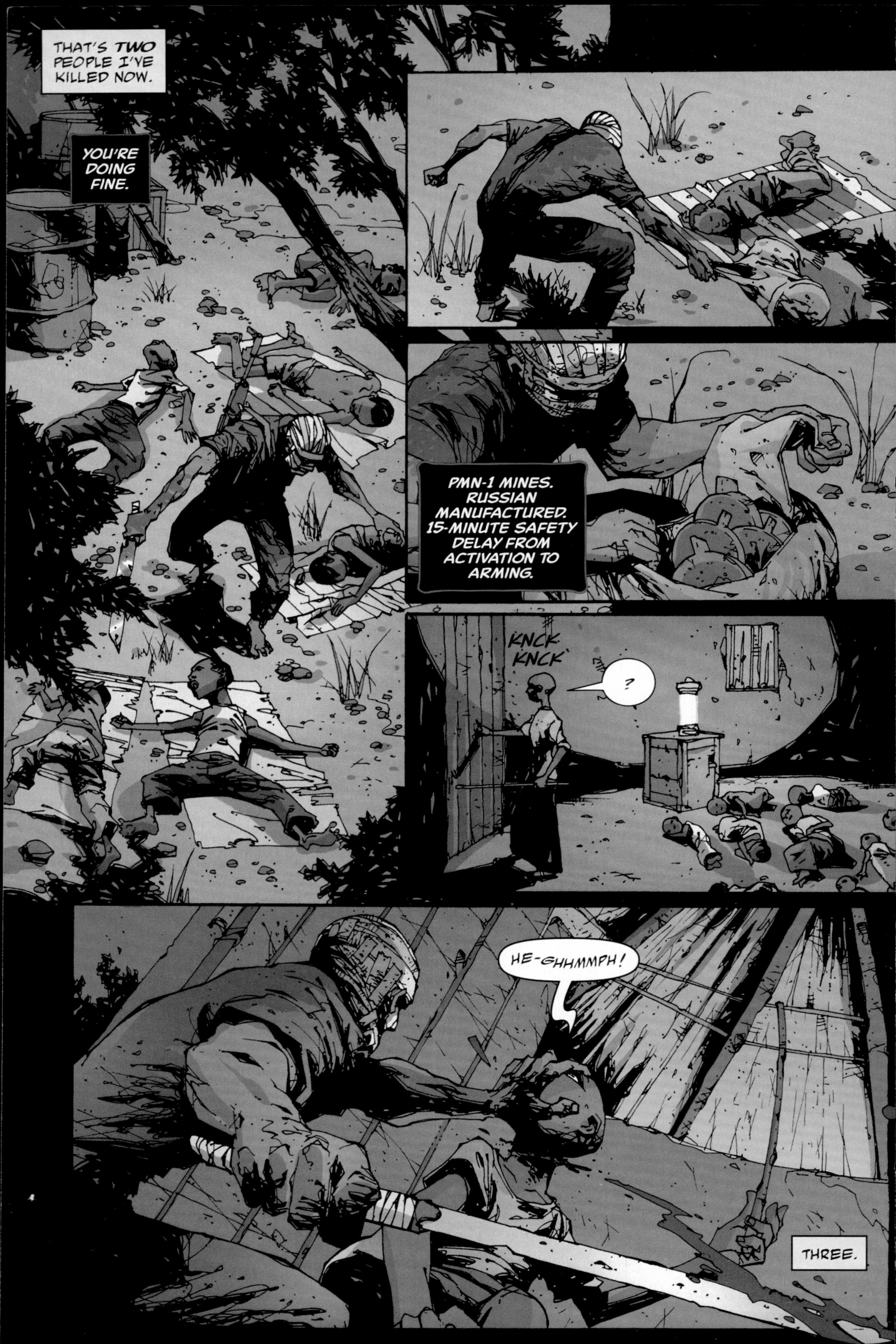
THAT'S TWO PEOPLE I'VE KILLED NOW.
YOU'RE DOING FINE.
PMN-1 MINES. RUSSIAN MANUFACTURED. 15-MINUTE SAFETY DELAY FROM ACTIVATION TO ARMING.
KNCK KNCK
?
HE-GHHMMPH!
THREE.

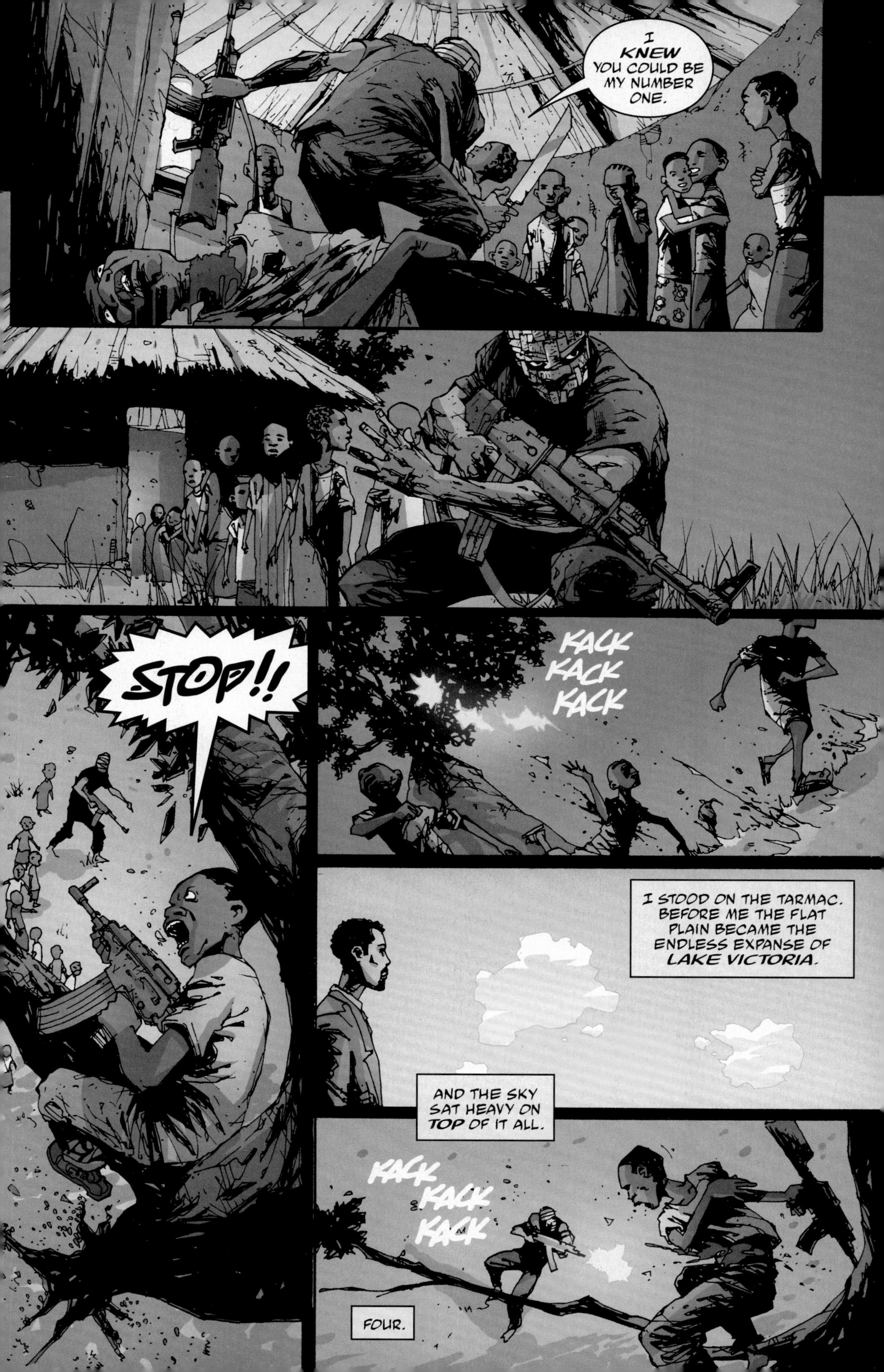
I KNEW YOU COULD BE MY NUMBER ONE.
STOP!!
KACK KACK KACK
I STOOD ON THE TARMAC. BEFORE ME THE FLAT PLAIN BECAME THE ENDLESS EXPANSE OF LAKE VICTORIA.
AND THE SKY SAT HEAVY ON TOP OF IT ALL.
KACK KACK KACK
FOUR.

CENTRAL AFRICAN SKY. WITH ITS MOUNTAIN RANGES OF CLOUDS. ITS SCORCHING COLORS. ITS FIERCE IMAGINATION.

ITS CONSTANT PROMISE OF DISTANT STORMS.

RUN, GIRLS! DON'T LOOK BACK. RUN!

WHEN THE FIRST WAVE OF REBELS HIT THE *LAND MINES* I STOP COUNTING THE DEAD.

I'M SORRY, BABY. I'M *SORRY*...IT'S GOING TO BE OKAY...I'VE GOT YOU.

GHGH--

ENOUGH, MOSES. THEY'RE COMING.

TIME TO START *RUNNING*.

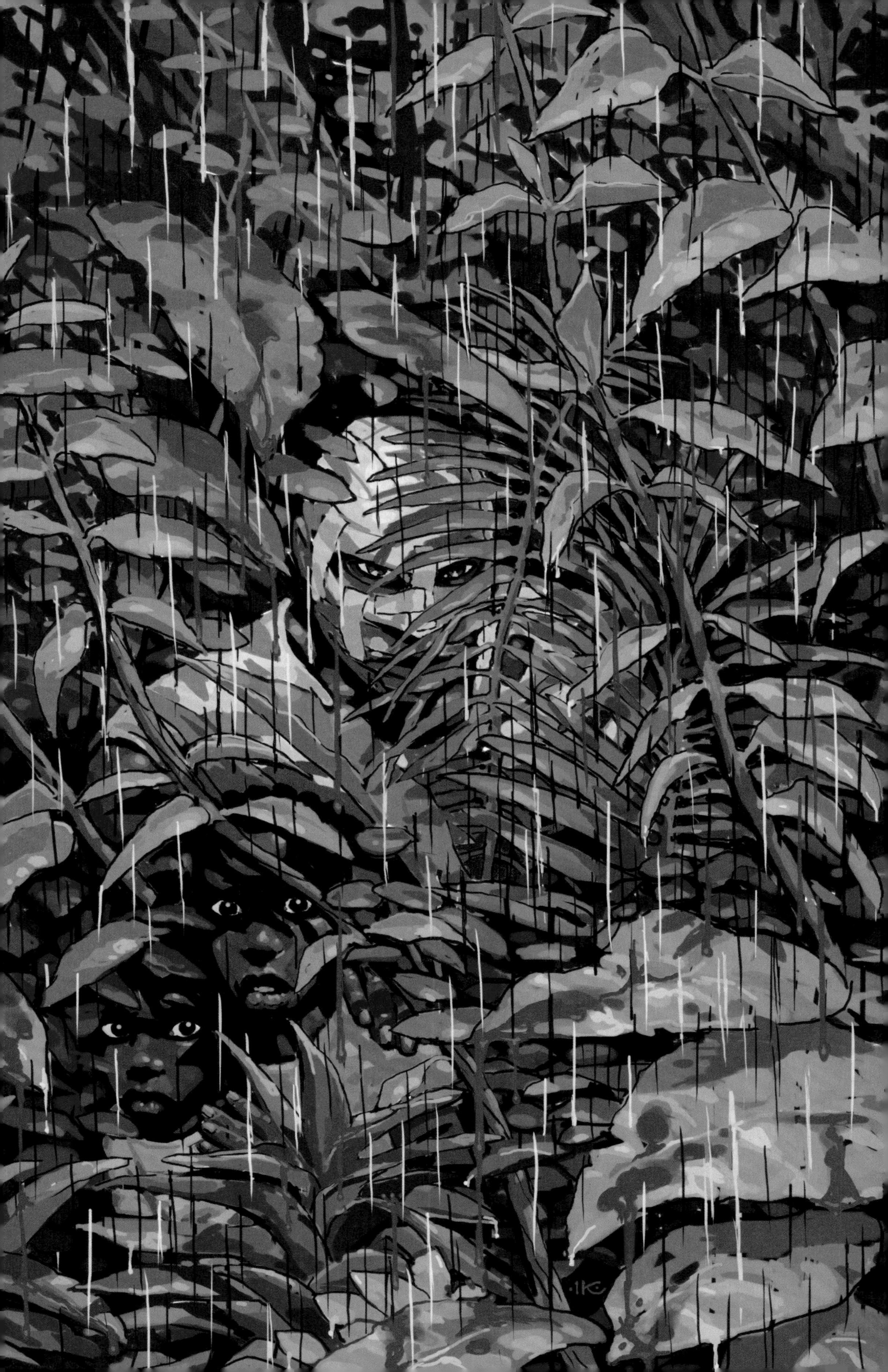

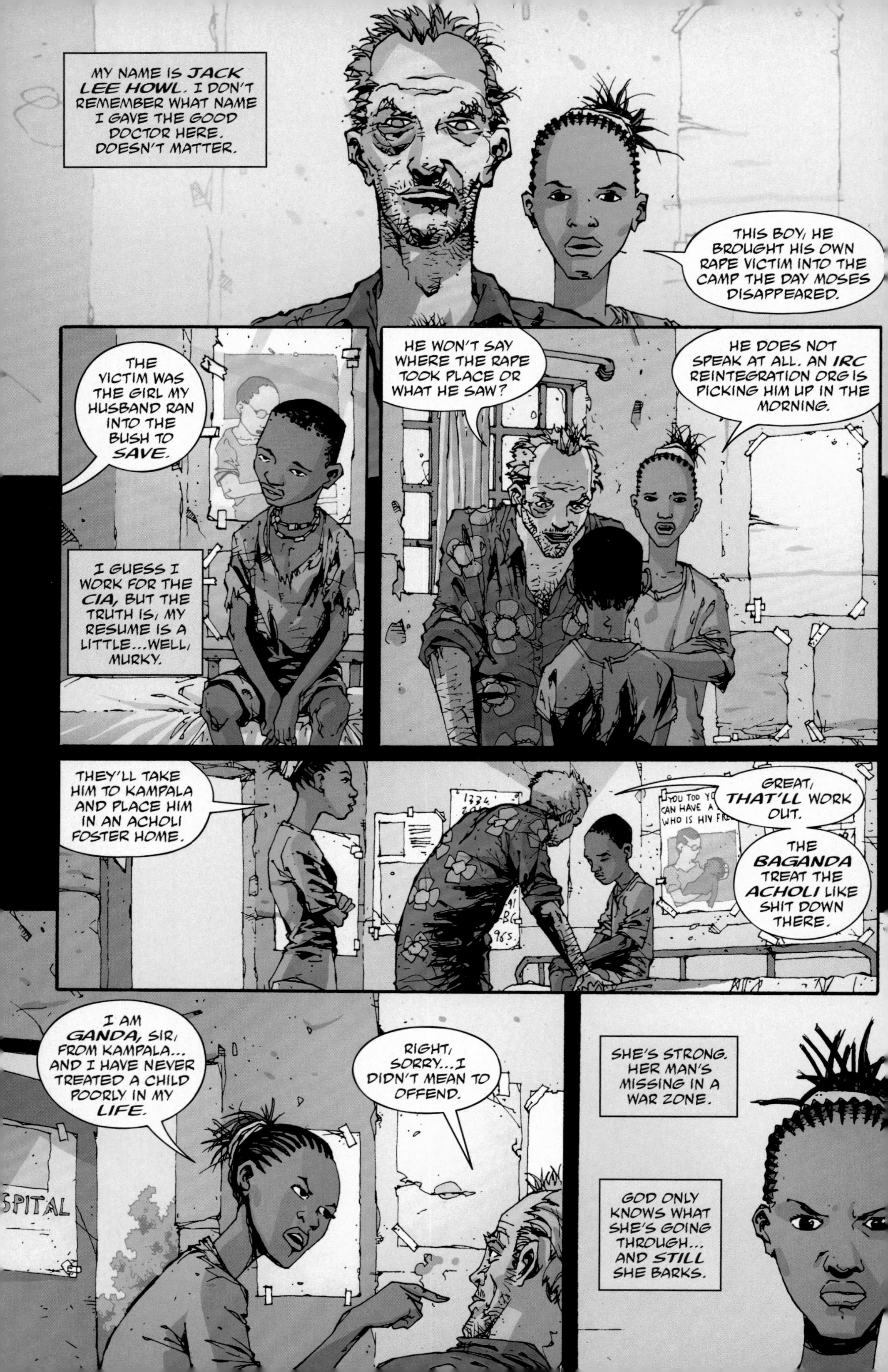

MY NAME IS JACK LEE HOWL. I DON'T REMEMBER WHAT NAME I GAVE THE GOOD DOCTOR HERE. DOESN'T MATTER.
THIS BOY, HE BROUGHT HIS OWN RAPE VICTIM INTO THE CAMP THE DAY MOSES DISAPPEARED.
THE VICTIM WAS THE GIRL MY HUSBAND RAN INTO THE BUSH TO SAVE.
I GUESS I WORK FOR THE CIA, BUT THE TRUTH IS, MY RESUME IS A LITTLE...WELL, MURKY.
HE WON'T SAY WHERE THE RAPE TOOK PLACE OR WHAT HE SAW?
HE DOES NOT SPEAK AT ALL. AN IRC REINTEGRATION ORG IS PICKING HIM UP IN THE MORNING.
THEY'LL TAKE HIM TO KAMPALA AND PLACE HIM IN AN ACHOLI FOSTER HOME.
GREAT, THAT'LL WORK OUT.
THE BAGANDA TREAT THE ACHOLI LIKE SHIT DOWN THERE.
I AM GANDA, SIR, FROM KAMPALA... AND I HAVE NEVER TREATED A CHILD POORLY IN MY LIFE.
RIGHT, SORRY...I DIDN'T MEAN TO OFFEND.
SHE'S STRONG. HER MAN'S MISSING IN A WAR ZONE.
GOD ONLY KNOWS WHAT SHE'S GOING THROUGH... AND STILL SHE BARKS.

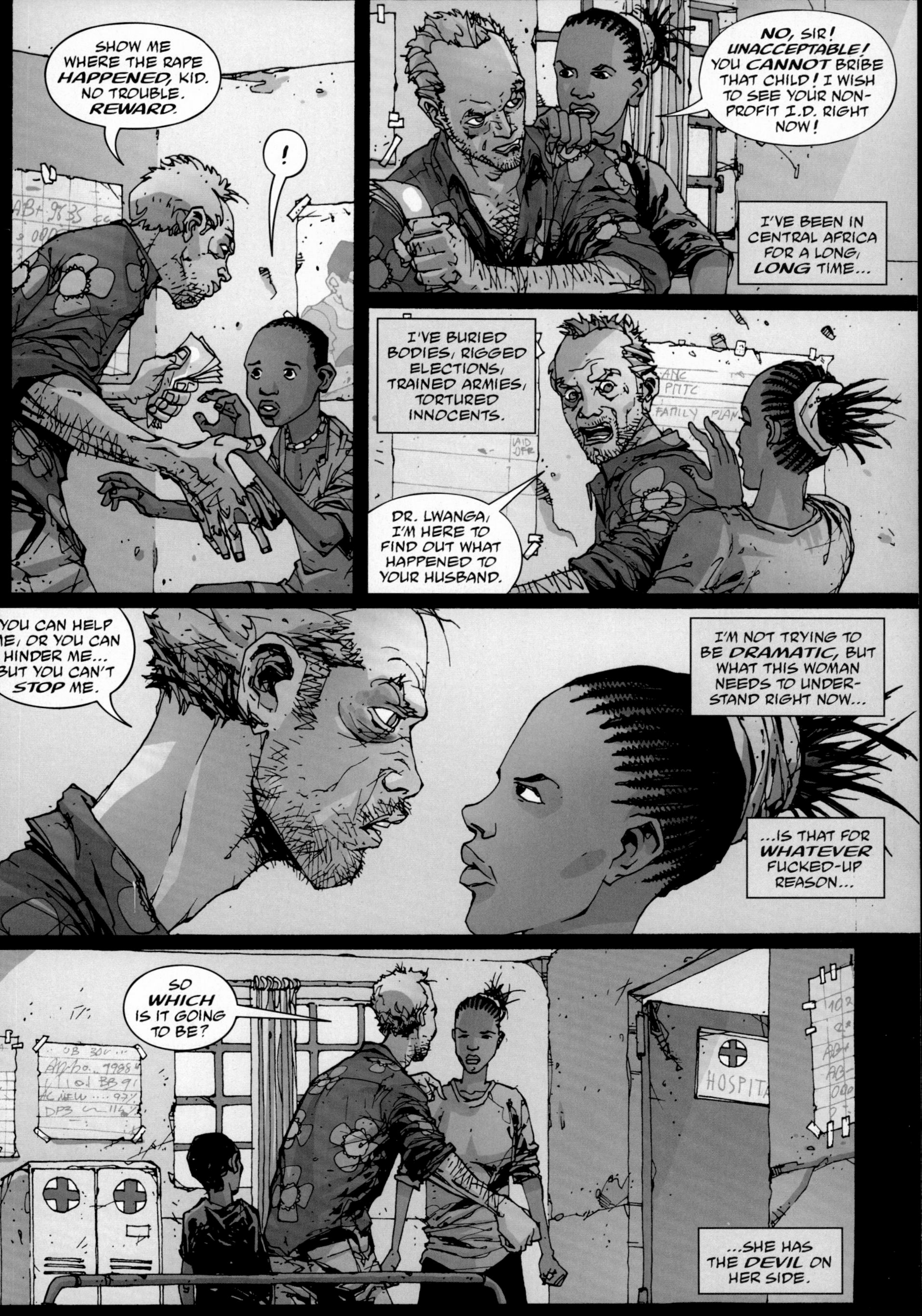
SHOW ME WHERE THE RAPE HAPPENED, KID. NO TROUBLE. REWARD.
!
NO, SIR! UNACCEPTABLE! YOU CANNOT BRIBE THAT CHILD! I WISH TO SEE YOUR NON-PROFIT I.D. RIGHT NOW!
I'VE BEEN IN CENTRAL AFRICA FOR A LONG, LONG TIME...
I'VE BURIED BODIES, RIGGED ELECTIONS, TRAINED ARMIES, TORTURED INNOCENTS.
DR. LWANGA, I'M HERE TO FIND OUT WHAT HAPPENED TO YOUR HUSBAND.
YOU CAN HELP ME, OR YOU CAN HINDER ME... BUT YOU CAN'T STOP ME.
I'M NOT TRYING TO BE DRAMATIC, BUT WHAT THIS WOMAN NEEDS TO UNDERSTAND RIGHT NOW...
...IS THAT FOR WHATEVER FUCKED-UP REASON...
SO WHICH IS IT GOING TO BE?
HOSPITA
...SHE HAS THE DEVIL ON HER SIDE.

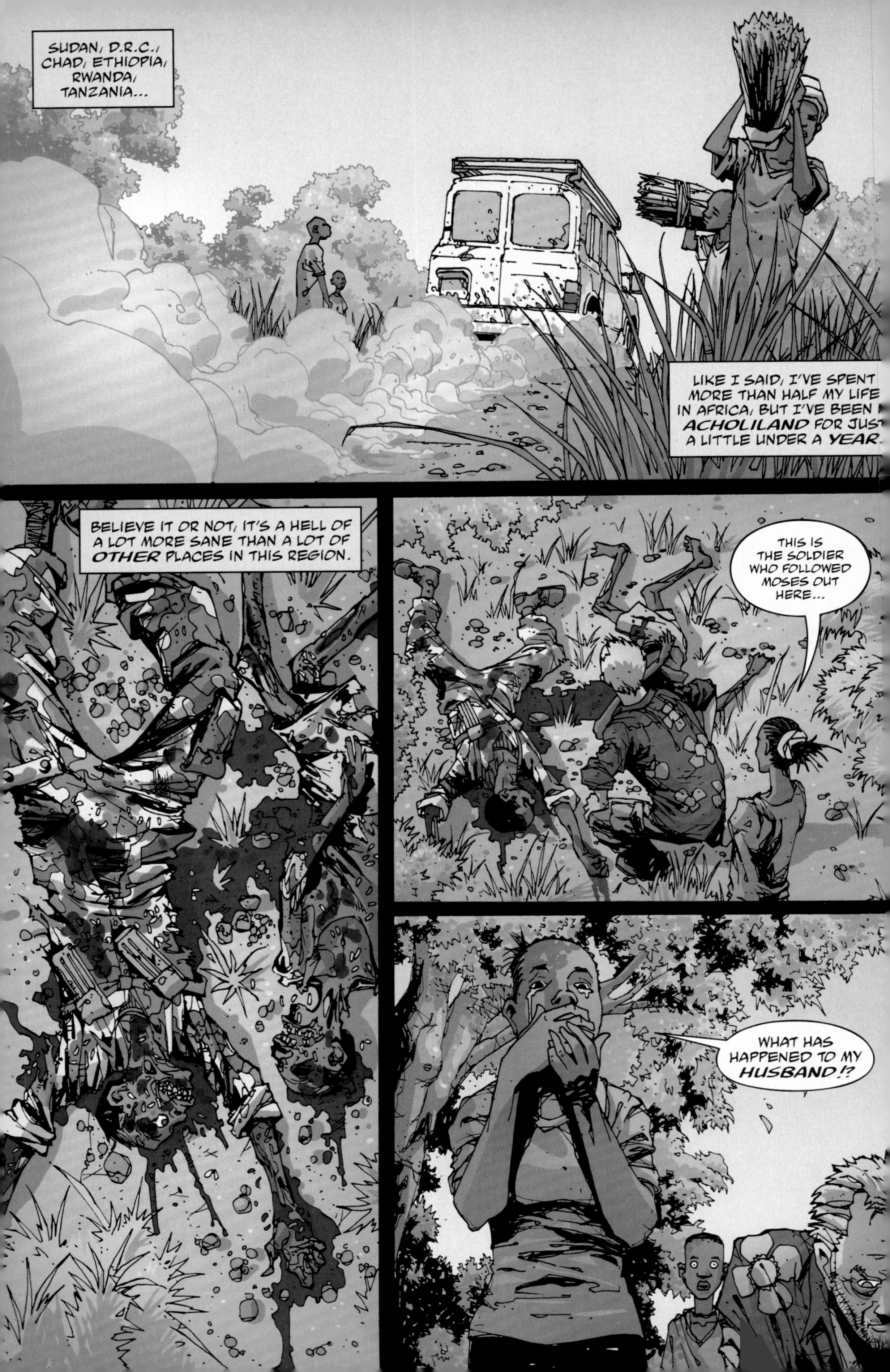
SUDAN, D.R.C., CHAD, ETHIOPIA, RWANDA, TANZANIA...
LIKE I SAID, I'VE SPENT MORE THAN HALF MY LIFE IN AFRICA, BUT I'VE BEEN IN ACHOLILAND FOR JUST A LITTLE UNDER A YEAR.
BELIEVE IT OR NOT, IT'S A HELL OF A LOT MORE SANE THAN A LOT OF OTHER PLACES IN THIS REGION.
THIS IS THE SOLDIER WHO FOLLOWED MOSES OUT HERE...
WHAT HAS HAPPENED TO MY HUSBAND!?

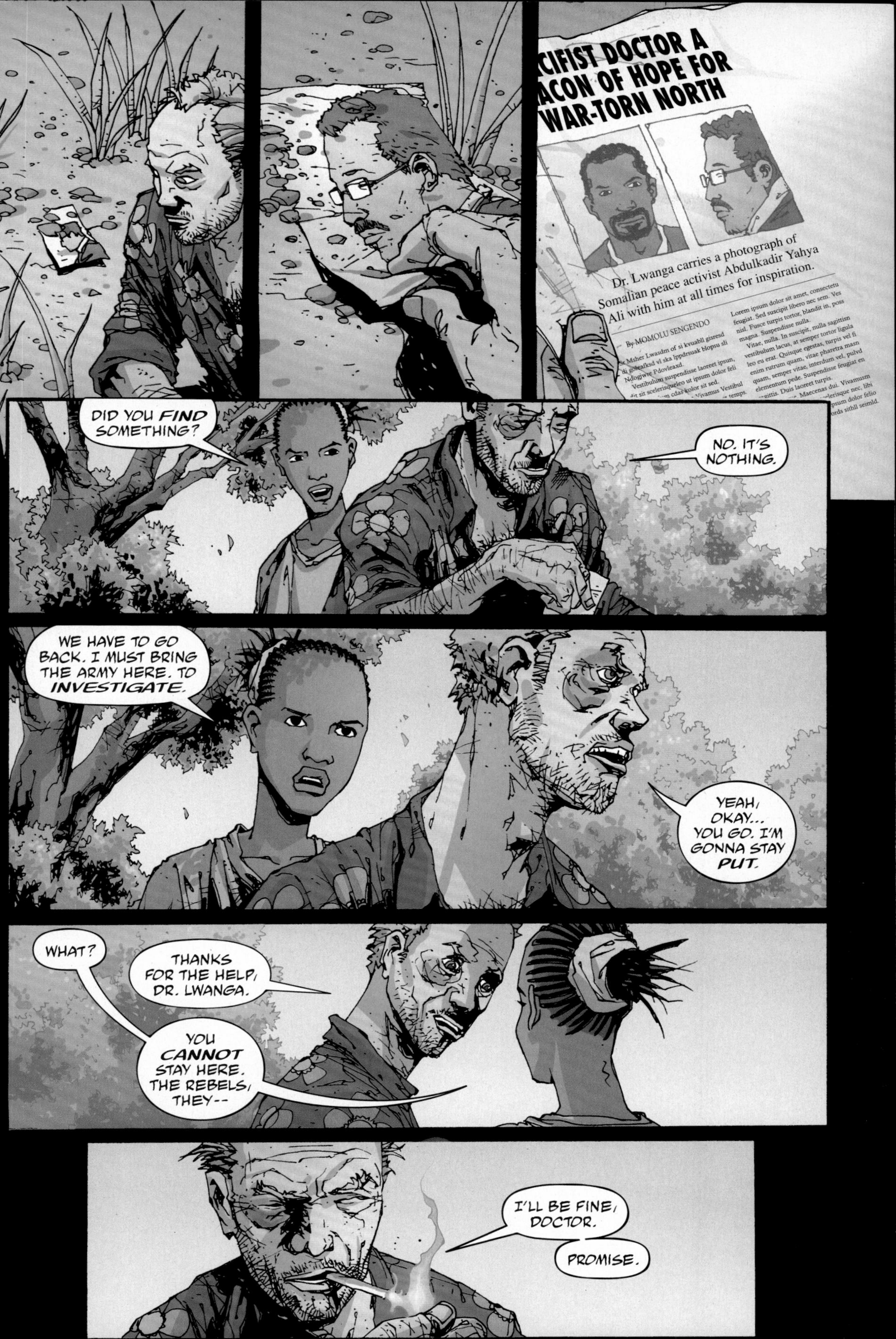

CIFIST DOCTOR A
ACON OF HOPE FOR
WAR-TORN NORTH
Dr. Lwanga carries a photograph of Somalian peace activist Abdulkadir Yahya Ali with him at all times for inspiration.
By MOMOLU SENGENDO
DID YOU FIND SOMETHING?
NO. IT'S NOTHING.
WE HAVE TO GO BACK. I MUST BRING THE ARMY HERE. TO INVESTIGATE.
YEAH, OKAY... YOU GO. I'M GONNA STAY PUT.
WHAT?
THANKS FOR THE HELP, DR. LWANGA.
YOU CANNOT STAY HERE. THE REBELS, THEY--
I'LL BE FINE, DOCTOR.
PROMISE.

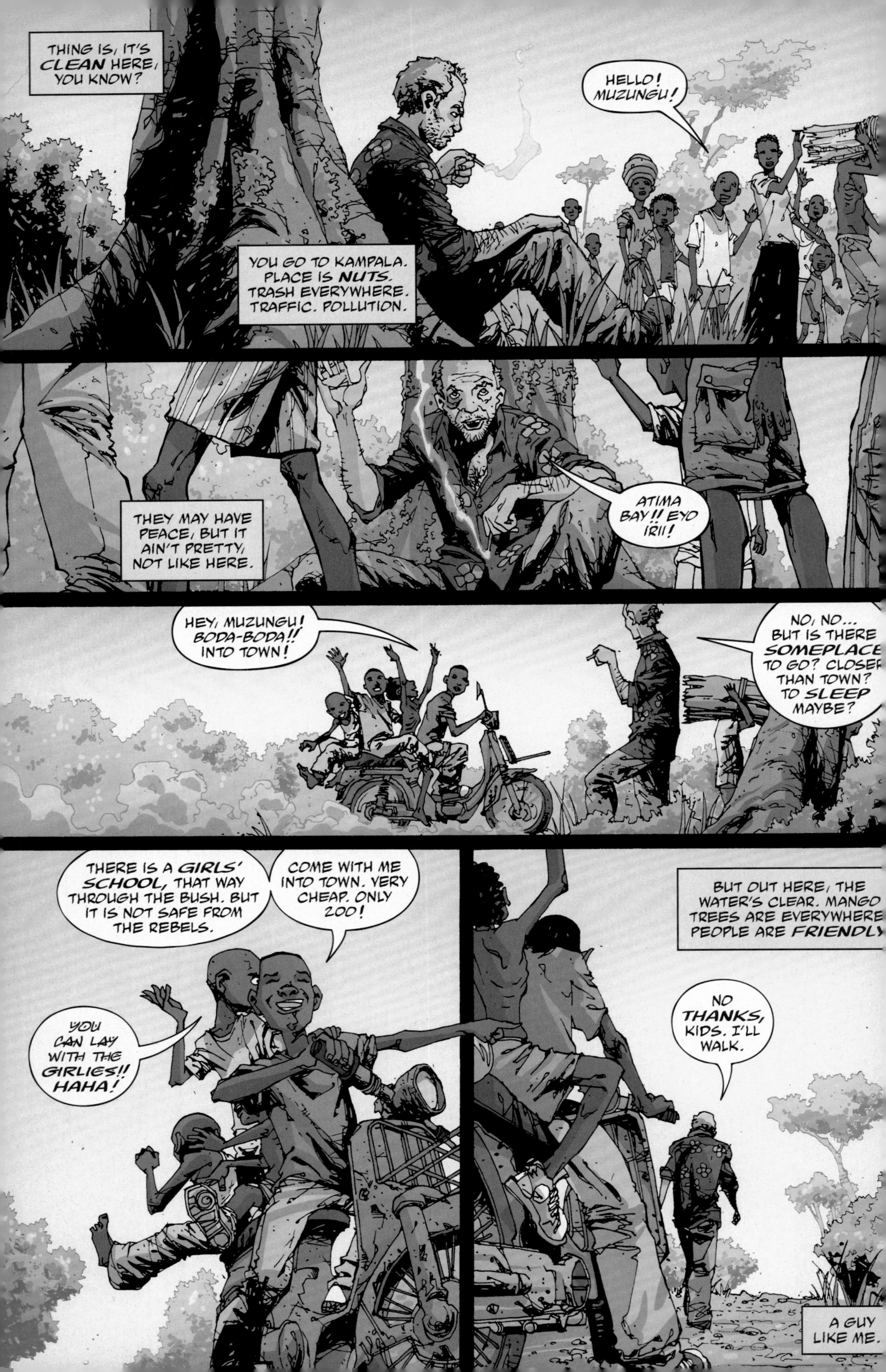
THING IS, IT'S CLEAN HERE, YOU KNOW?
HELLO! MUZUNGU!
YOU GO TO KAMPALA. PLACE IS NUTS. TRASH EVERYWHERE. TRAFFIC. POLLUTION.
THEY MAY HAVE PEACE, BUT IT AIN'T PRETTY, NOT LIKE HERE.
ATIMA BAY!! EYO IRII!
HEY, MUZUNGU! BODA-BODA!! INTO TOWN!
NO, NO... BUT IS THERE SOMEPLACE TO GO? CLOSER THAN TOWN? TO SLEEP MAYBE?
THERE IS A GIRLS' SCHOOL, THAT WAY THROUGH THE BUSH. BUT IT IS NOT SAFE FROM THE REBELS.
COME WITH ME INTO TOWN. VERY CHEAP. ONLY 200!
YOU CAN LAY WITH THE GIRLIES!! HAHA!
BUT OUT HERE, THE WATER'S CLEAR. MANGO TREES ARE EVERYWHERE. PEOPLE ARE FRIENDLY.
NO THANKS, KIDS. I'LL WALK.
A GUY LIKE ME.

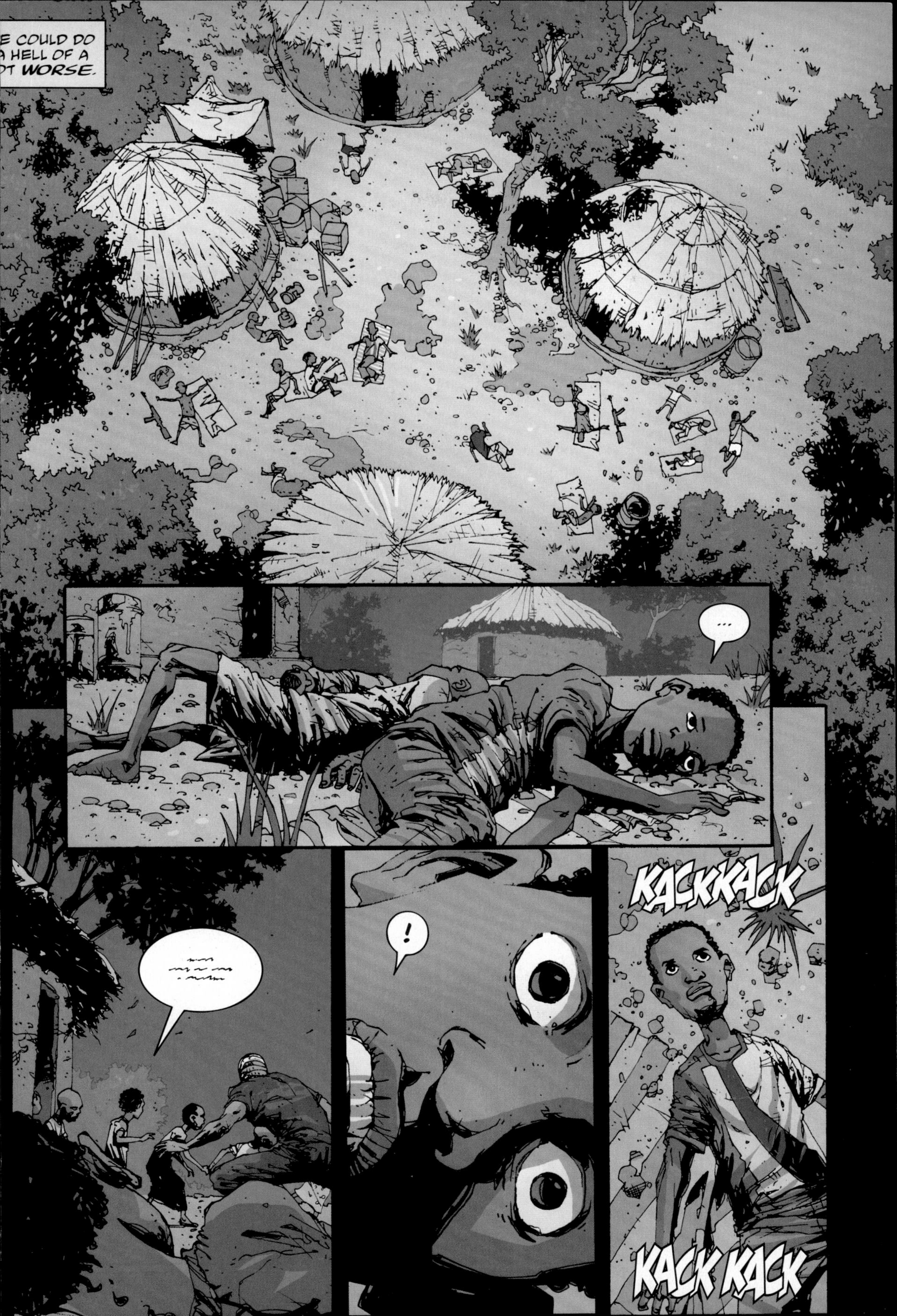
E COULD DO
A HELL OF A
OT WORSE.
...
!
KACK KACK
KACK KACK

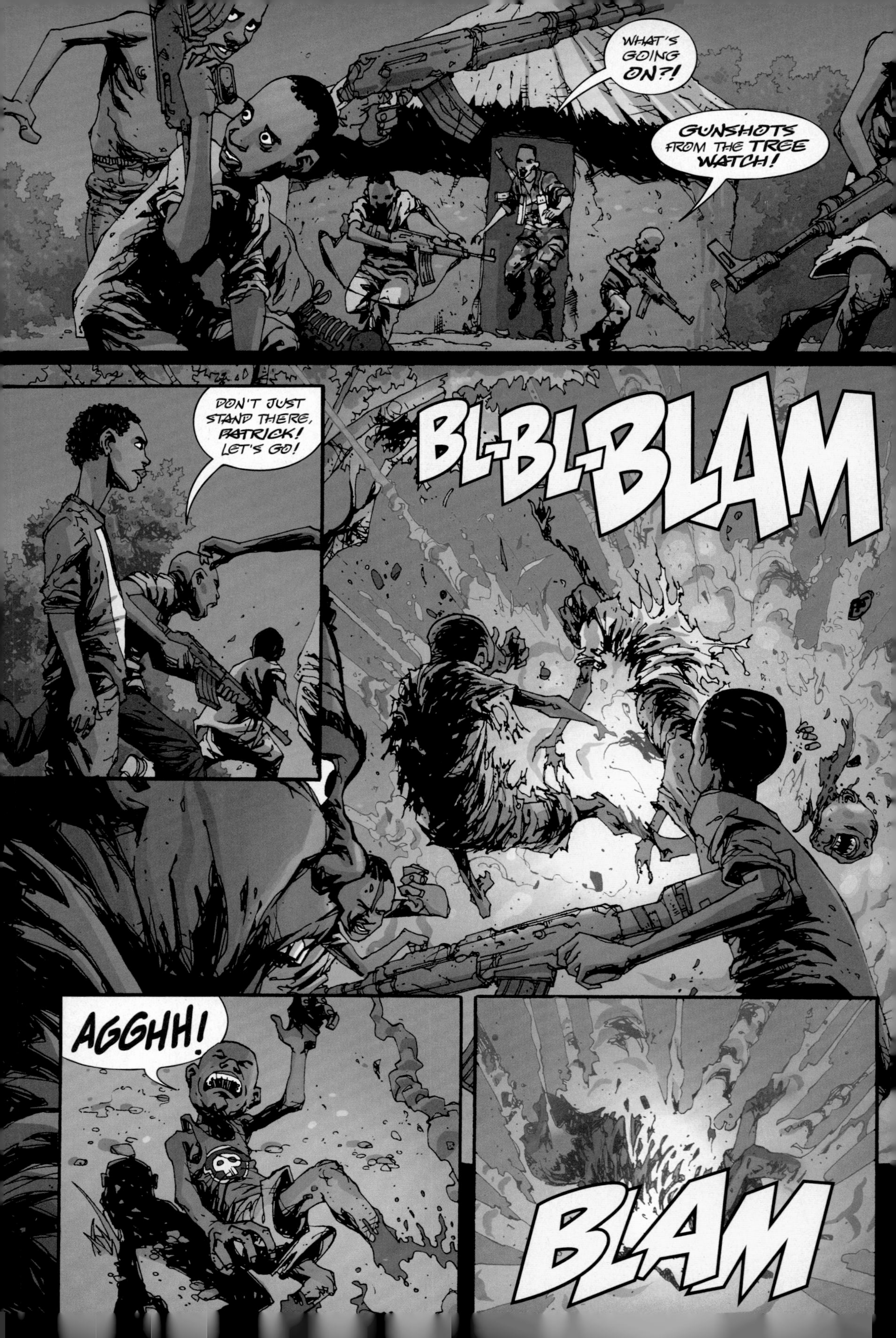

WHAT'S GOING ON?!
GUNSHOTS FROM THE TREE WATCH!
DON'T JUST STAND THERE, PATRICK! LET'S GO!
BL-BL-BLAM
AGGHH!
BLAM

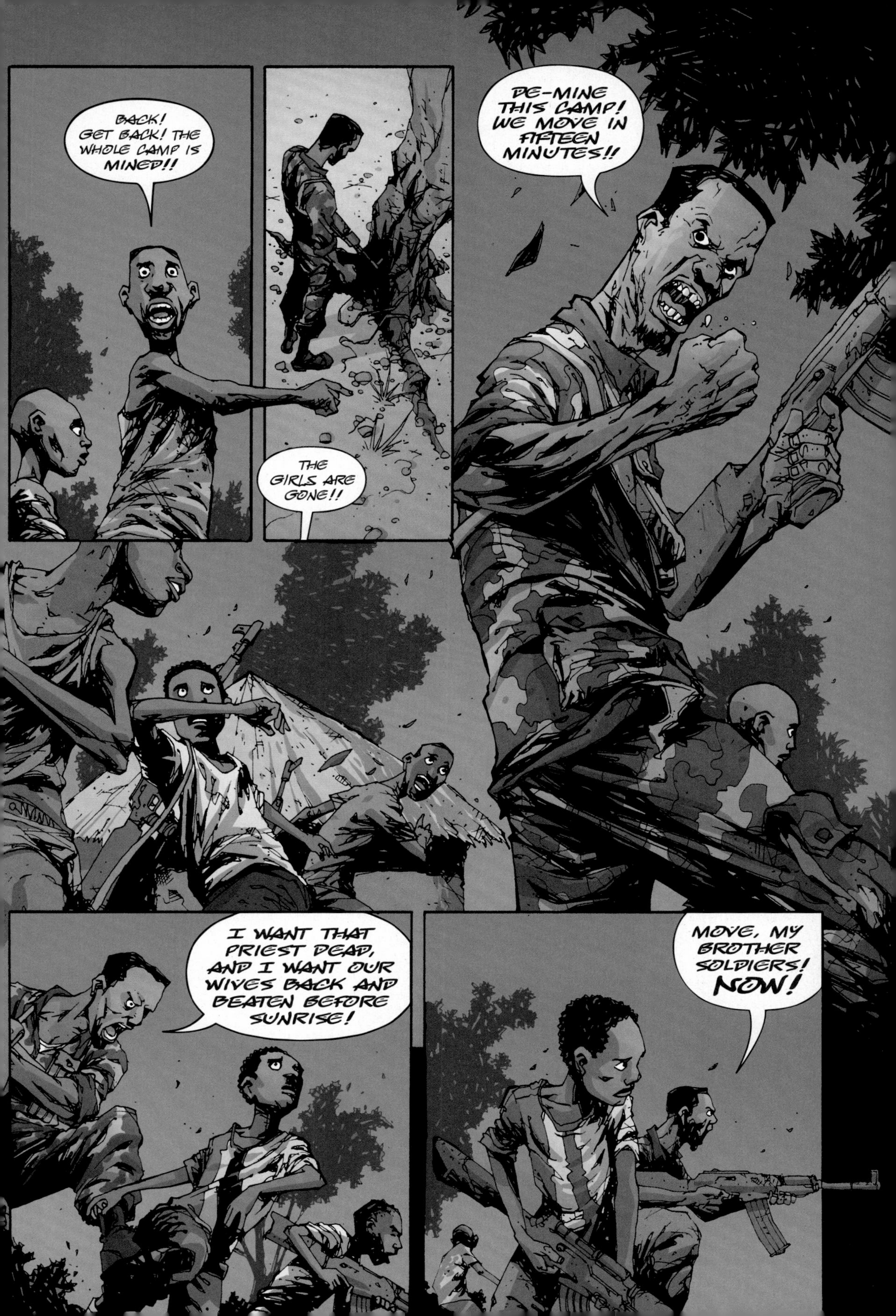
BACK! GET BACK! THE WHOLE CAMP IS MINED!!
THE GIRLS ARE GONE!!
DE-MINE THIS CAMP! WE MOVE IN FIFTEEN MINUTES!!
I WANT THAT PRIEST DEAD, AND I WANT OUR WIVES BACK AND BEATEN BEFORE SUNRISE!
MOVE, MY BROTHER SOLDIERS! NOW!

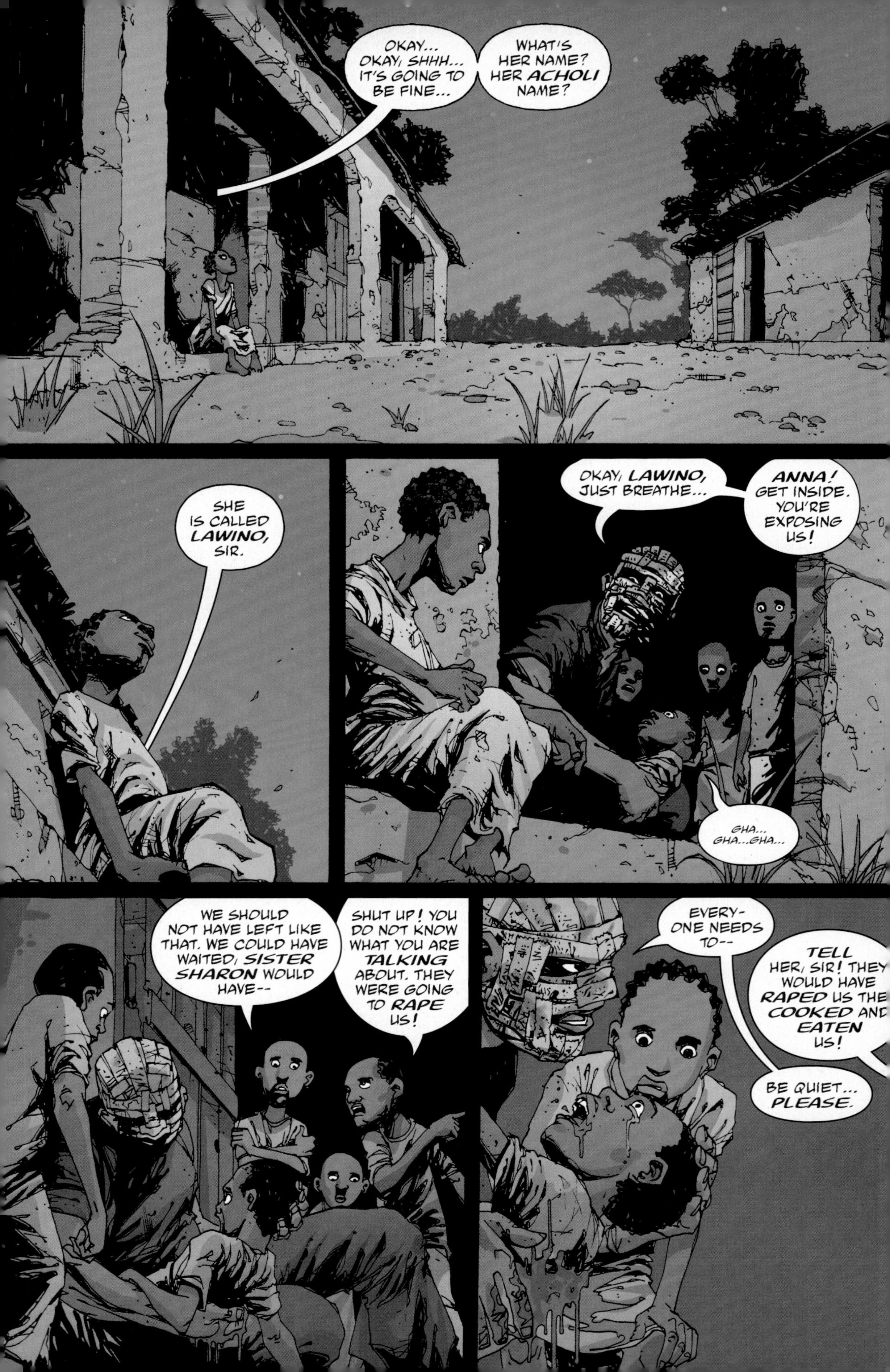
OKAY... OKAY, SHHH... IT'S GOING TO BE FINE...
WHAT'S HER NAME? HER ACHOLI NAME?
SHE IS CALLED LAWINO, SIR.
OKAY, LAWINO, JUST BREATHE...
ANNA! GET INSIDE. YOU'RE EXPOSING US!
GHA... GHA...GHA...
WE SHOULD NOT HAVE LEFT LIKE THAT. WE COULD HAVE WAITED, SISTER SHARON WOULD HAVE--
SHUT UP! YOU DO NOT KNOW WHAT YOU ARE TALKING ABOUT. THEY WERE GOING TO RAPE US!
EVERY-ONE NEEDS TO--
TELL HER, SIR! THEY WOULD HAVE RAPED US THE COOKED AND EATEN US!
BE QUIET... PLEASE.

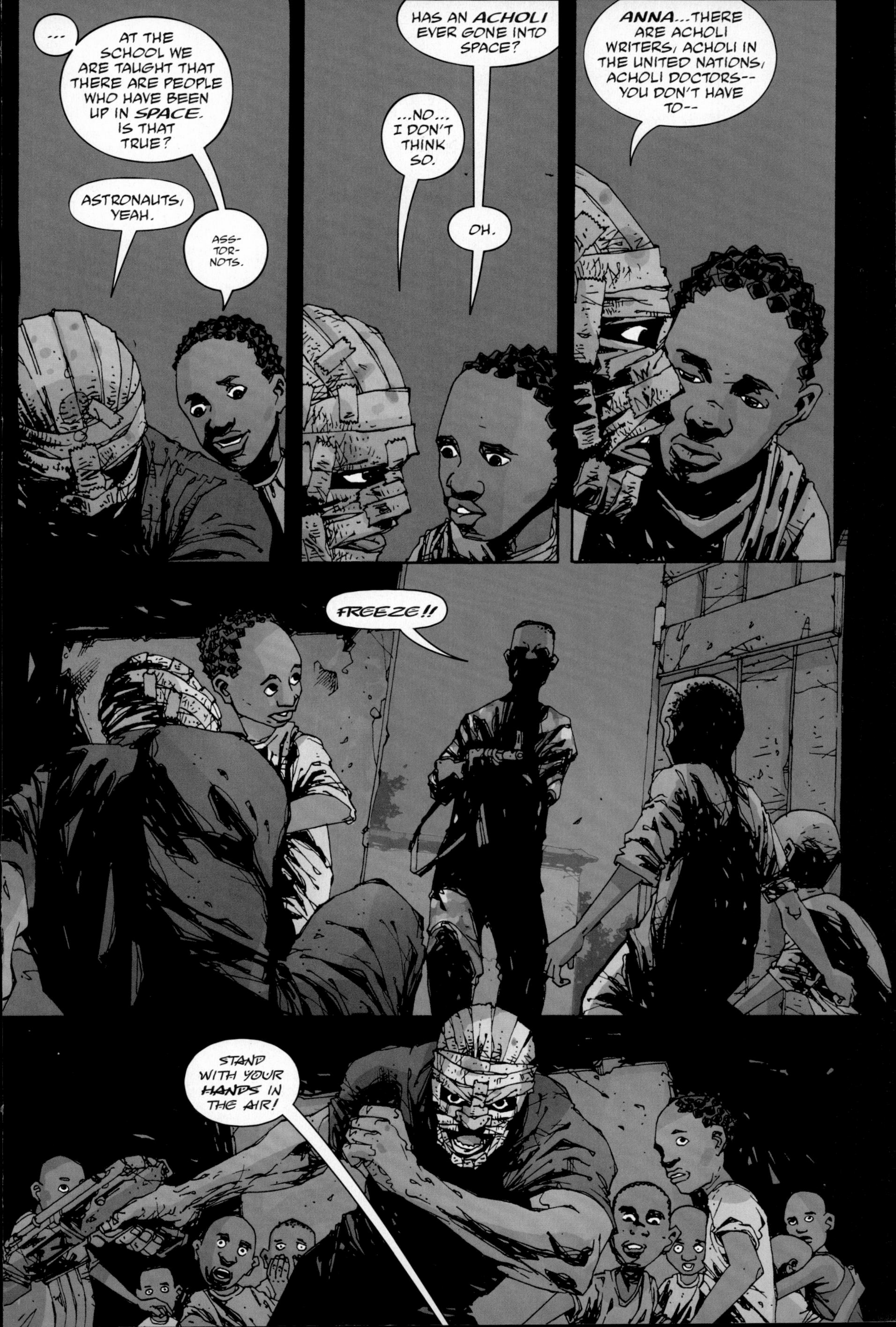
...
AT THE SCHOOL WE ARE TAUGHT THAT THERE ARE PEOPLE WHO HAVE BEEN UP IN SPACE. IS THAT TRUE?
ASTRONAUTS, YEAH.
ASS-TOR-NOTS.
HAS AN ACHOLI EVER GONE INTO SPACE?
...NO... I DON'T THINK SO.
OH.
ANNA...THERE ARE ACHOLI WRITERS, ACHOLI IN THE UNITED NATIONS, ACHOLI DOCTORS-- YOU DON'T HAVE TO--
FREEZE!!
STAND WITH YOUR HANDS IN THE AIR!

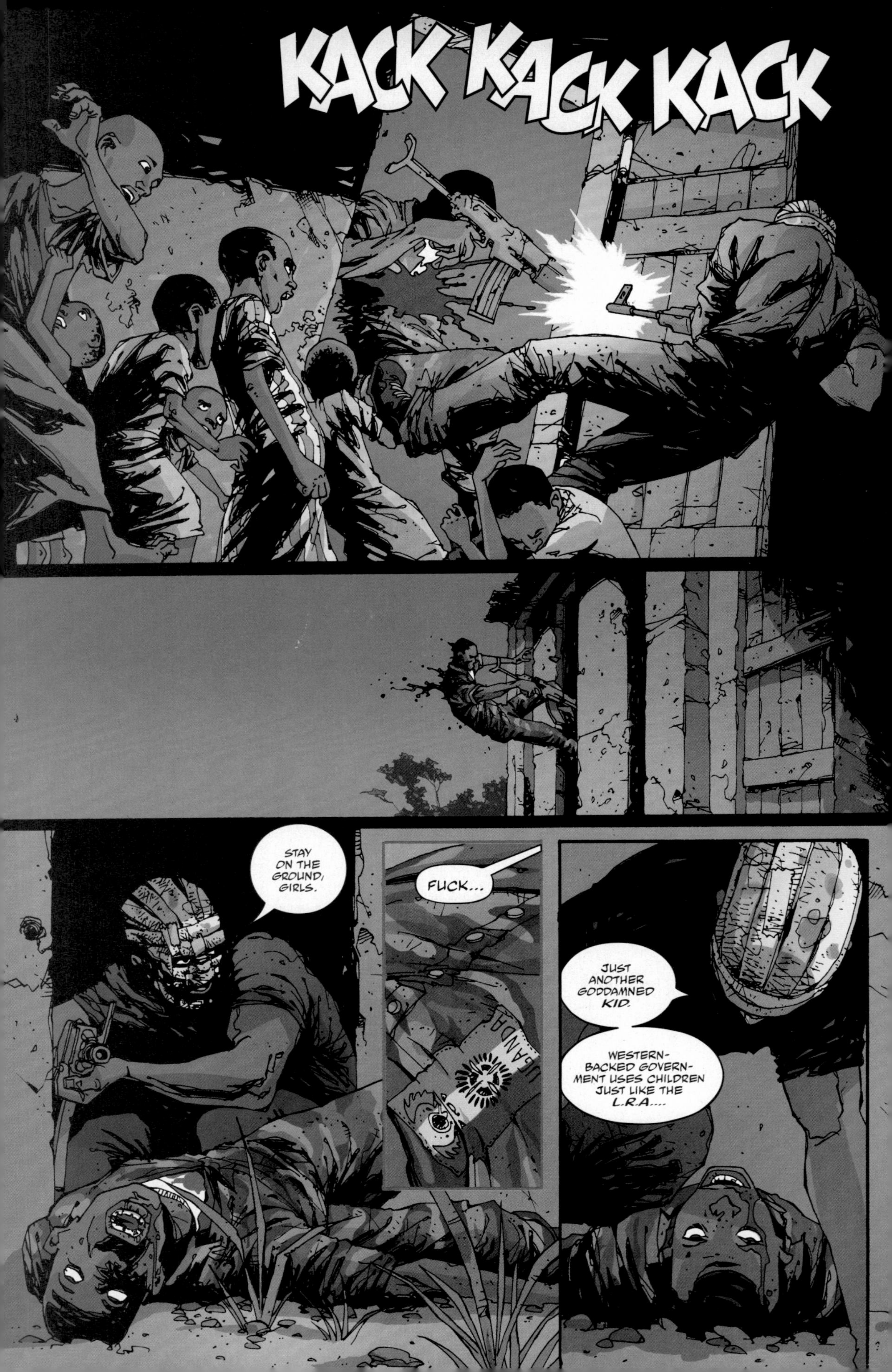
KACK KACK KACK
STAY ON THE GROUND, GIRLS.
FUCK...
JUST ANOTHER GODDAMNED KID.
WESTERN-BACKED GOVERNMENT USES CHILDREN JUST LIKE THE L.R.A....

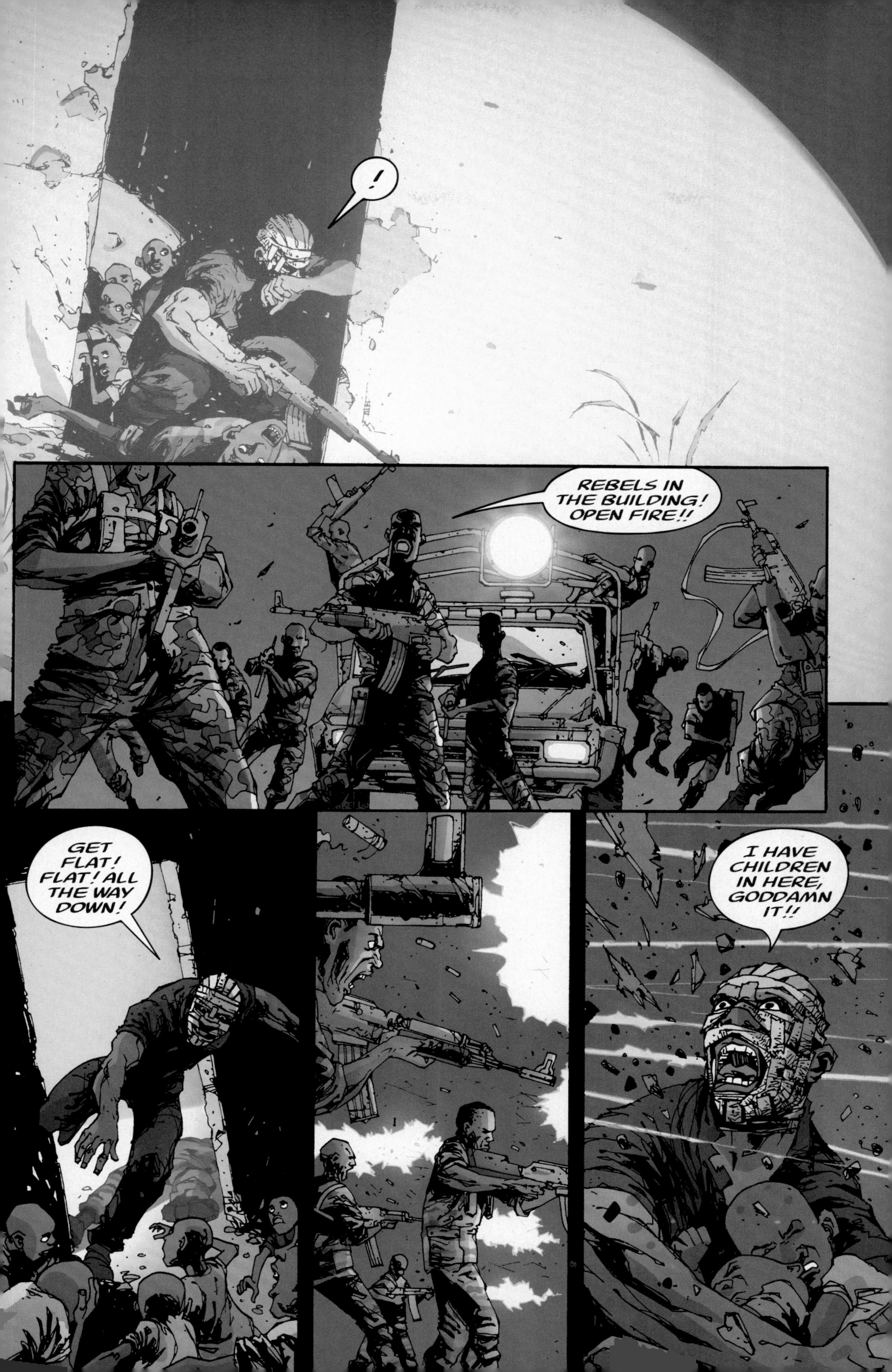
!
REBELS IN THE BUILDING! OPEN FIRE!!
GET FLAT! FLAT! ALL THE WAY DOWN!
I HAVE CHILDREN IN HERE, GODDAMN IT!!

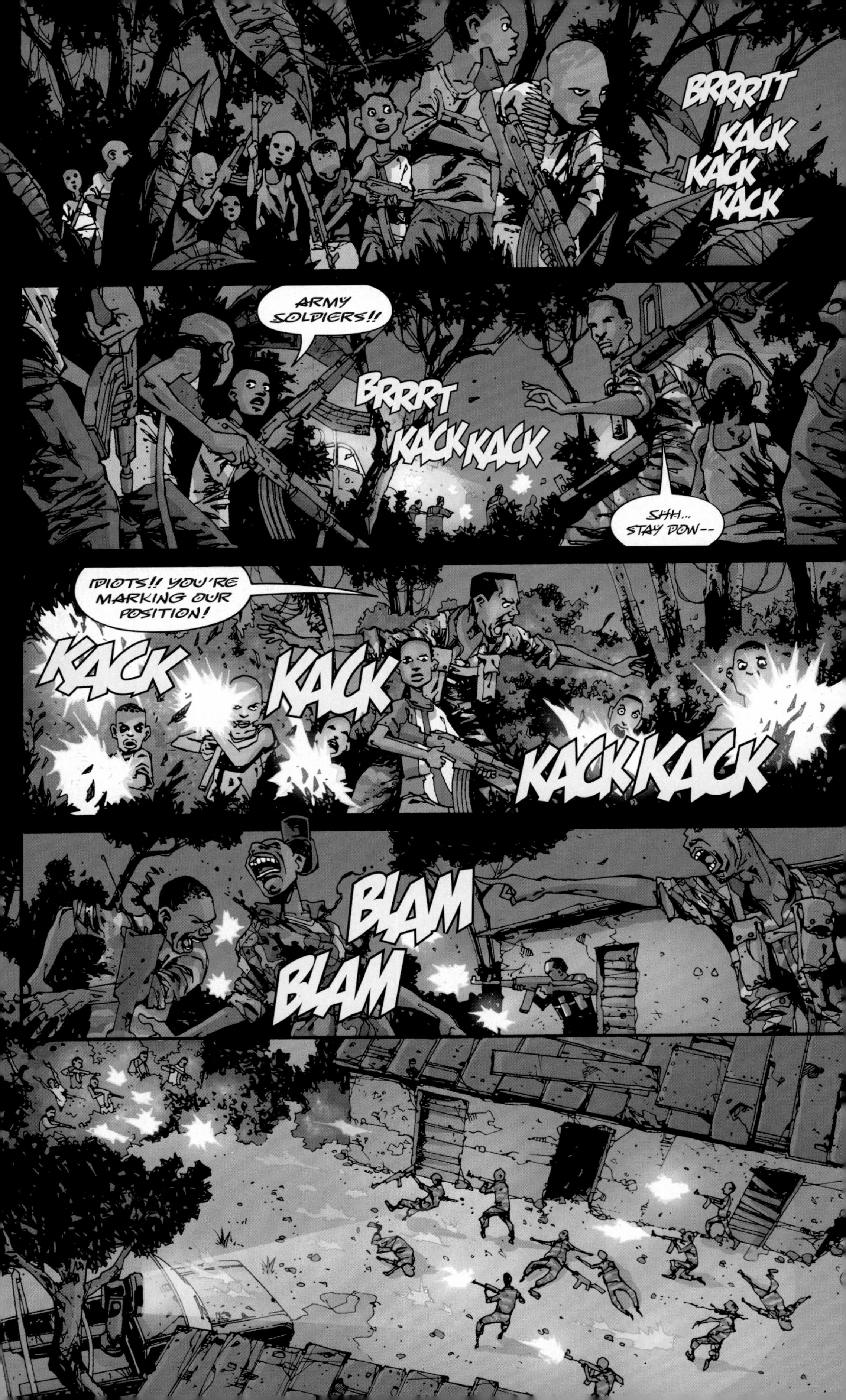
BRRRITT
KACK
KACK
KACK
ARMY SOLDIERS!!
BRRRRT
KACK KACK
SHH... STAY DOW--
IDIOTS!! YOU'RE MARKING OUR POSITION!
KACK
KACK
KACK KACK
BLAM
BLAM

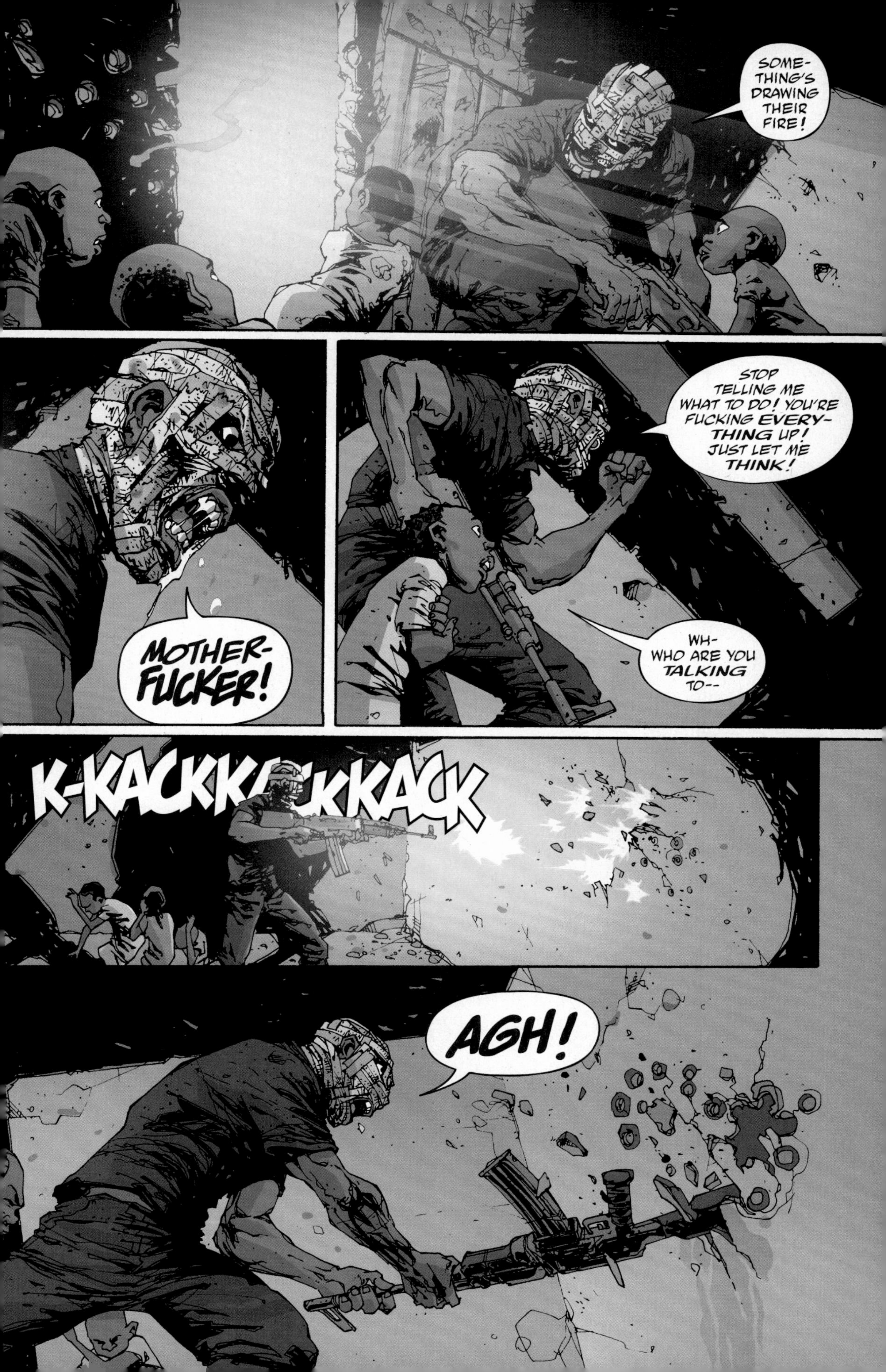
SOME-THING'S DRAWING THEIR FIRE!
MOTHER-FUCKER!
STOP TELLING ME WHAT TO DO! YOU'RE FUCKING EVERY-THING UP! JUST LET ME THINK!
WH-WHO ARE YOU TALKING TO--
K-KACKKACKKACK
AGH!

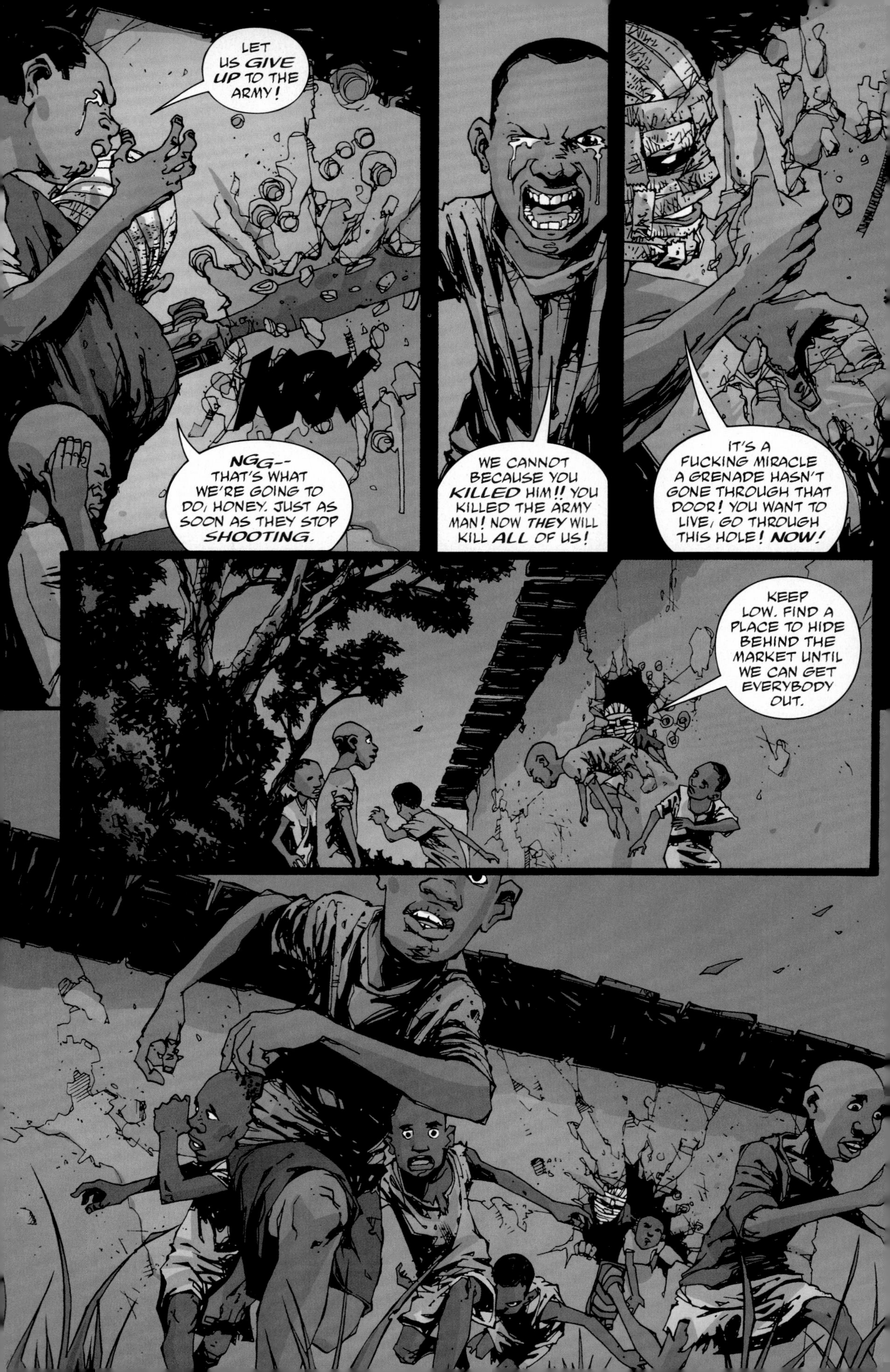
LET US GIVE UP TO THE ARMY!
KRAK
NGG-- THAT'S WHAT WE'RE GOING TO DO, HONEY. JUST AS SOON AS THEY STOP SHOOTING.
WE CANNOT BECAUSE YOU KILLED HIM!! YOU KILLED THE ARMY MAN! NOW THEY WILL KILL ALL OF US!
IT'S A FUCKING MIRACLE A GRENADE HASN'T GONE THROUGH THAT DOOR! YOU WANT TO LIVE, GO THROUGH THIS HOLE! NOW!
KEEP LOW. FIND A PLACE TO HIDE BEHIND THE MARKET UNTIL WE CAN GET EVERYBODY OUT.

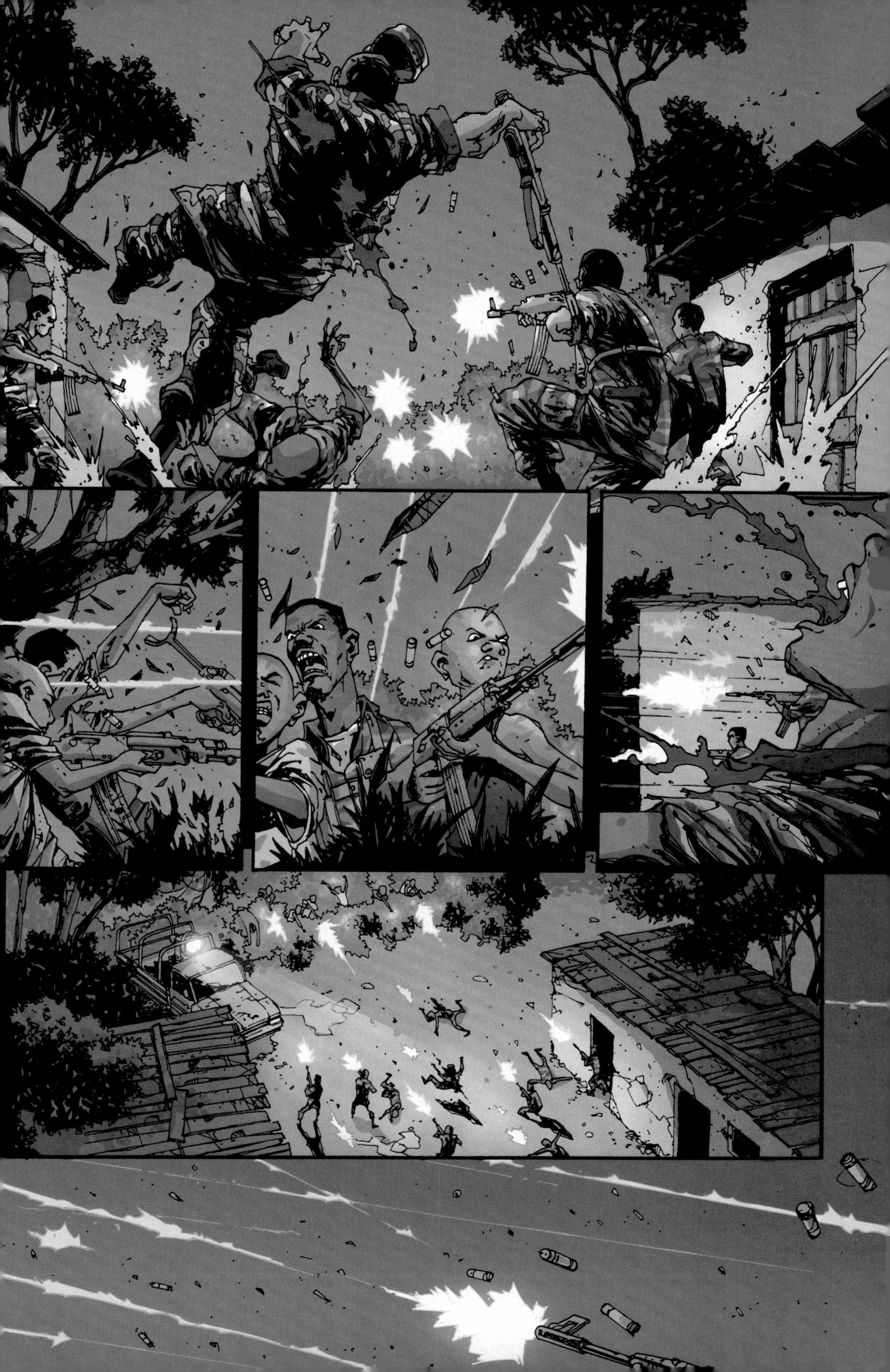

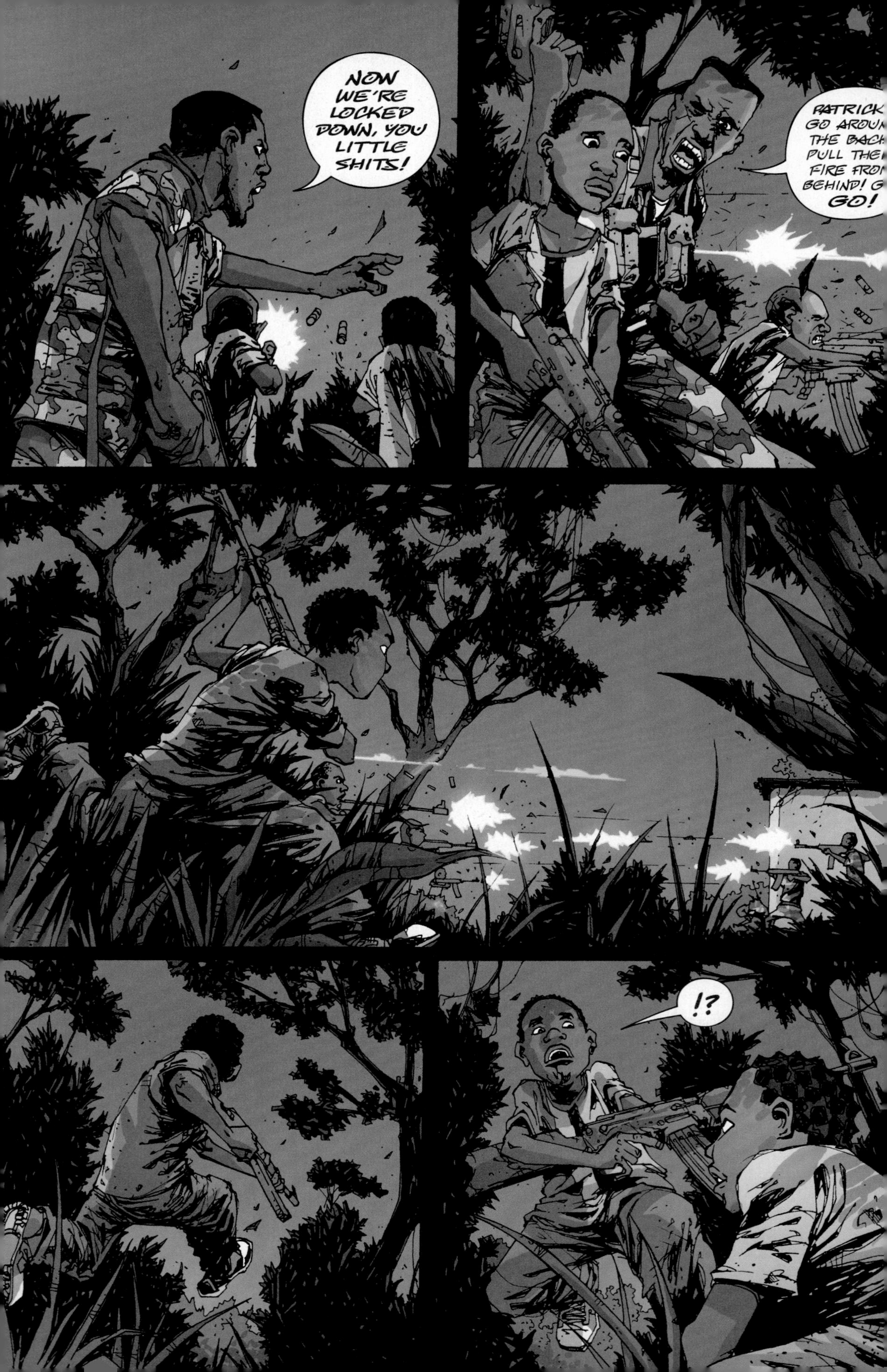

NOW WE'RE LOCKED DOWN, YOU LITTLE SHITS!
PATRICK GO AROUN THE BACK PULL THE FIRE FROM BEHIND! G GO!
!?

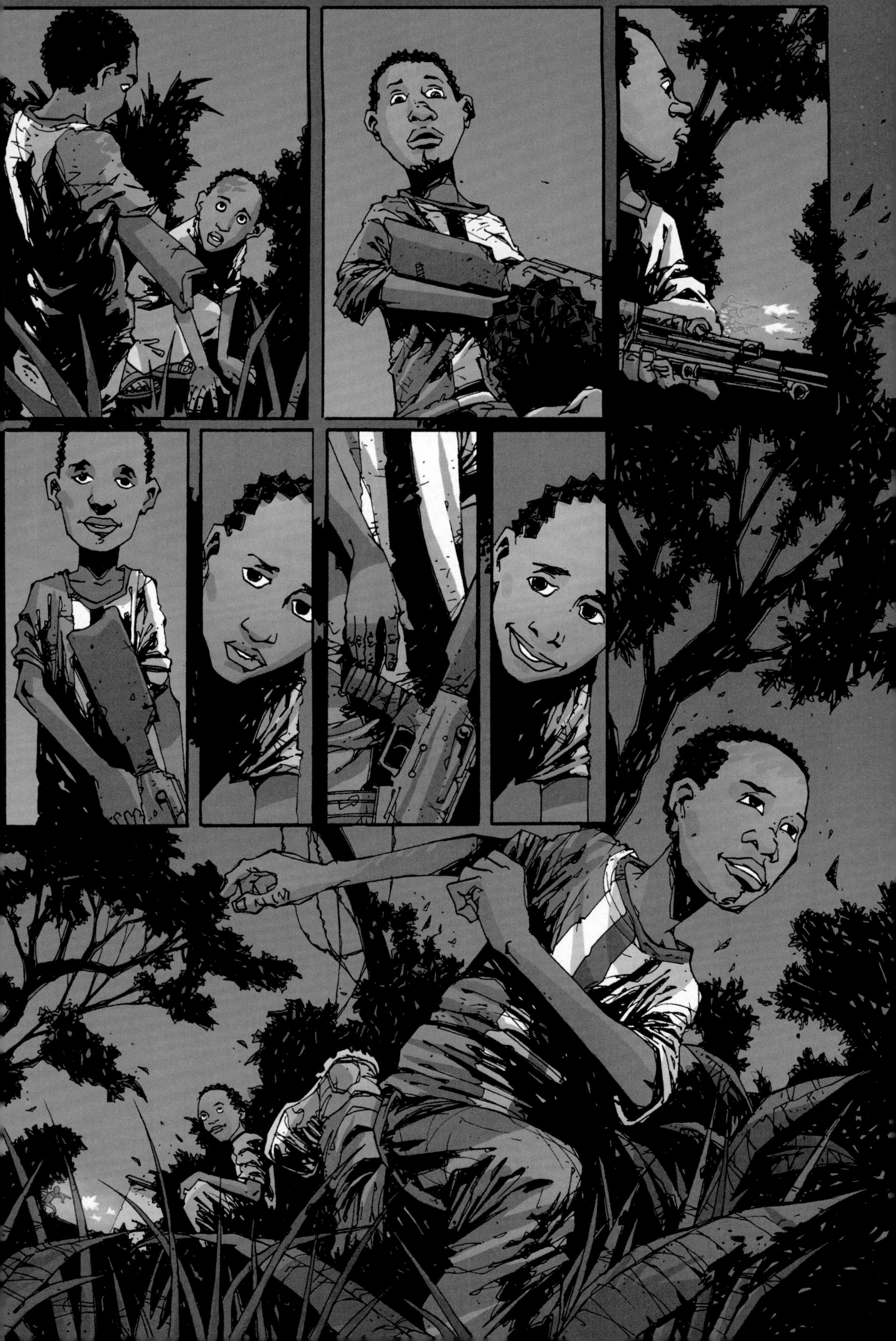

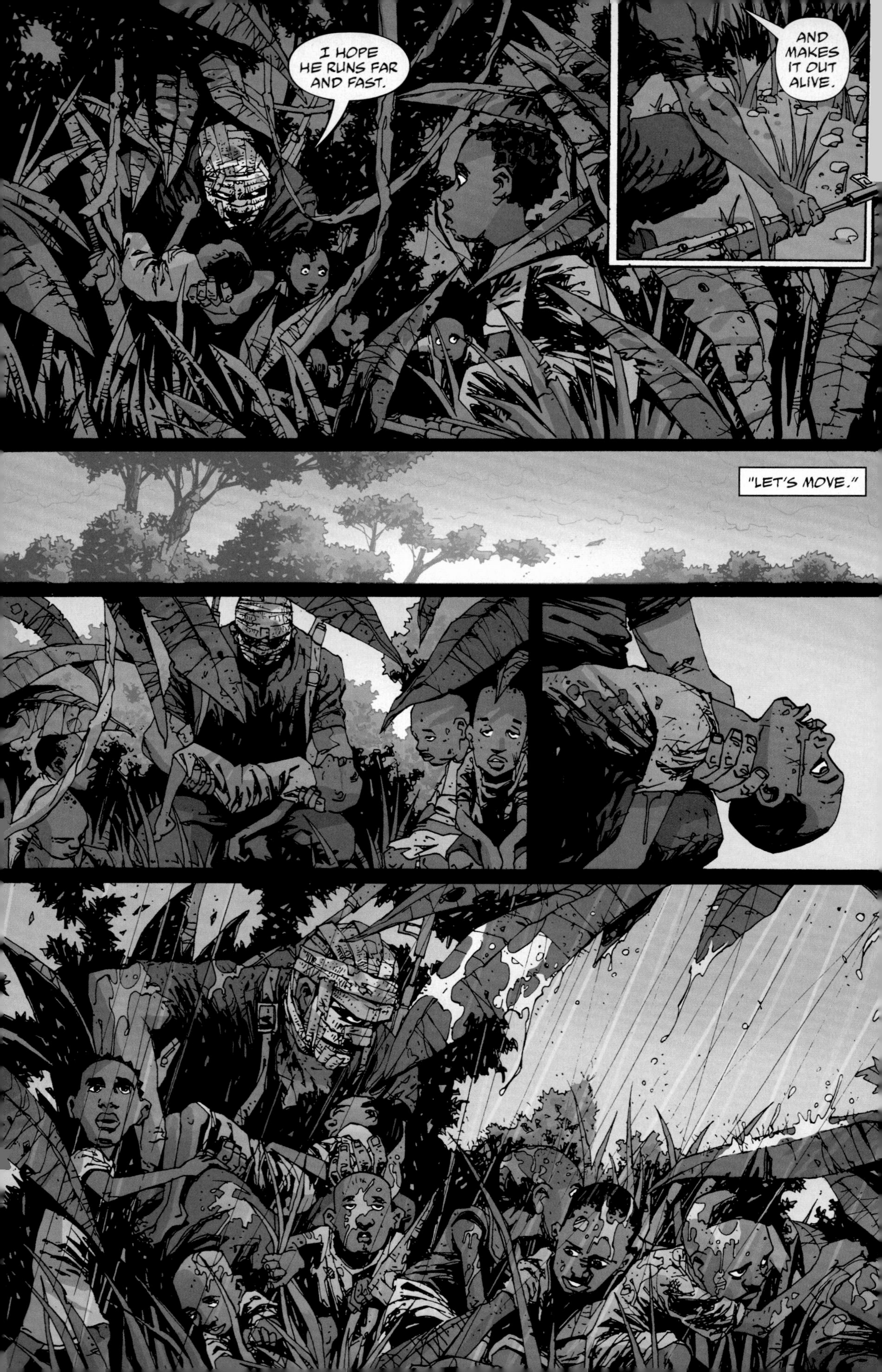
I HOPE HE RUNS FAR AND FAST.
AND MAKES IT OUT ALIVE.
"LET'S MOVE."

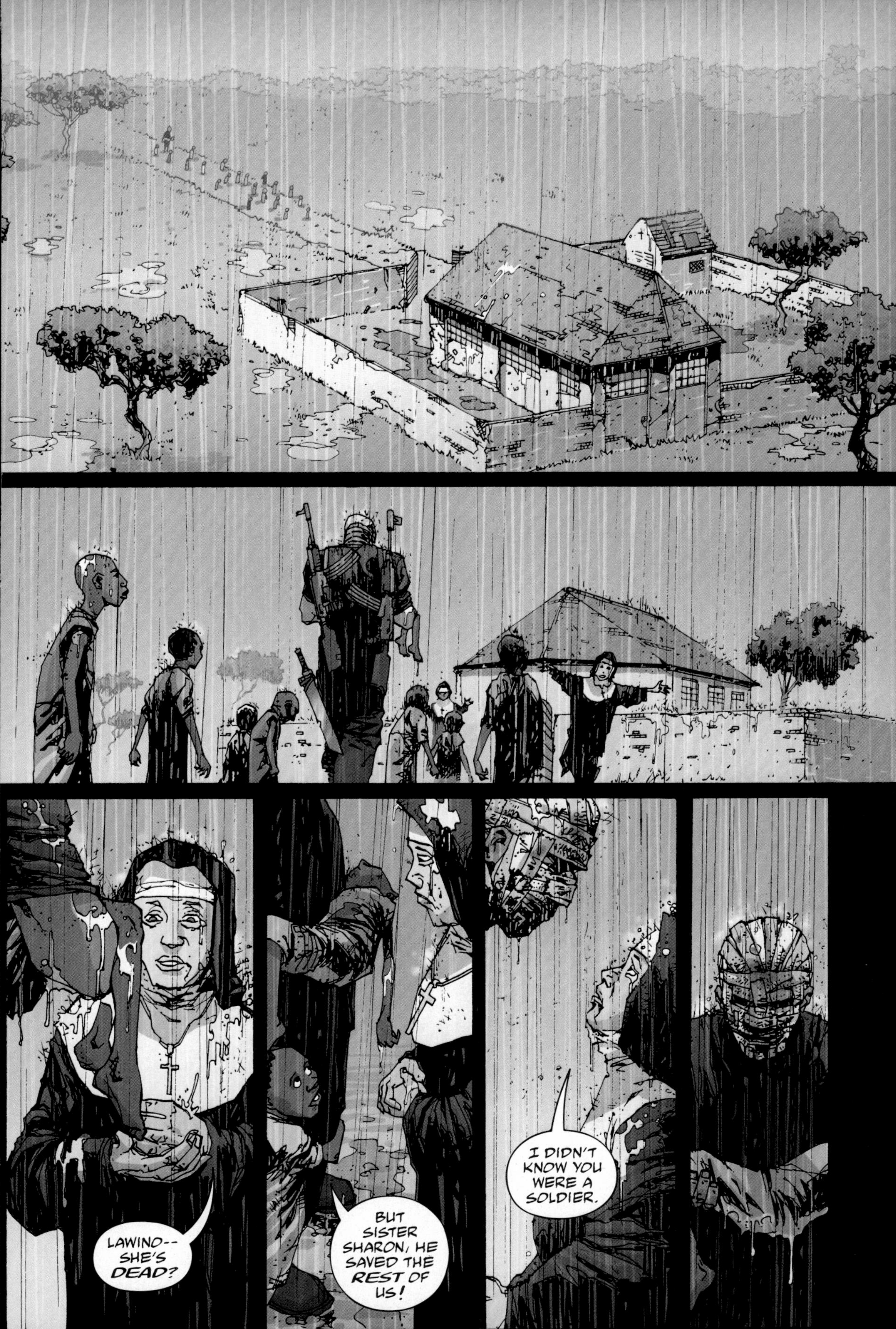
LAWINO--SHE'S DEAD?
BUT SISTER SHARON, HE SAVED THE REST OF US!
I DIDN'T KNOW YOU WERE A SOLDIER.

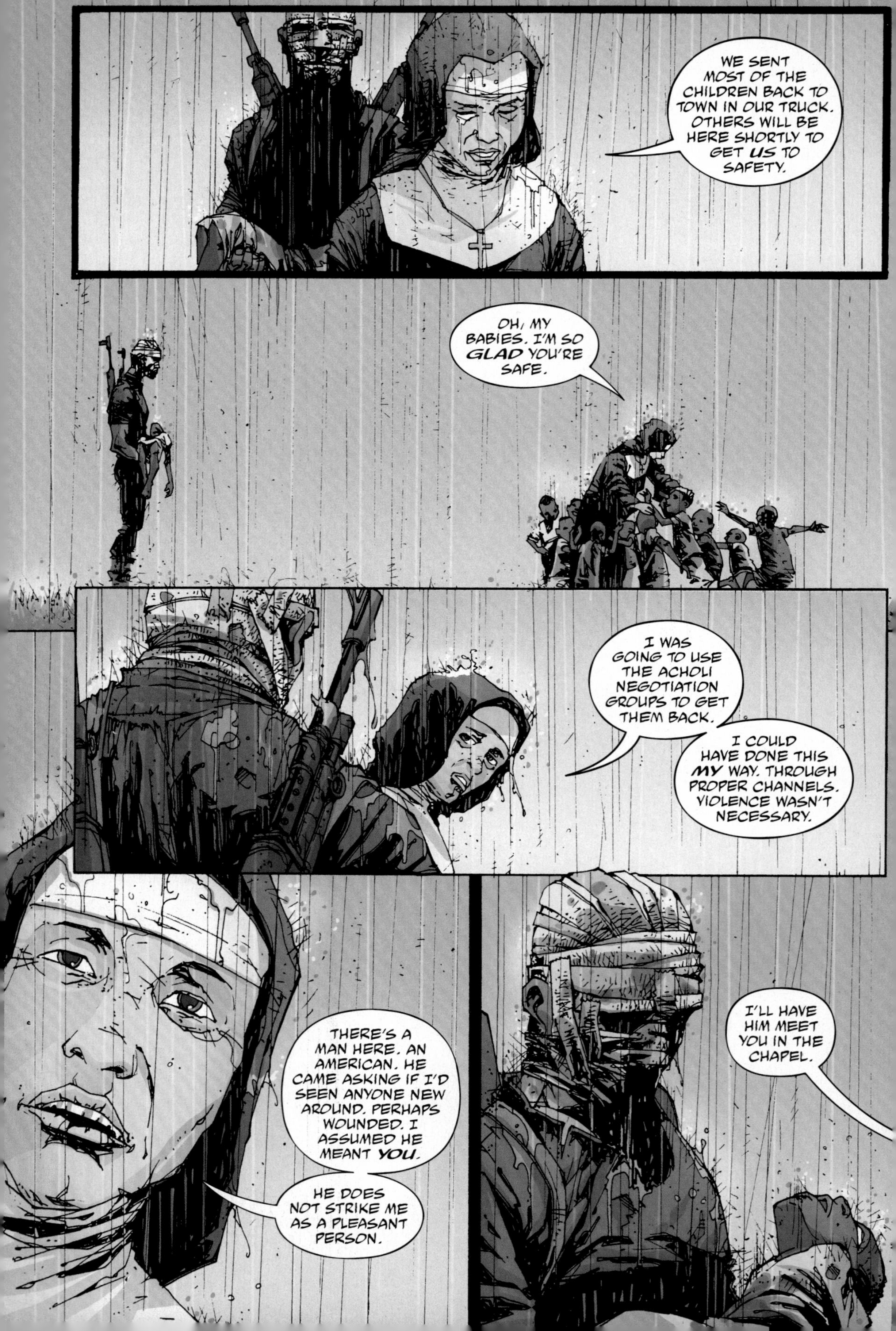
WE SENT MOST OF THE CHILDREN BACK TO TOWN IN OUR TRUCK. OTHERS WILL BE HERE SHORTLY TO GET US TO SAFETY.
OH, MY BABIES. I'M SO GLAD YOU'RE SAFE.
I WAS GOING TO USE THE ACHOLI NEGOTIATION GROUPS TO GET THEM BACK.
I COULD HAVE DONE THIS MY WAY. THROUGH PROPER CHANNELS. VIOLENCE WASN'T NECESSARY.
THERE'S A MAN HERE. AN AMERICAN. HE CAME ASKING IF I'D SEEN ANYONE NEW AROUND. PERHAPS WOUNDED. I ASSUMED HE MEANT YOU.
HE DOES NOT STRIKE ME AS A PLEASANT PERSON.
I'LL HAVE HIM MEET YOU IN THE CHAPEL.

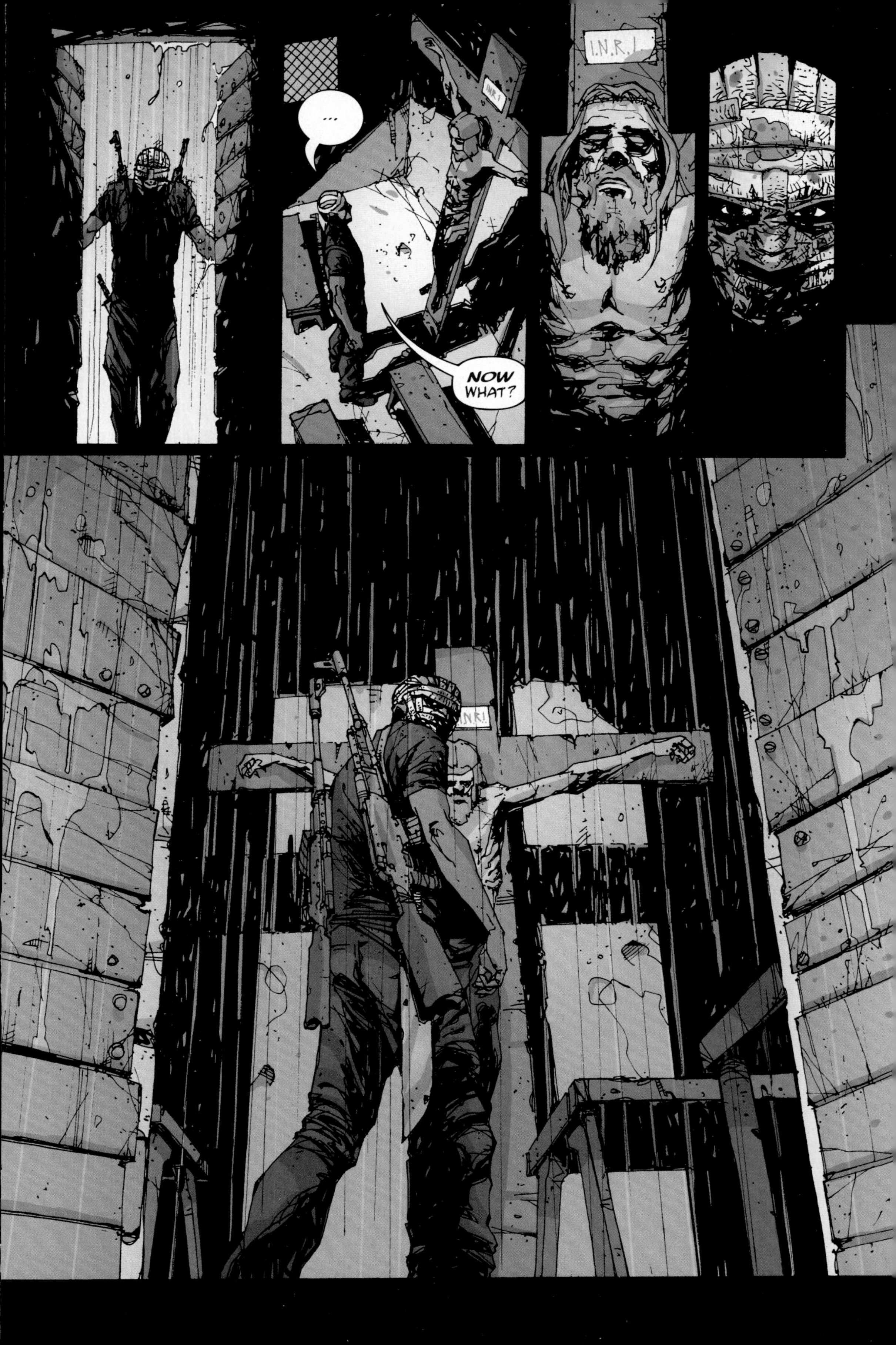

I.N.R.I.
...
NOW WHAT?
I.N.R.I.

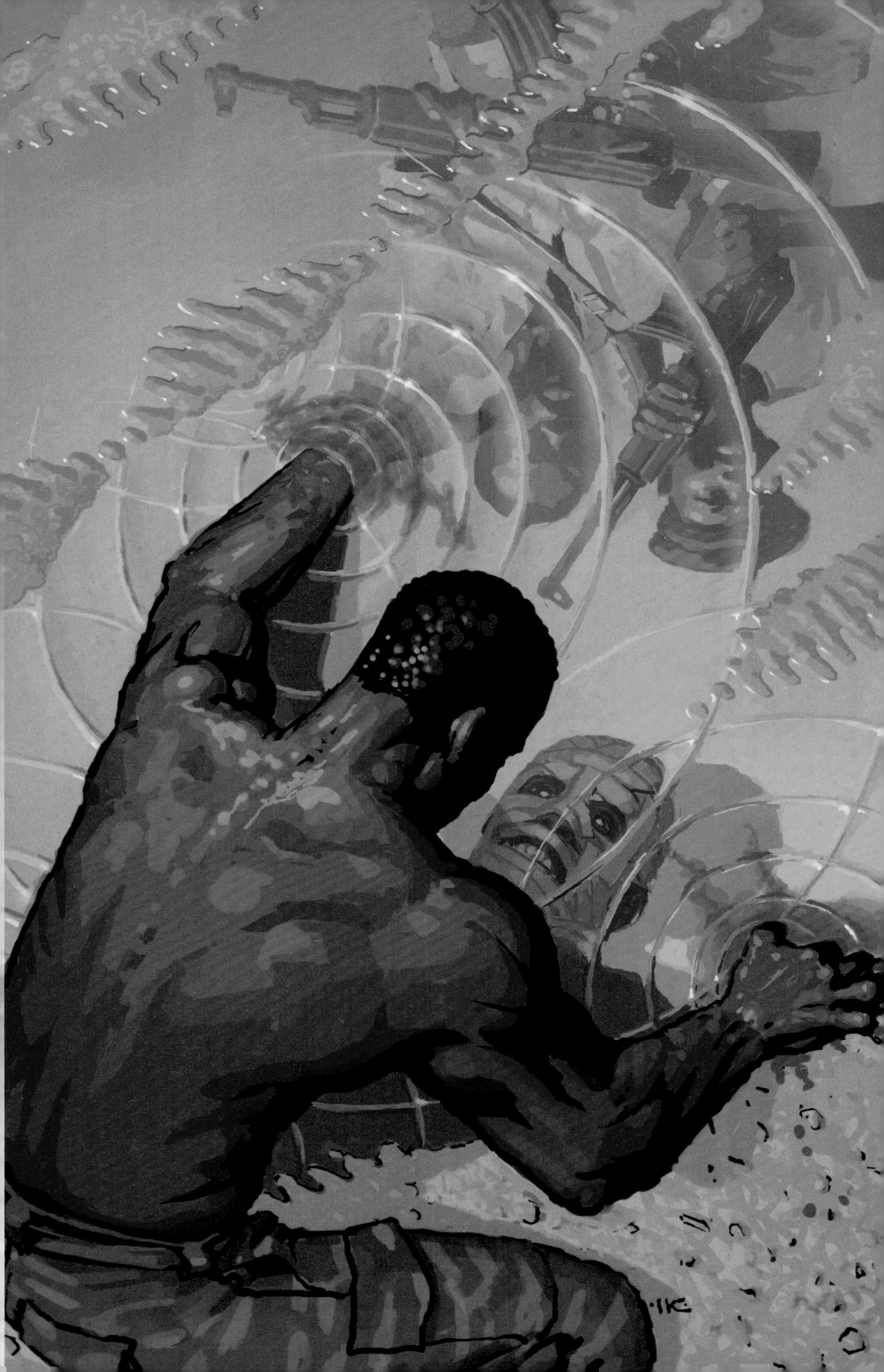

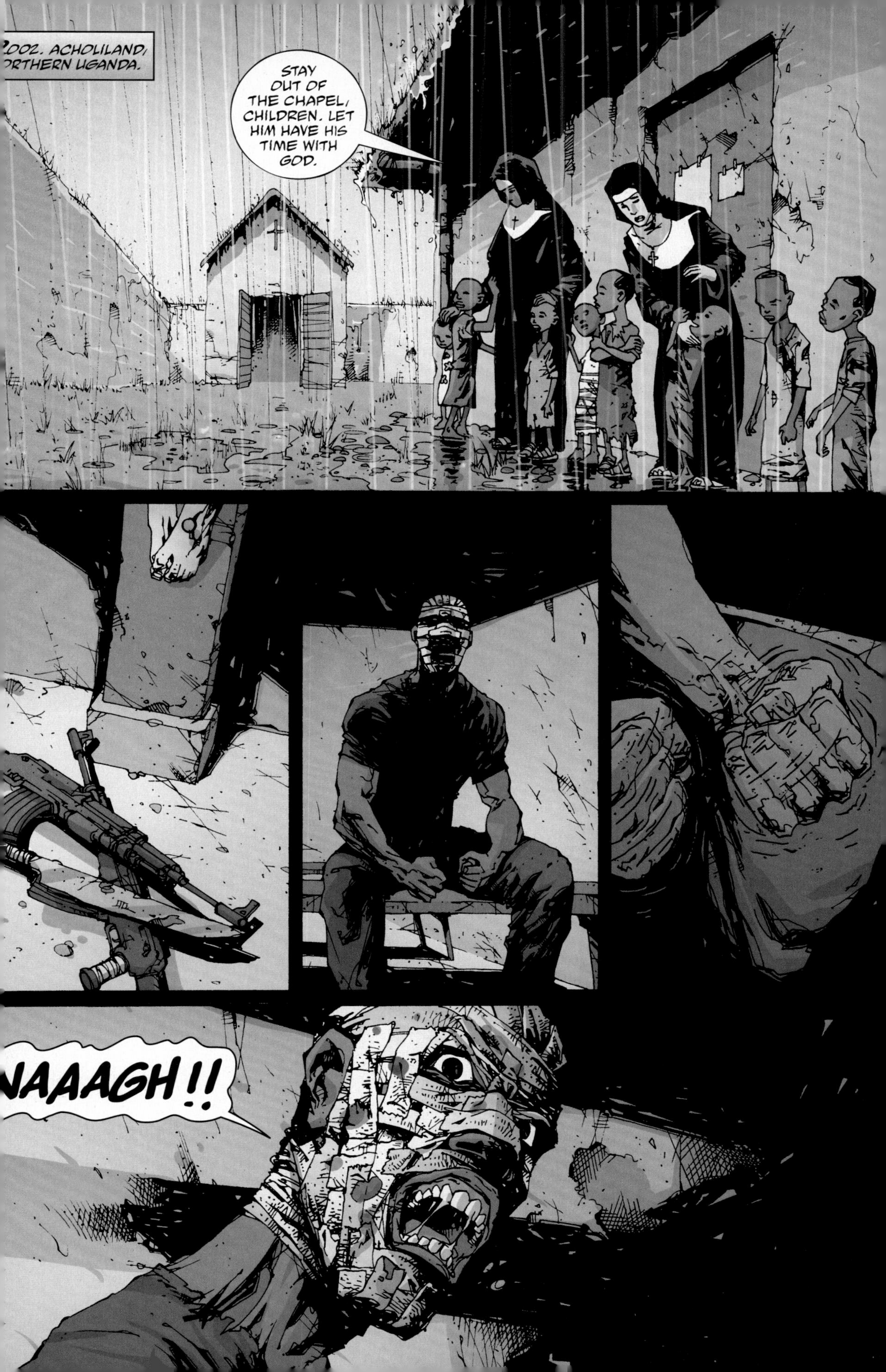

2002. ACHOLILAND, NORTHERN UGANDA.
STAY OUT OF THE CHAPEL, CHILDREN. LET HIM HAVE HIS TIME WITH GOD.
NAAAGH!!

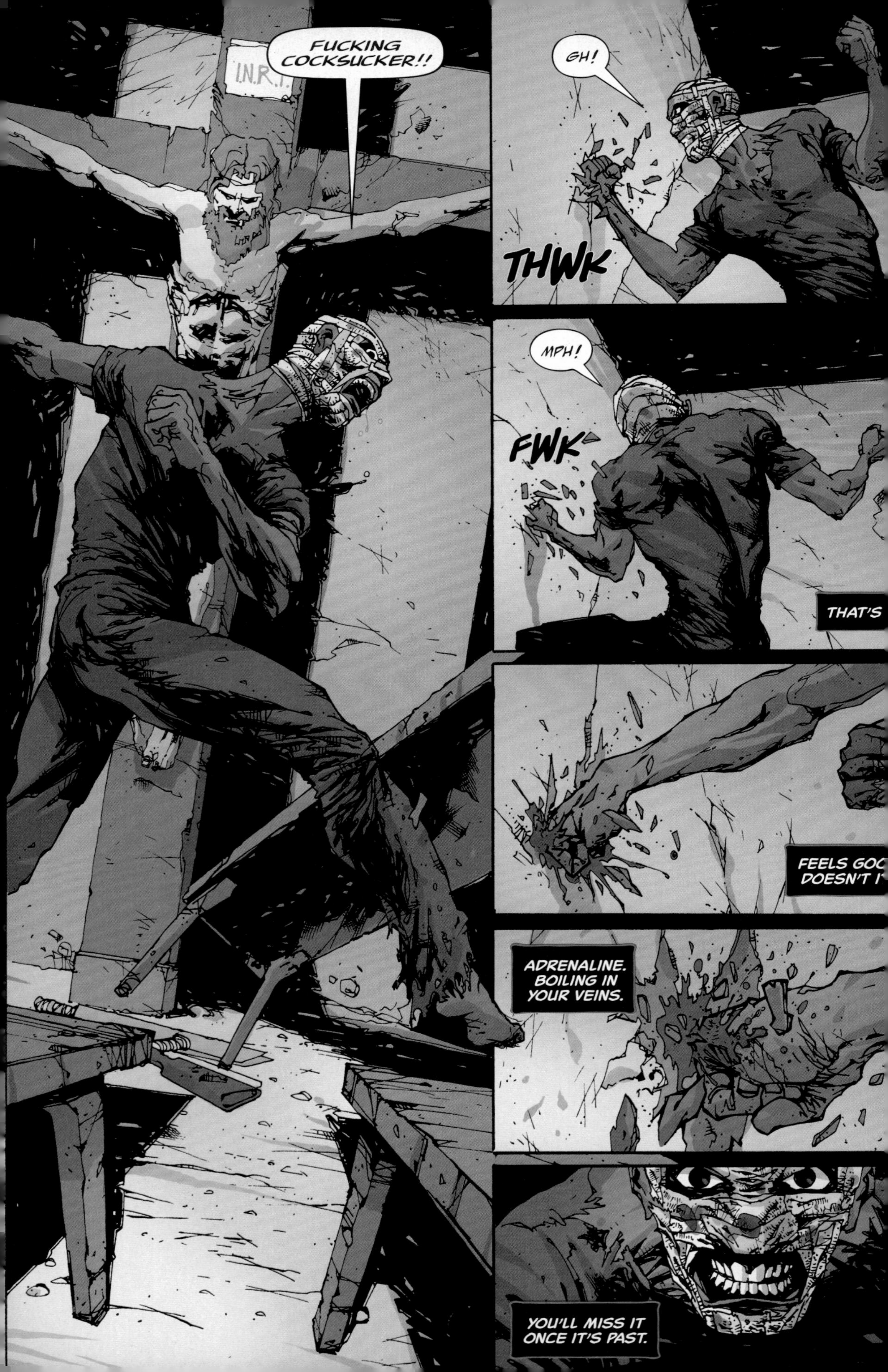
FUCKING COCKSUCKER!!
I.N.R.I.
GH!
THWK
MPH!
FWK
THAT'S
FEELS GOO
DOESN'T I
ADRENALINE. BOILING IN YOUR VEINS.
YOU'LL MISS IT ONCE IT'S PAST.

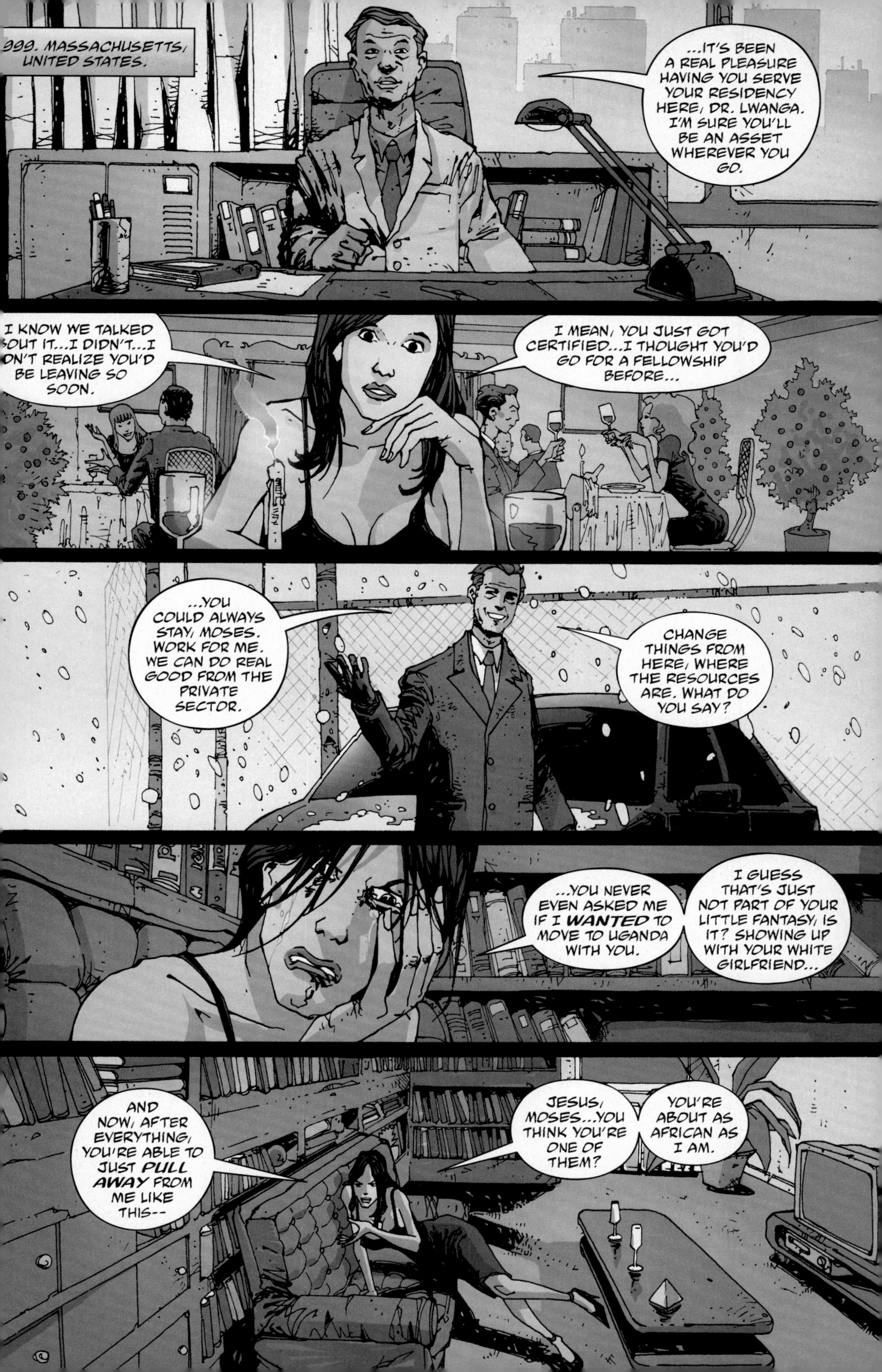
999. MASSACHUSETTS, UNITED STATES.
...IT'S BEEN A REAL PLEASURE HAVING YOU SERVE YOUR RESIDENCY HERE, DR. LWANGA. I'M SURE YOU'LL BE AN ASSET WHEREVER YOU GO.
I KNOW WE TALKED BOUT IT...I DIDN'T...I DN'T REALIZE YOU'D BE LEAVING SO SOON.
I MEAN, YOU JUST GOT CERTIFIED...I THOUGHT YOU'D GO FOR A FELLOWSHIP BEFORE...
...YOU COULD ALWAYS STAY, MOSES. WORK FOR ME. WE CAN DO REAL GOOD FROM THE PRIVATE SECTOR.
CHANGE THINGS FROM HERE, WHERE THE RESOURCES ARE. WHAT DO YOU SAY?
...YOU NEVER EVEN ASKED ME IF I ***WANTED*** TO MOVE TO UGANDA WITH YOU.
I GUESS THAT'S JUST NOT PART OF YOUR LITTLE FANTASY, IS IT? SHOWING UP WITH YOUR WHITE GIRLFRIEND...
AND NOW, AFTER EVERYTHING, YOU'RE ABLE TO JUST ***PULL AWAY*** FROM ME LIKE THIS--
JESUS, MOSES...YOU THINK YOU'RE ONE OF THEM?
YOU'RE ABOUT AS AFRICAN AS I AM.

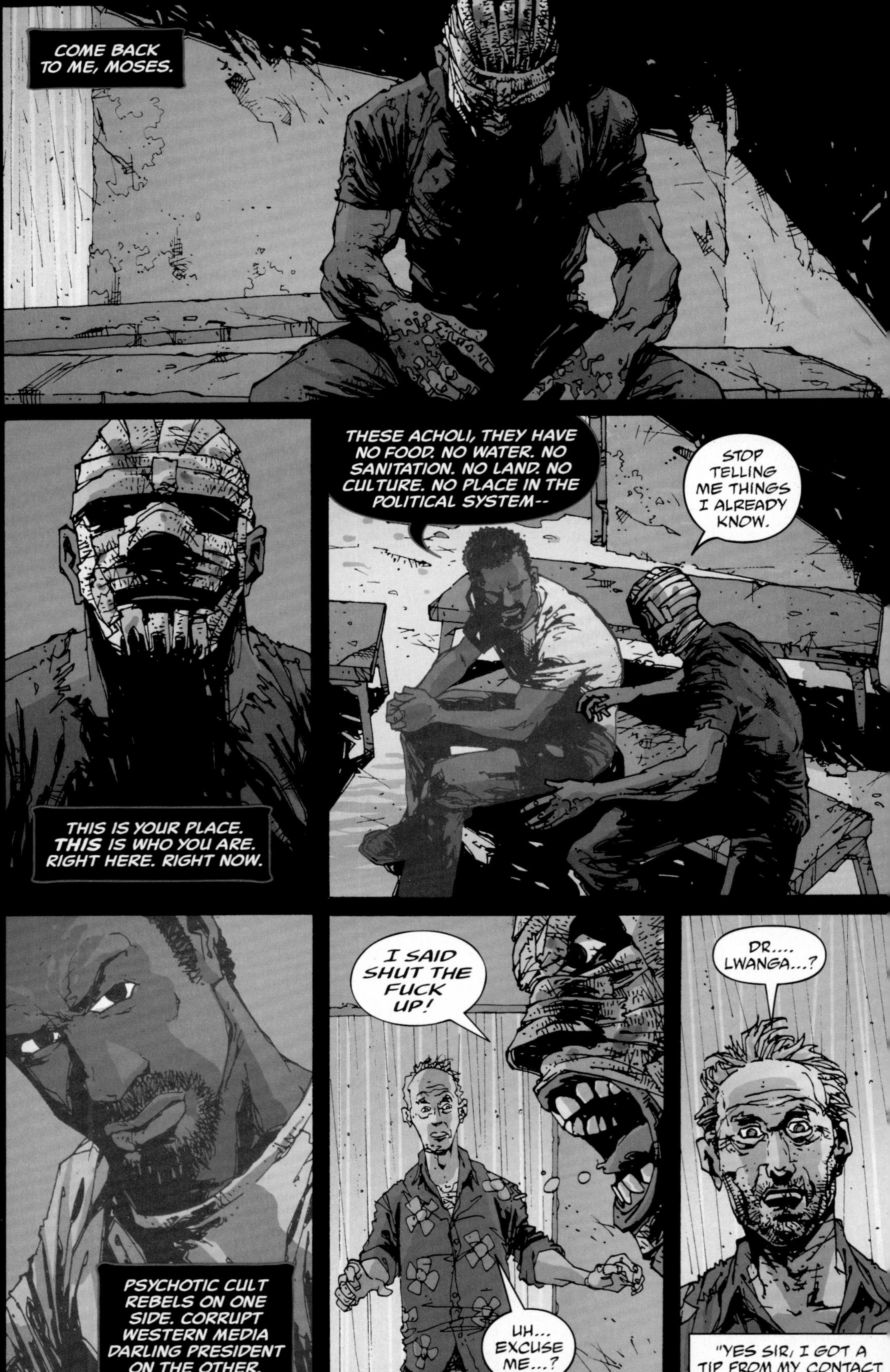
COME BACK TO ME, MOSES.
THESE ACHOLI, THEY HAVE NO FOOD. NO WATER. NO SANITATION. NO LAND. NO CULTURE. NO PLACE IN THE POLITICAL SYSTEM--
STOP TELLING ME THINGS I ALREADY KNOW.
THIS IS YOUR PLACE. THIS IS WHO YOU ARE. RIGHT HERE. RIGHT NOW.
PSYCHOTIC CULT REBELS ON ONE SIDE. CORRUPT WESTERN MEDIA DARLING PRESIDENT ON THE OTHER.
I SAID SHUT THE FUCK UP!
UH... EXCUSE ME...?
DR.... LWANGA...?
"YES SIR, I GOT A TIP FROM MY CONTACT IN KATANGA..."

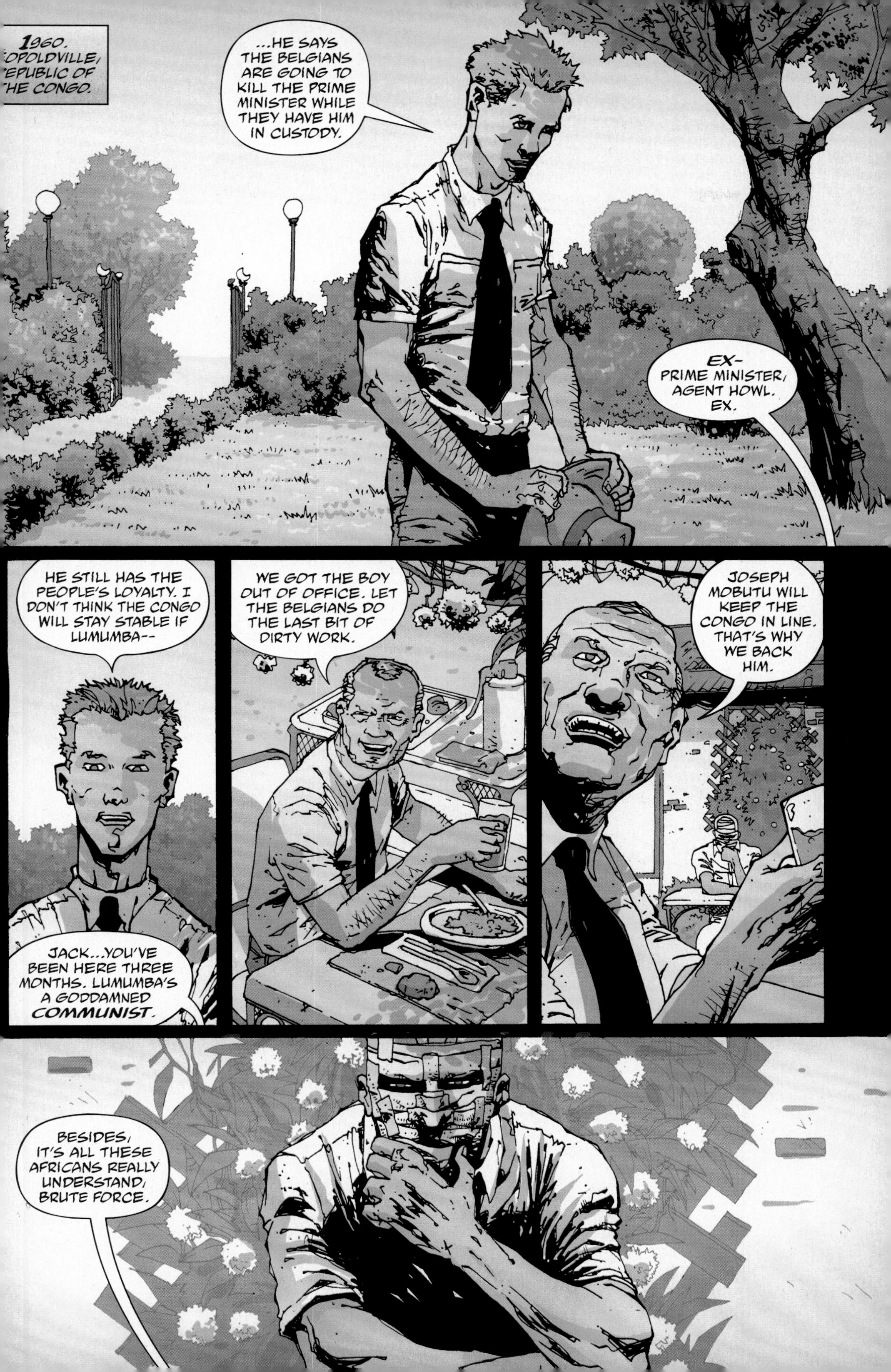
1960. EOPOLDVILLE, EPUBLIC OF THE CONGO.
...HE SAYS THE BELGIANS ARE GOING TO KILL THE PRIME MINISTER WHILE THEY HAVE HIM IN CUSTODY.
EX- PRIME MINISTER, AGENT HOWL. EX.
HE STILL HAS THE PEOPLE'S LOYALTY. I DON'T THINK THE CONGO WILL STAY STABLE IF LUMUMBA--
JACK...YOU'VE BEEN HERE THREE MONTHS. LUMUMBA'S A GODDAMNED COMMUNIST.
WE GOT THE BOY OUT OF OFFICE. LET THE BELGIANS DO THE LAST BIT OF DIRTY WORK.
JOSEPH MOBUTU WILL KEEP THE CONGO IN LINE. THAT'S WHY WE BACK HIM.
BESIDES, IT'S ALL THESE AFRICANS REALLY UNDERSTAND, BRUTE FORCE.

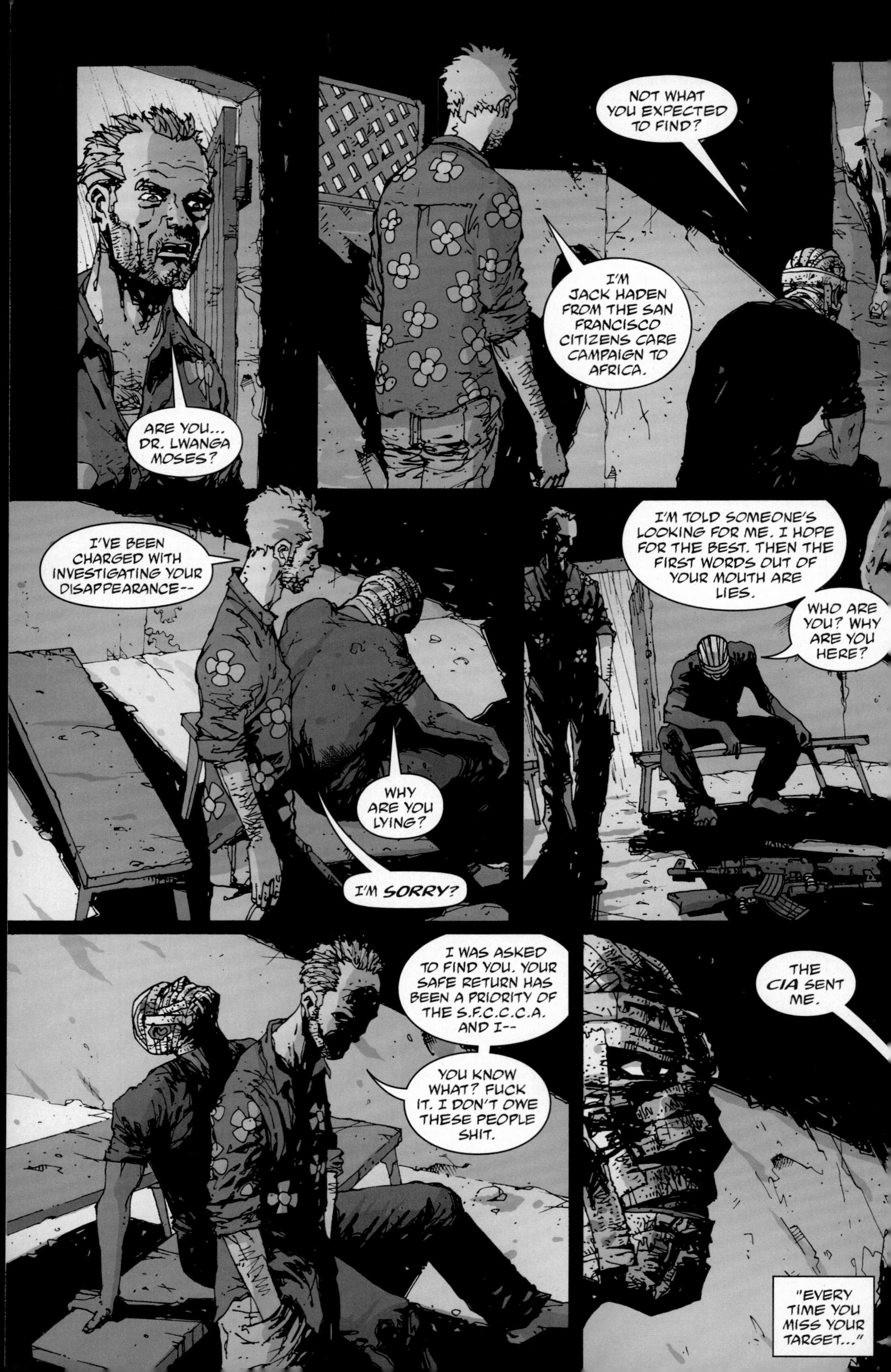
ARE YOU... DR. LWANGA MOSES?
I'M JACK HADEN FROM THE SAN FRANCISCO CITIZENS CARE CAMPAIGN TO AFRICA.
NOT WHAT YOU EXPECTED TO FIND?
I'VE BEEN CHARGED WITH INVESTIGATING YOUR DISAPPEARANCE--
WHY ARE YOU LYING?
I'M SORRY?
I'M TOLD SOMEONE'S LOOKING FOR ME. I HOPE FOR THE BEST. THEN THE FIRST WORDS OUT OF YOUR MOUTH ARE LIES.
WHO ARE YOU? WHY ARE YOU HERE?
I WAS ASKED TO FIND YOU. YOUR SAFE RETURN HAS BEEN A PRIORITY OF THE S.F.C.C.C.A. AND I--
YOU KNOW WHAT? FUCK IT. I DON'T OWE THESE PEOPLE SHIT.
THE CIA SENT ME.
"EVERY TIME YOU MISS YOUR TARGET..."

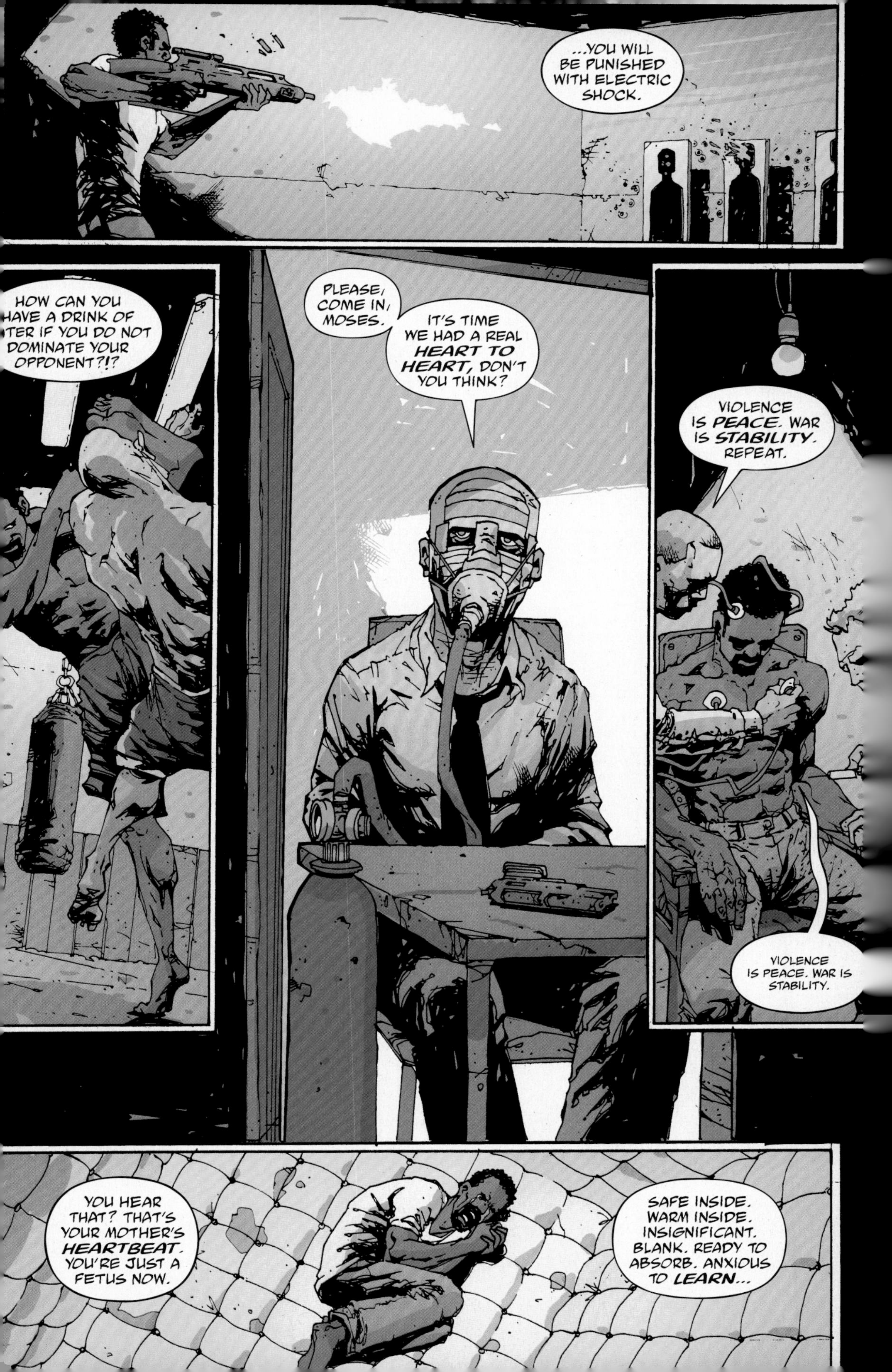
...YOU WILL BE PUNISHED WITH ELECTRIC SHOCK.
HOW CAN YOU HAVE A DRINK OF TER IF YOU DO NOT DOMINATE YOUR OPPONENT?!?
PLEASE, COME IN, MOSES.
IT'S TIME WE HAD A REAL HEART TO HEART, DON'T YOU THINK?
VIOLENCE IS PEACE. WAR IS STABILITY. REPEAT.
VIOLENCE IS PEACE. WAR IS STABILITY.
YOU HEAR THAT? THAT'S YOUR MOTHER'S HEARTBEAT. YOU'RE JUST A FETUS NOW.
SAFE INSIDE. WARM INSIDE. INSIGNIFICANT. BLANK. READY TO ABSORB. ANXIOUS TO LEARN...

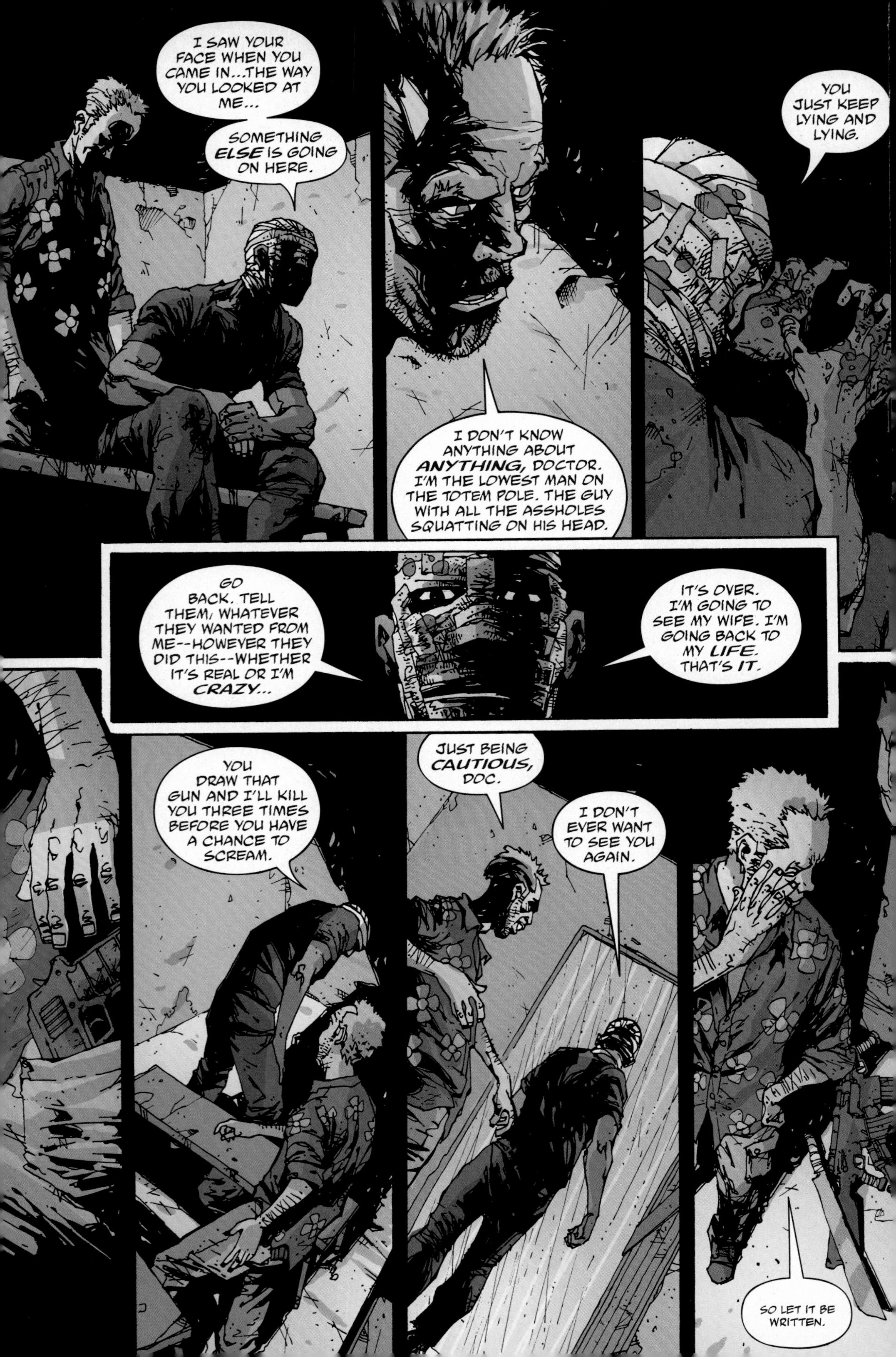
I SAW YOUR FACE WHEN YOU CAME IN...THE WAY YOU LOOKED AT ME...
SOMETHING ELSE IS GOING ON HERE.
I DON'T KNOW ANYTHING ABOUT ANYTHING, DOCTOR. I'M THE LOWEST MAN ON THE TOTEM POLE. THE GUY WITH ALL THE ASSHOLES SQUATTING ON HIS HEAD.
YOU JUST KEEP LYING AND LYING.
GO BACK. TELL THEM, WHATEVER THEY WANTED FROM ME--HOWEVER THEY DID THIS--WHETHER IT'S REAL OR I'M CRAZY...
IT'S OVER. I'M GOING TO SEE MY WIFE. I'M GOING BACK TO MY LIFE. THAT'S IT.
YOU DRAW THAT GUN AND I'LL KILL YOU THREE TIMES BEFORE YOU HAVE A CHANCE TO SCREAM.
JUST BEING CAUTIOUS, DOC.
I DON'T EVER WANT TO SEE YOU AGAIN.
SO LET IT BE WRITTEN.

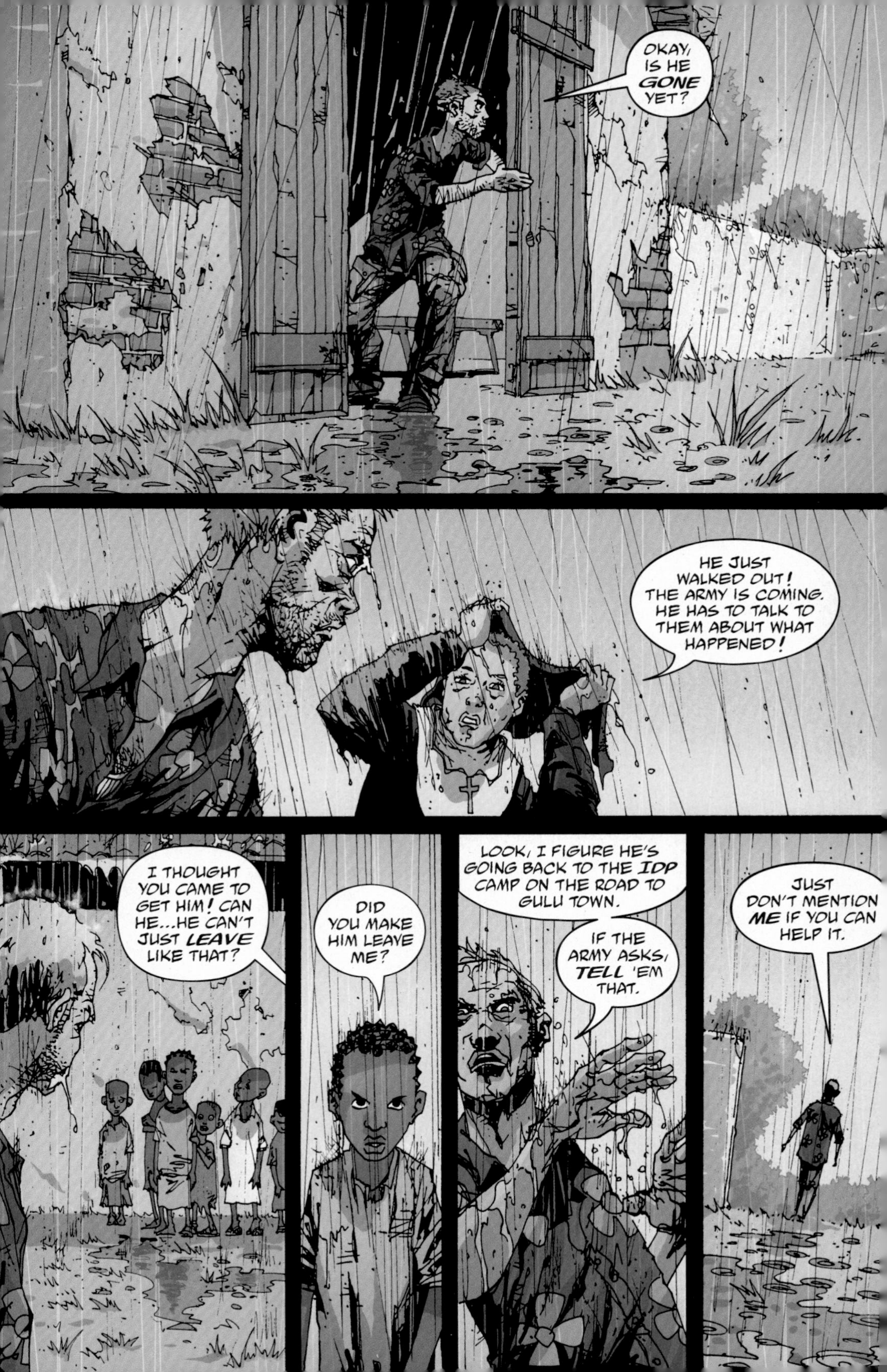

OKAY, IS HE GONE YET?
HE JUST WALKED OUT! THE ARMY IS COMING. HE HAS TO TALK TO THEM ABOUT WHAT HAPPENED!
I THOUGHT YOU CAME TO GET HIM! CAN HE...HE CAN'T JUST LEAVE LIKE THAT?
DID YOU MAKE HIM LEAVE ME?
LOOK, I FIGURE HE'S GOING BACK TO THE IDP CAMP ON THE ROAD TO GULU TOWN.
IF THE ARMY ASKS, TELL 'EM THAT.
JUST DON'T MENTION ME IF YOU CAN HELP IT.

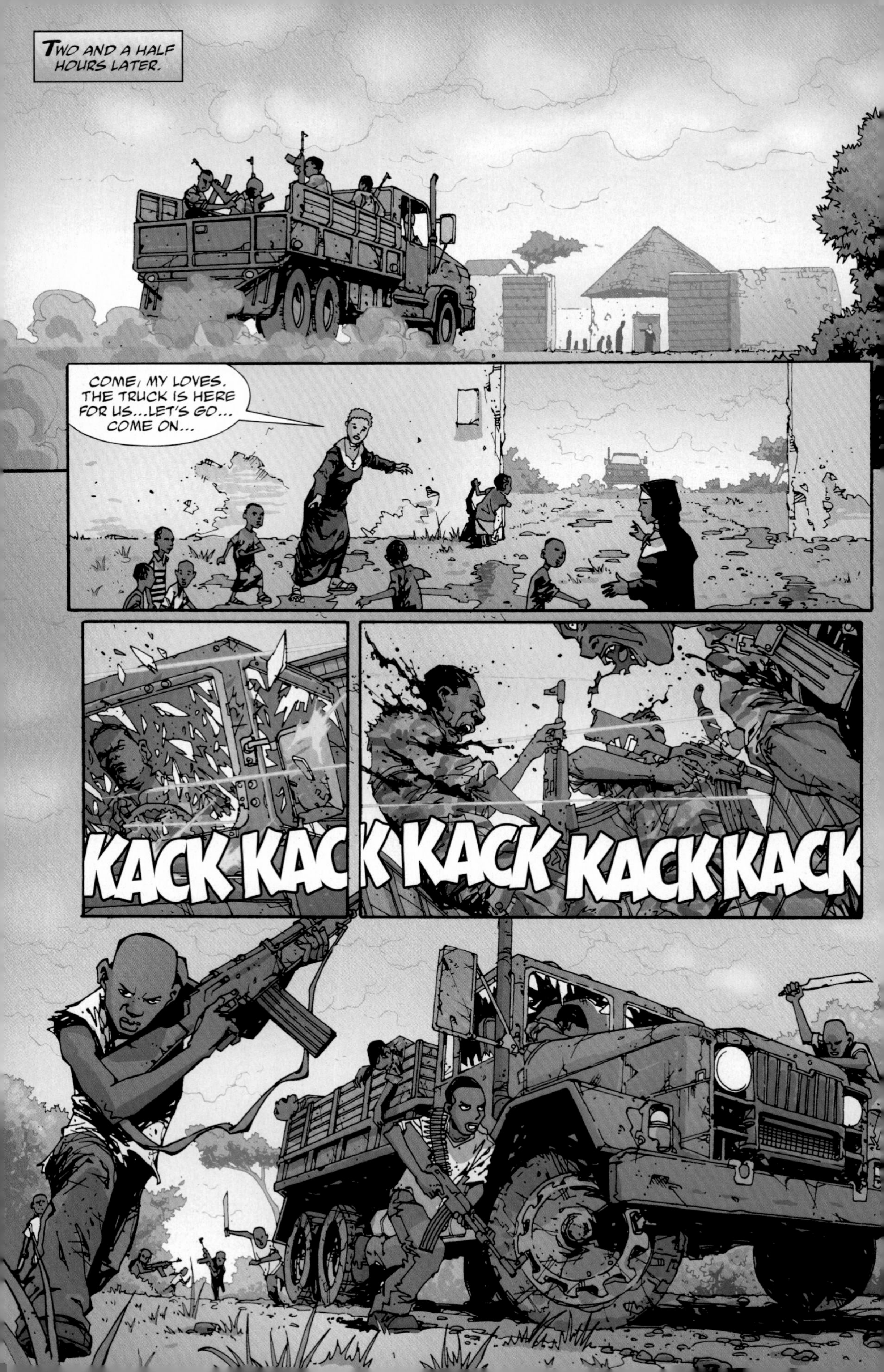
TWO AND A HALF HOURS LATER.
COME, MY LOVES. THE TRUCK IS HERE FOR US...LET'S GO... COME ON...
KACK KACK KACK KACK KACK KACK

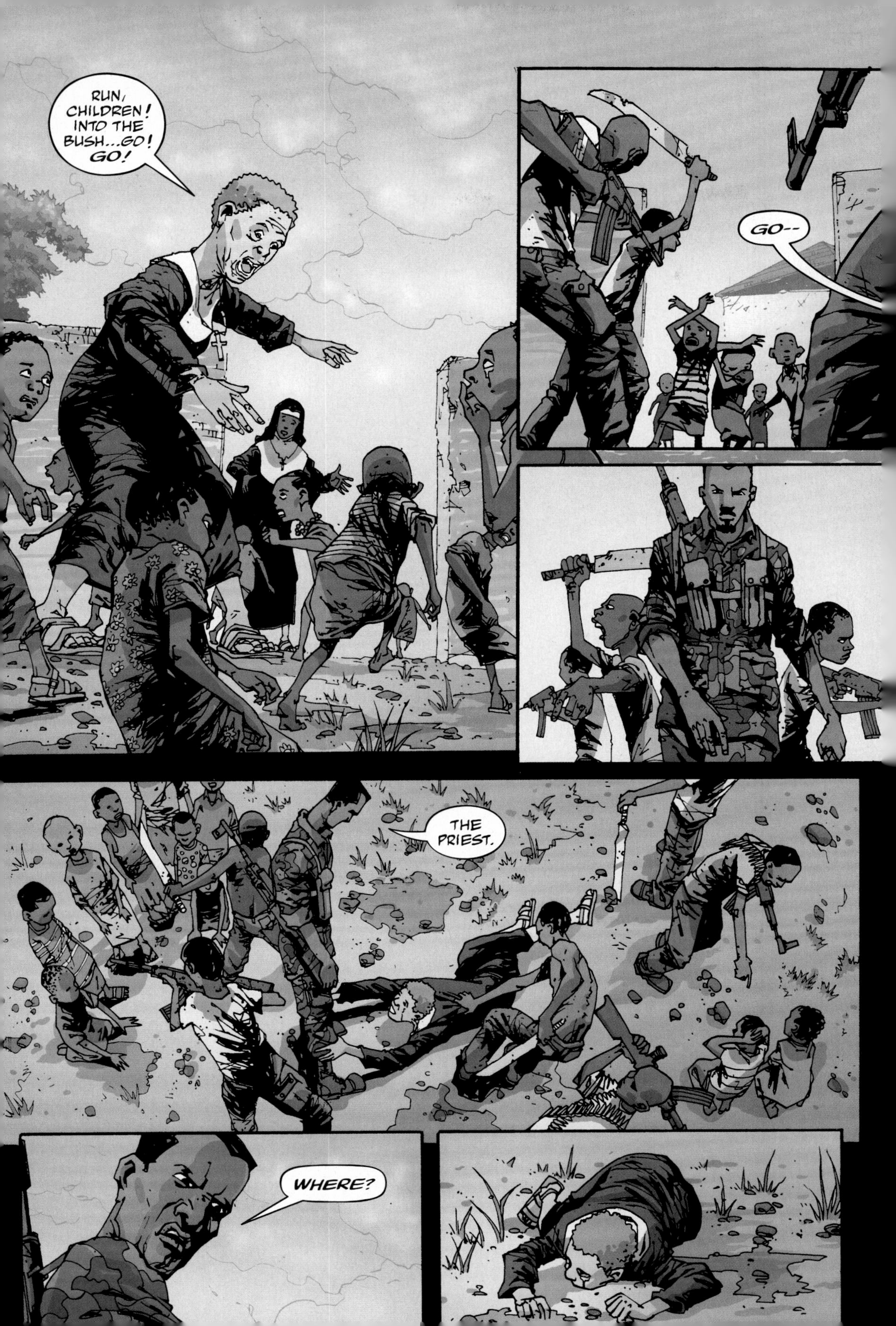
RUN, CHILDREN! INTO THE BUSH...GO! GO!
GO--
THE PRIEST.
WHERE?

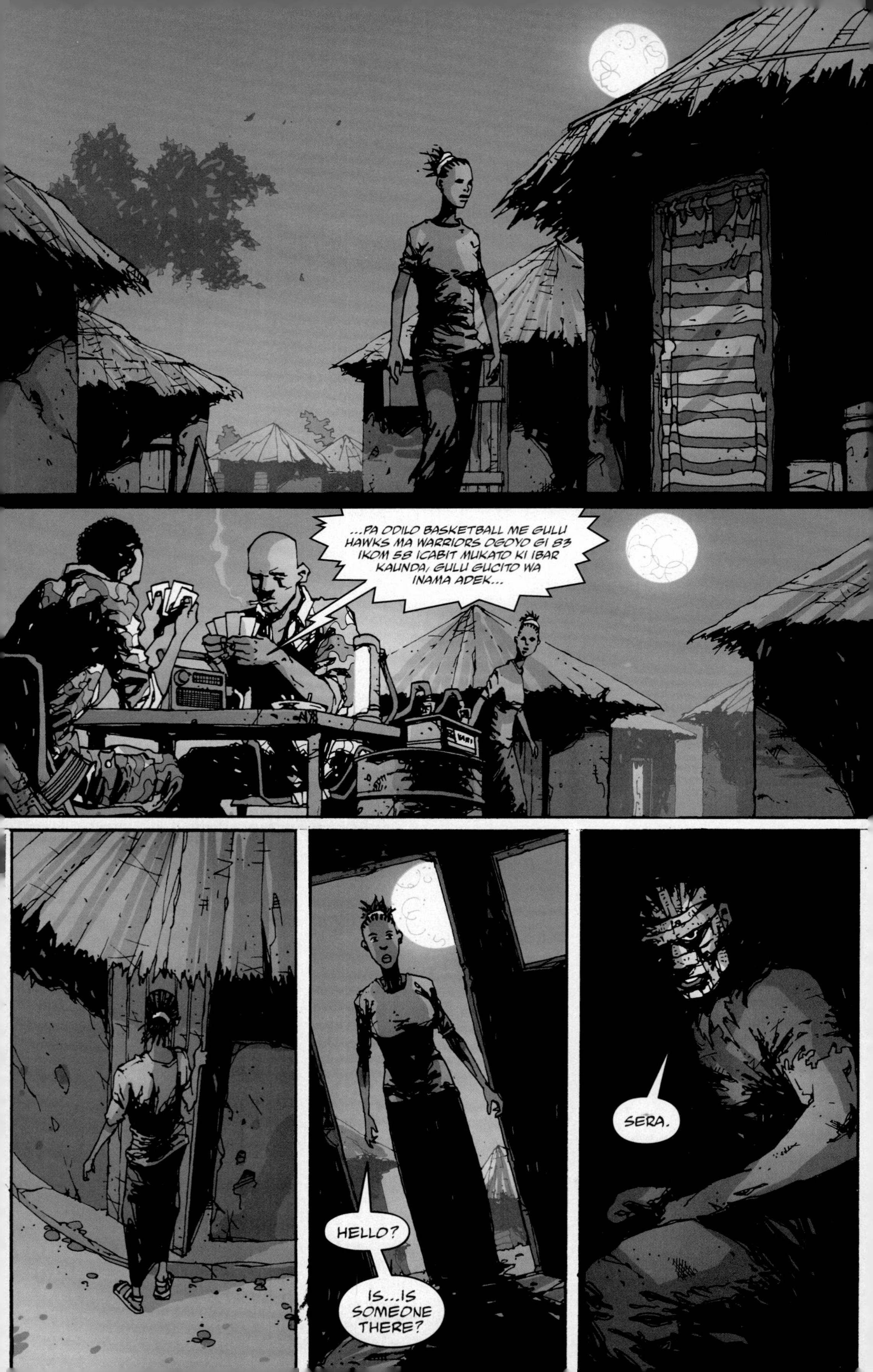
...PA ODILO BASKETBALL ME GULU HAWKS MA WARRIORS OGOYO GI 83 IKOM 58 ICABIT MUKATO KI IBAR KAUNDA, GULU GUCITO WA INAMA ADEK...
HELLO?
IS...IS SOMEONE THERE?
SERA.

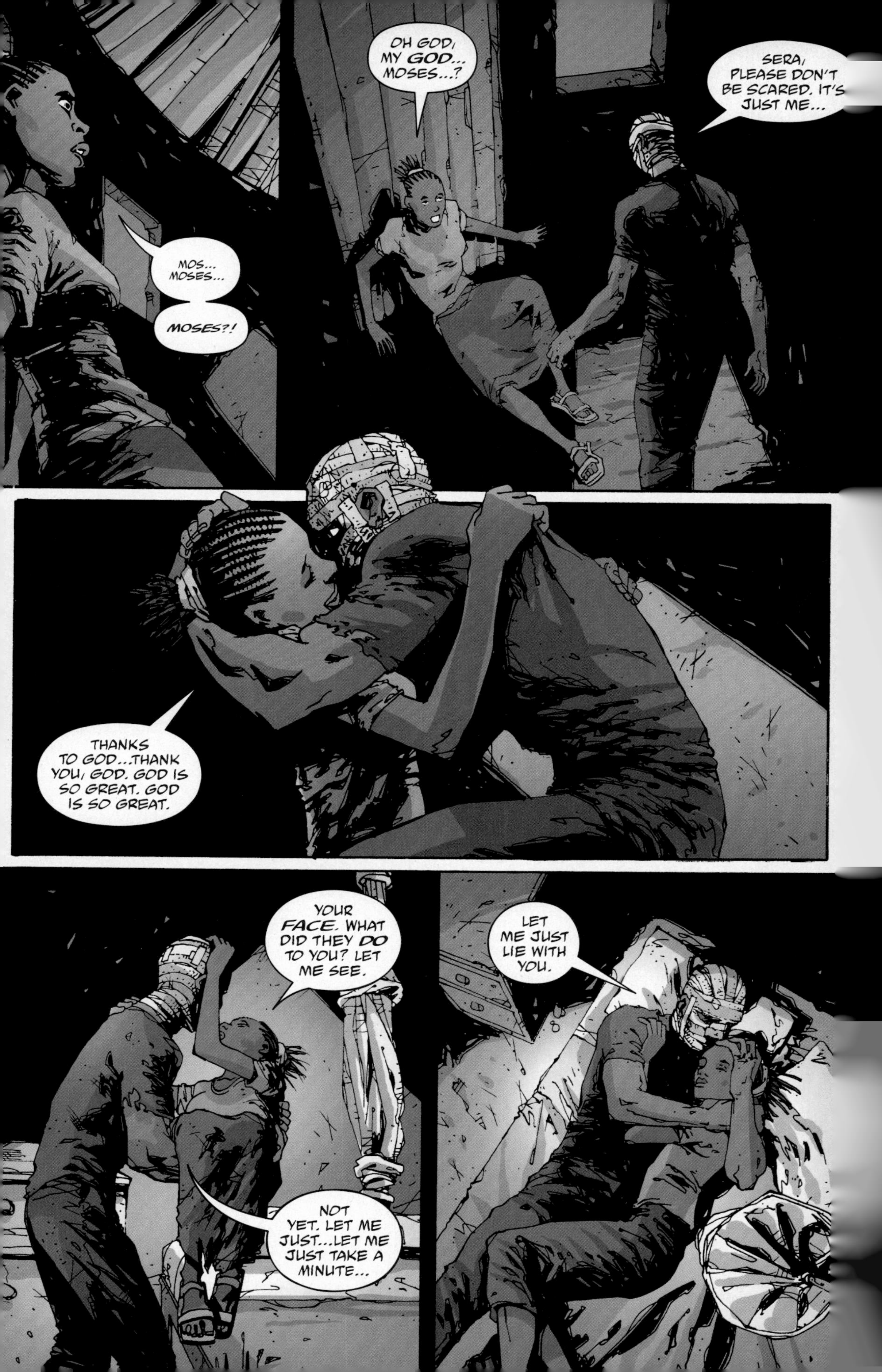
MOS... MOSES...
MOSES?!
OH GOD, MY GOD... MOSES...?
SERA, PLEASE DON'T BE SCARED. IT'S JUST ME...
THANKS TO GOD...THANK YOU, GOD. GOD IS SO GREAT. GOD IS SO GREAT.
YOUR FACE. WHAT DID THEY DO TO YOU? LET ME SEE.
NOT YET. LET ME JUST...LET ME JUST TAKE A MINUTE...
LET ME JUST LIE WITH YOU.

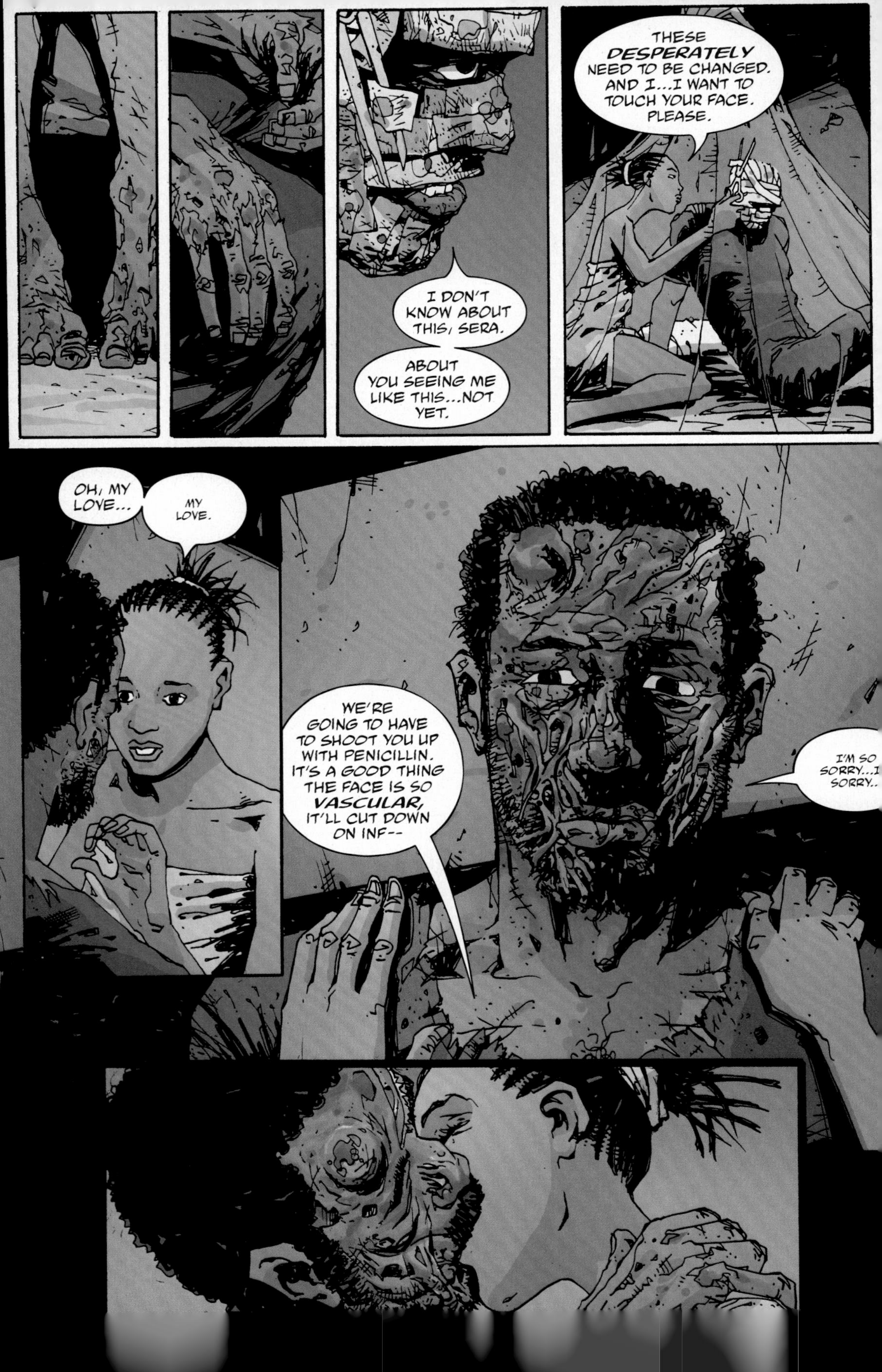
I DON'T KNOW ABOUT THIS, SERA.
ABOUT YOU SEEING ME LIKE THIS...NOT YET.
THESE *DESPERATELY* NEED TO BE CHANGED. AND I...I WANT TO TOUCH YOUR FACE. PLEASE.
OH, MY LOVE...
MY LOVE.
WE'RE GOING TO HAVE TO SHOOT YOU UP WITH PENICILLIN. IT'S A GOOD THING THE FACE IS SO *VASCULAR,* IT'LL CUT DOWN ON INF--
I'M SO SORRY...I SORRY...

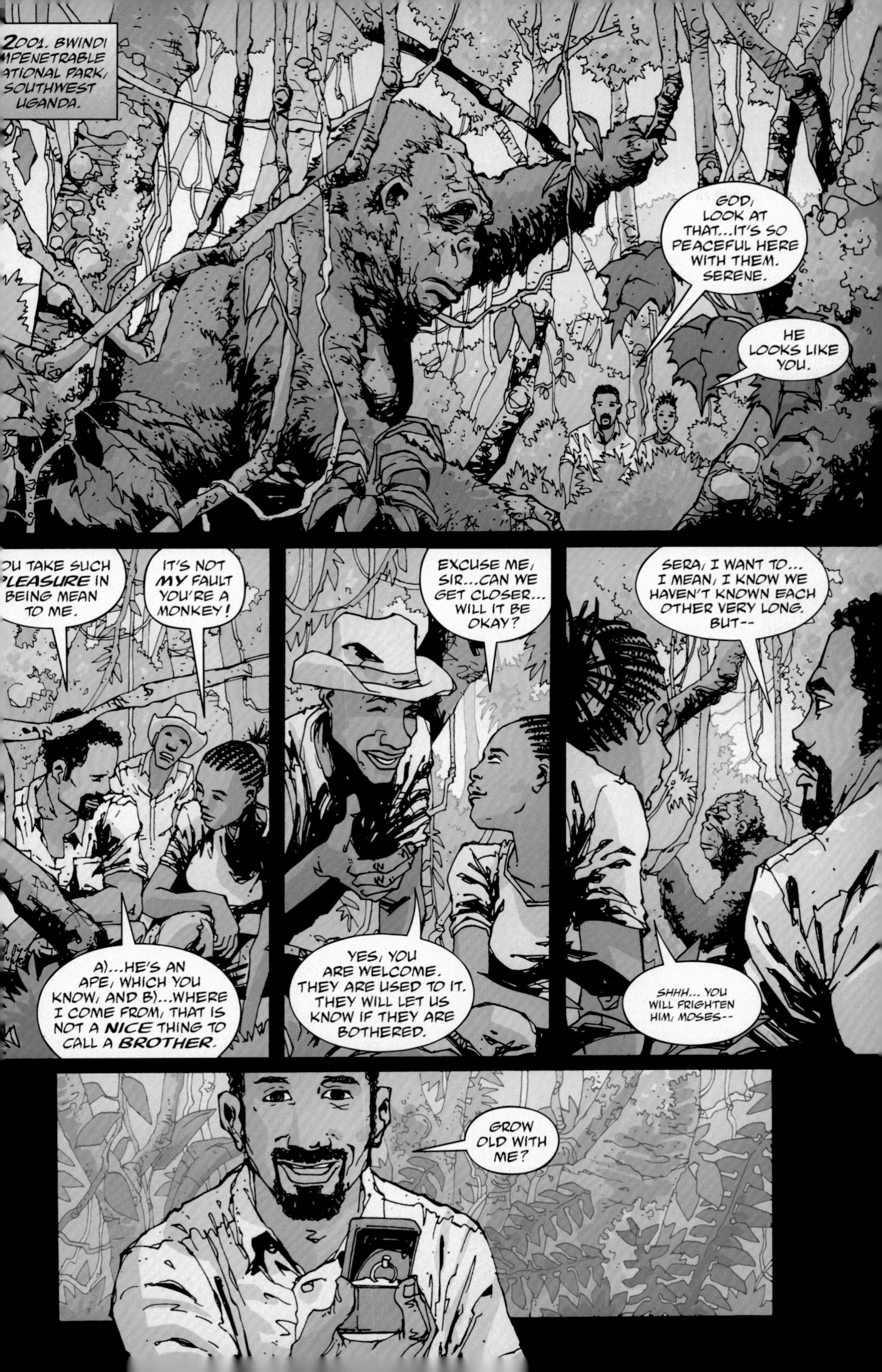
2001. BWINDI IMPENETRABLE NATIONAL PARK, SOUTHWEST UGANDA.
GOD, LOOK AT THAT...IT'S SO PEACEFUL HERE WITH THEM. SERENE.
HE LOOKS LIKE YOU.
YOU TAKE SUCH PLEASURE IN BEING MEAN TO ME.
IT'S NOT MY FAULT YOU'RE A MONKEY!
A)...HE'S AN APE, WHICH YOU KNOW, AND B)...WHERE I COME FROM, THAT IS NOT A NICE THING TO CALL A BROTHER.
EXCUSE ME, SIR...CAN WE GET CLOSER... WILL IT BE OKAY?
YES, YOU ARE WELCOME. THEY ARE USED TO IT. THEY WILL LET US KNOW IF THEY ARE BOTHERED.
SERA, I WANT TO... I MEAN, I KNOW WE HAVEN'T KNOWN EACH OTHER VERY LONG. BUT--
SHHH... YOU WILL FRIGHTEN HIM, MOSES--
GROW OLD WITH ME?

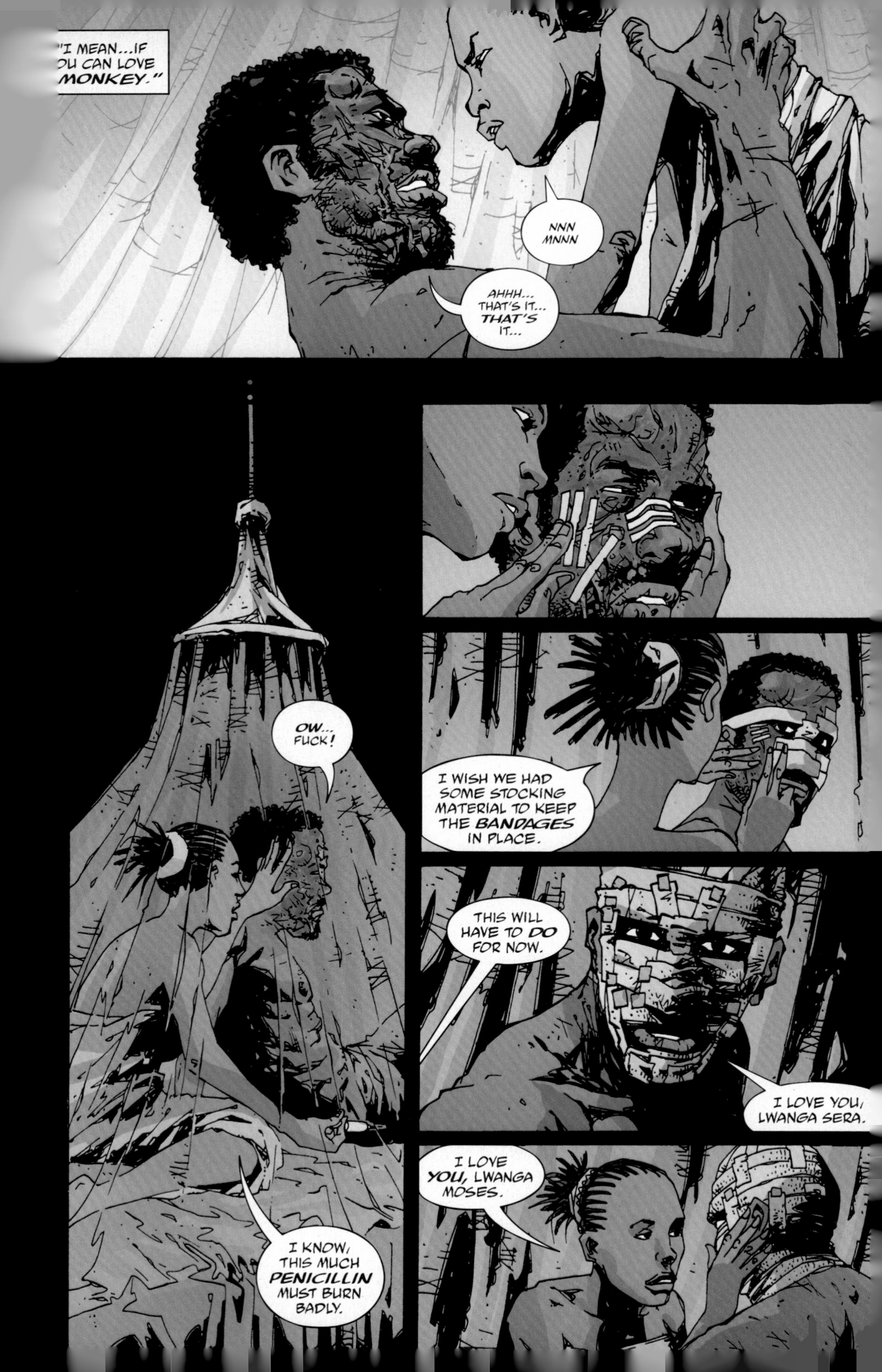
"I MEAN...IF
YOU CAN LOVE
MONKEY."
NNN MNNN
AHHH... THAT'S IT... THAT'S IT...
OW... FUCK!
I KNOW, THIS MUCH PENICILLIN MUST BURN BADLY.
I WISH WE HAD SOME STOCKING MATERIAL TO KEEP THE BANDAGES IN PLACE.
THIS WILL HAVE TO DO FOR NOW.
I LOVE YOU, LWANGA SERA.
I LOVE YOU, LWANGA MOSES.

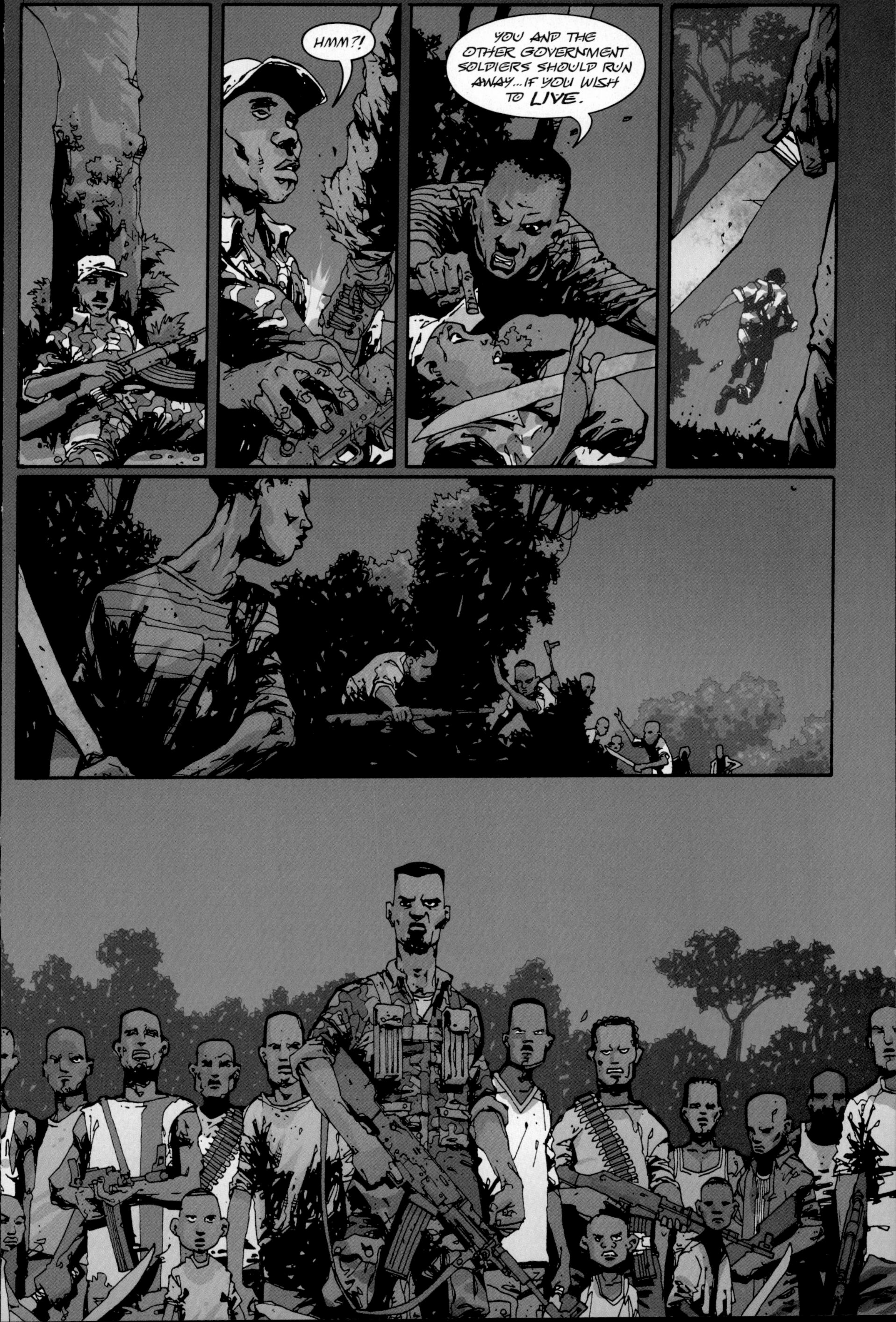
HMM?!
YOU AND THE OTHER GOVERNMENT SOLDIERS SHOULD RUN AWAY... IF YOU WISH TO LIVE.

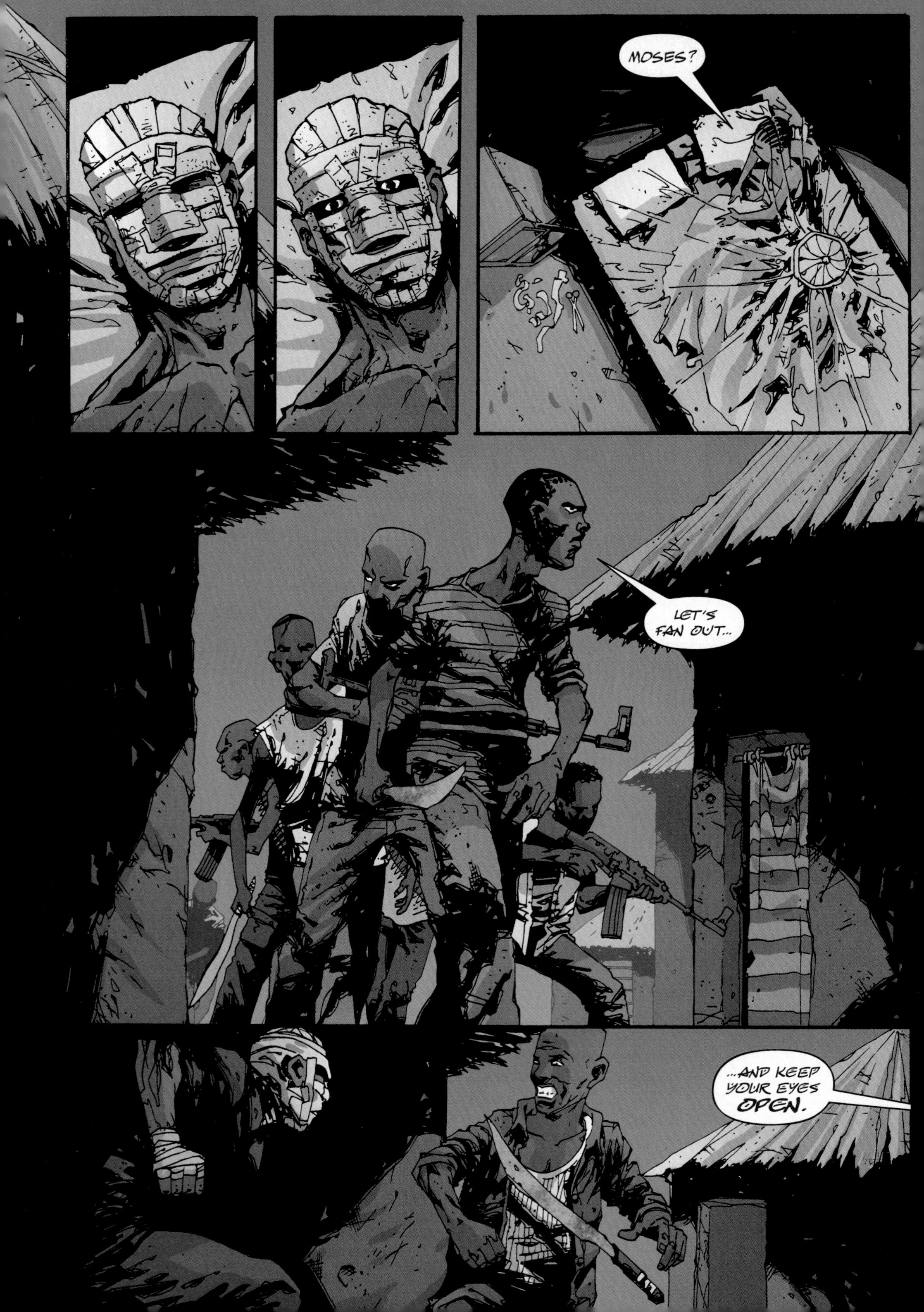
MOSES?
LET'S FAN OUT...
...AND KEEP YOUR EYES OPEN.

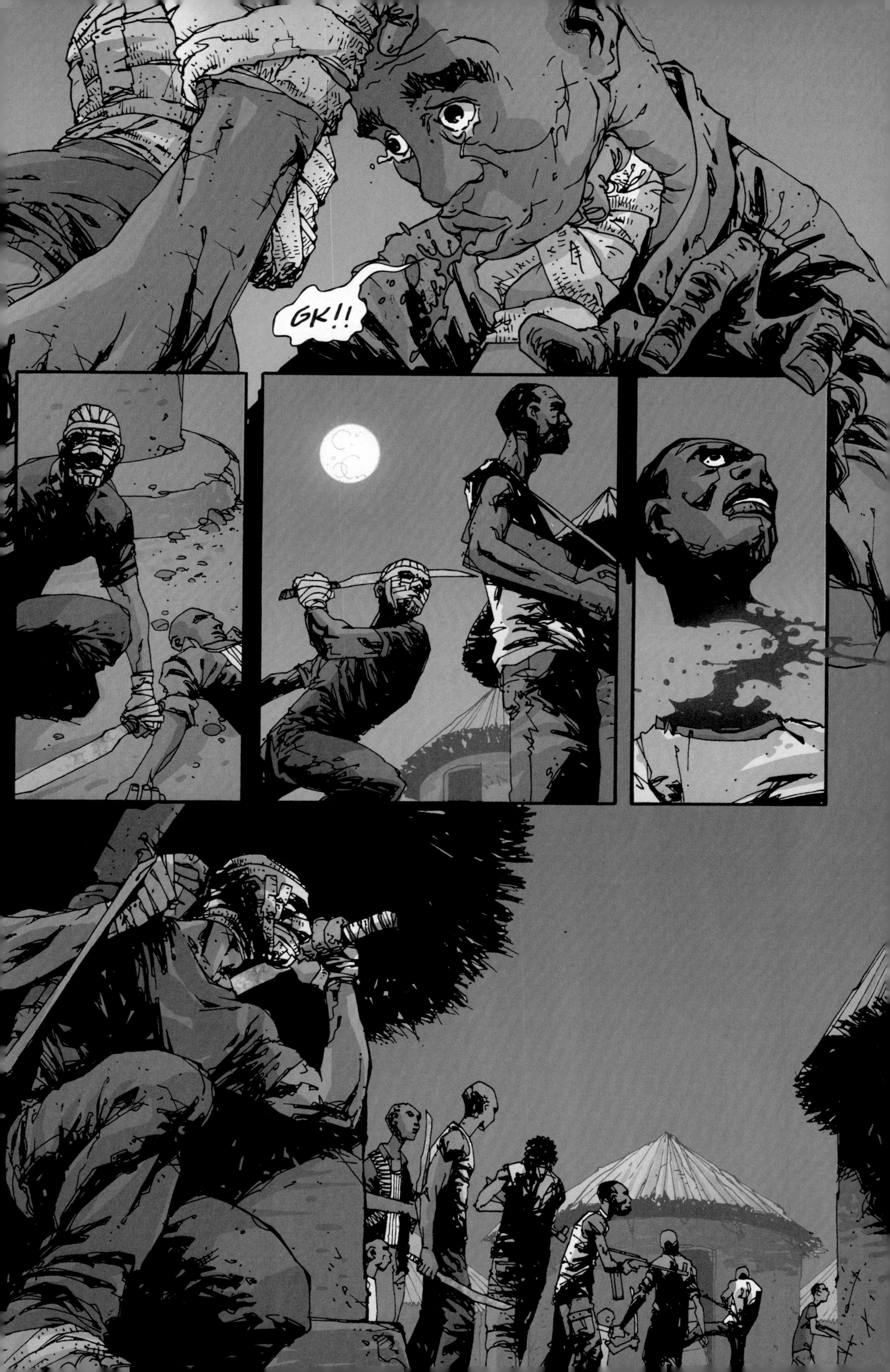
GK!!

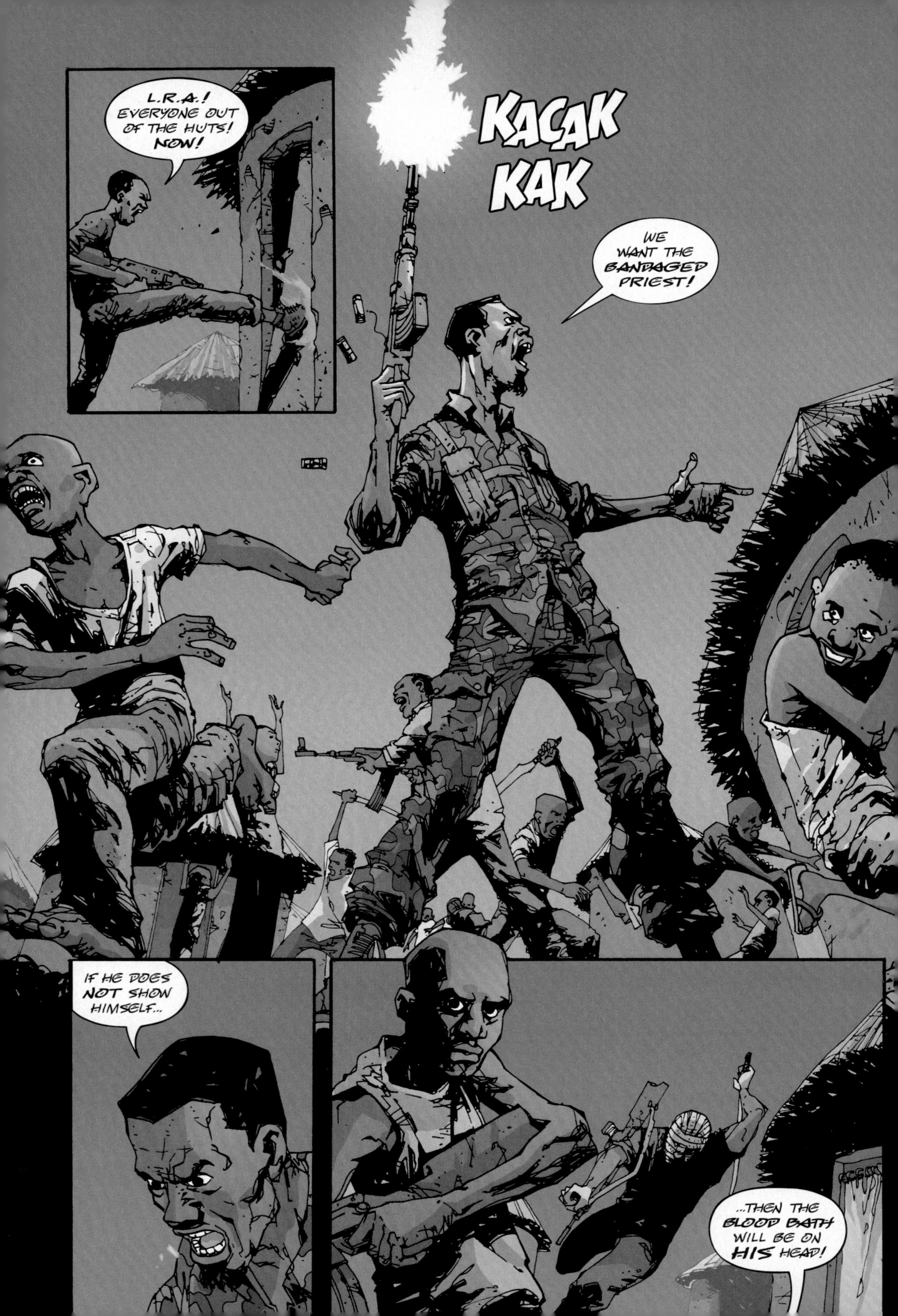
L.R.A.! EVERYONE OUT OF THE HUTS! NOW!
KACAK KAK
WE WANT THE BANDAGED PRIEST!
IF HE DOES NOT SHOW HIMSELF...
...THEN THE BLOOD BATH WILL BE ON HIS HEAD!

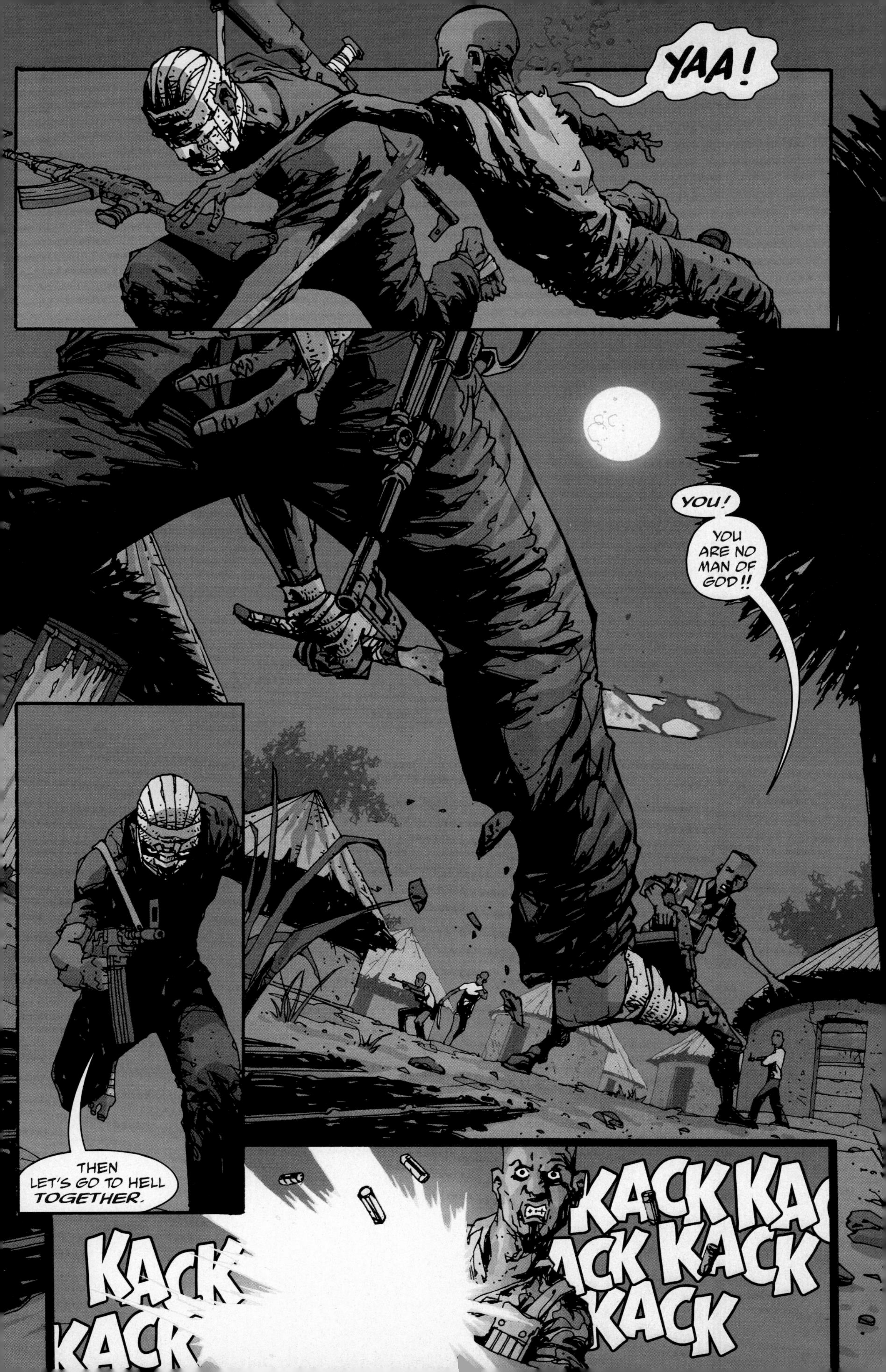

YAA!
YOU!
YOU ARE NO MAN OF GOD!!
THEN LET'S GO TO HELL TOGETHER.
KACK KACK
KACK KACK KACK KACK KACK

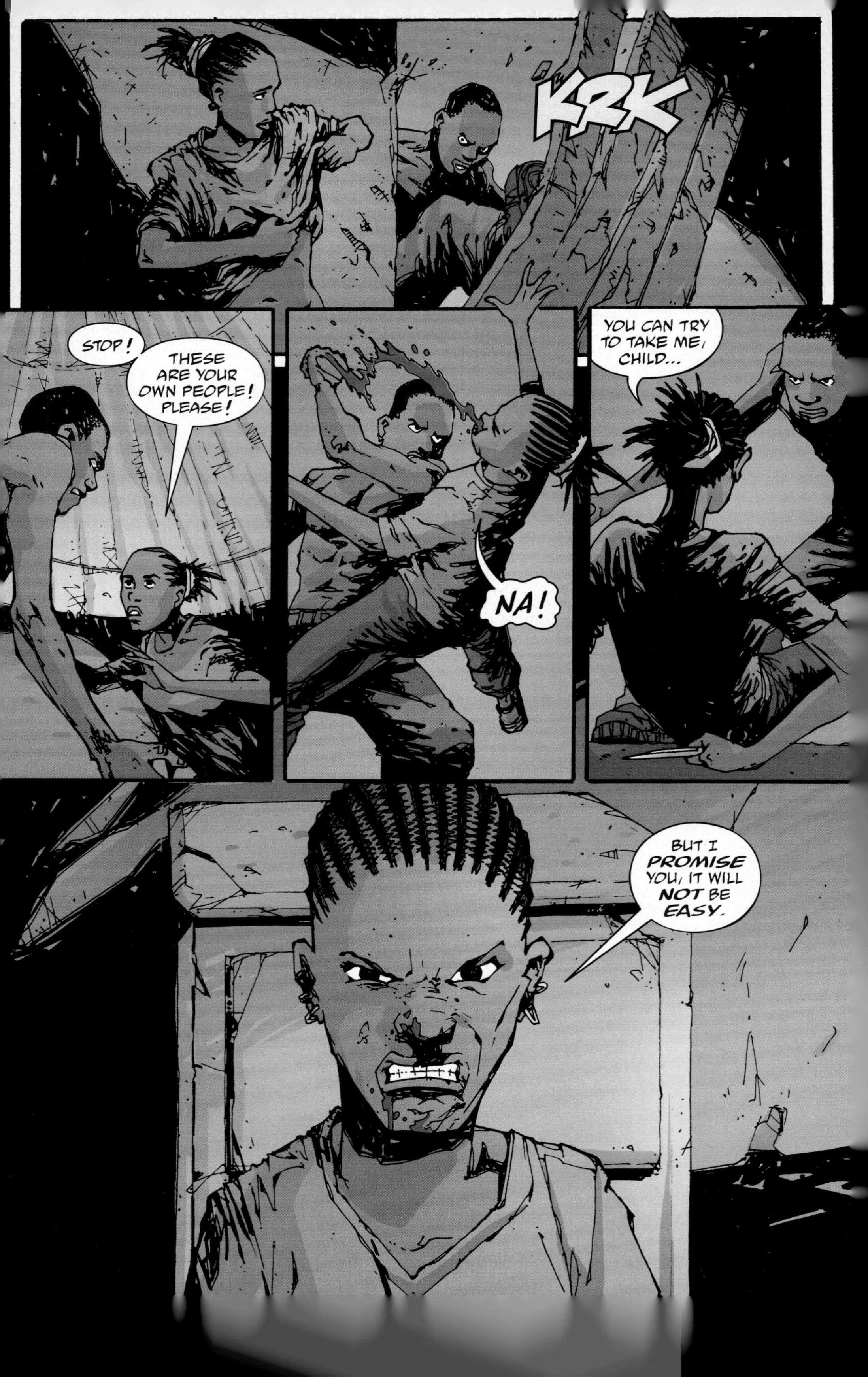
KRK
STOP!
THESE ARE YOUR OWN PEOPLE! PLEASE!
NA!
YOU CAN TRY TO TAKE ME, CHILD...
BUT I PROMISE YOU, IT WILL NOT BE EASY.

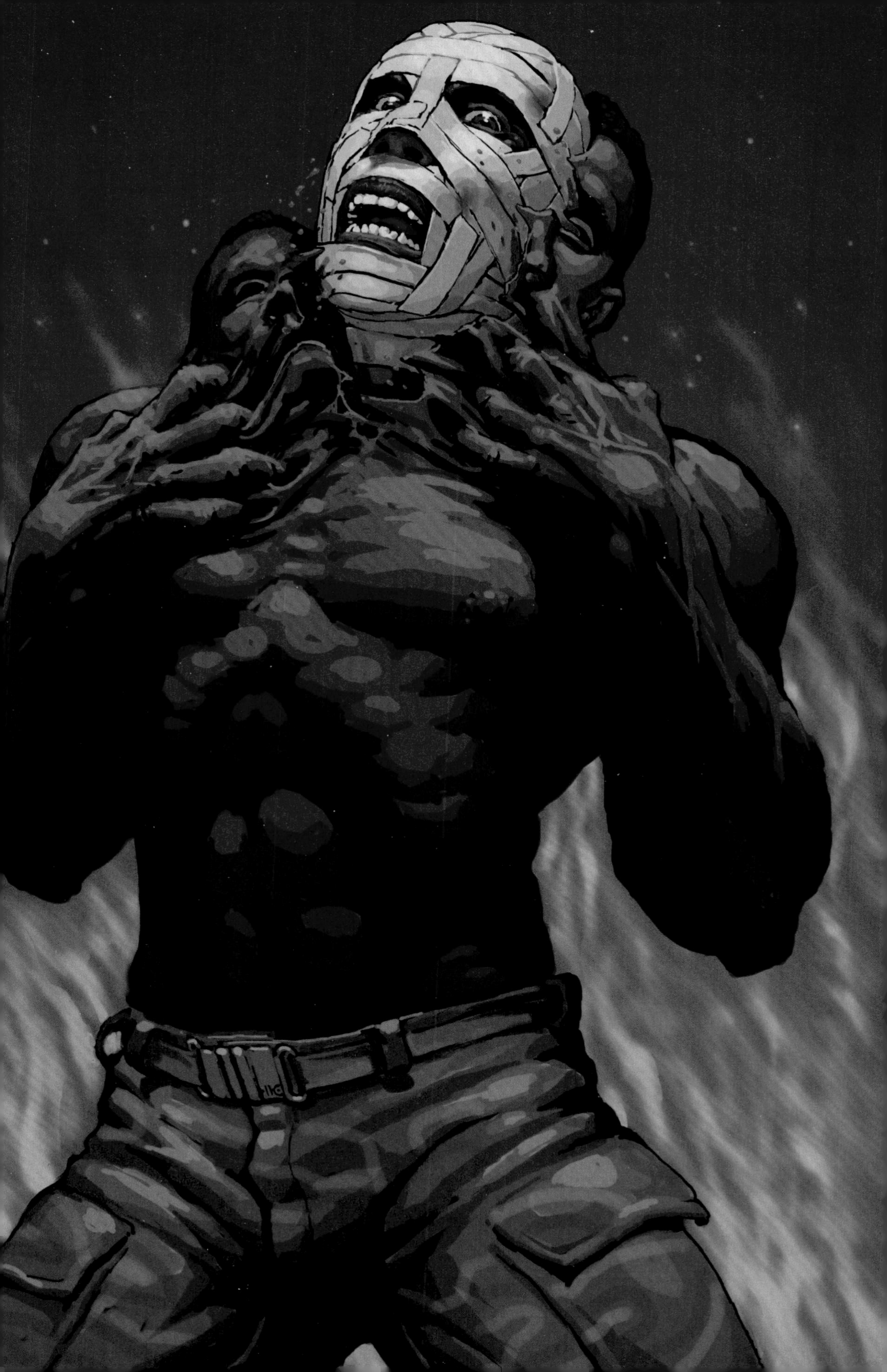

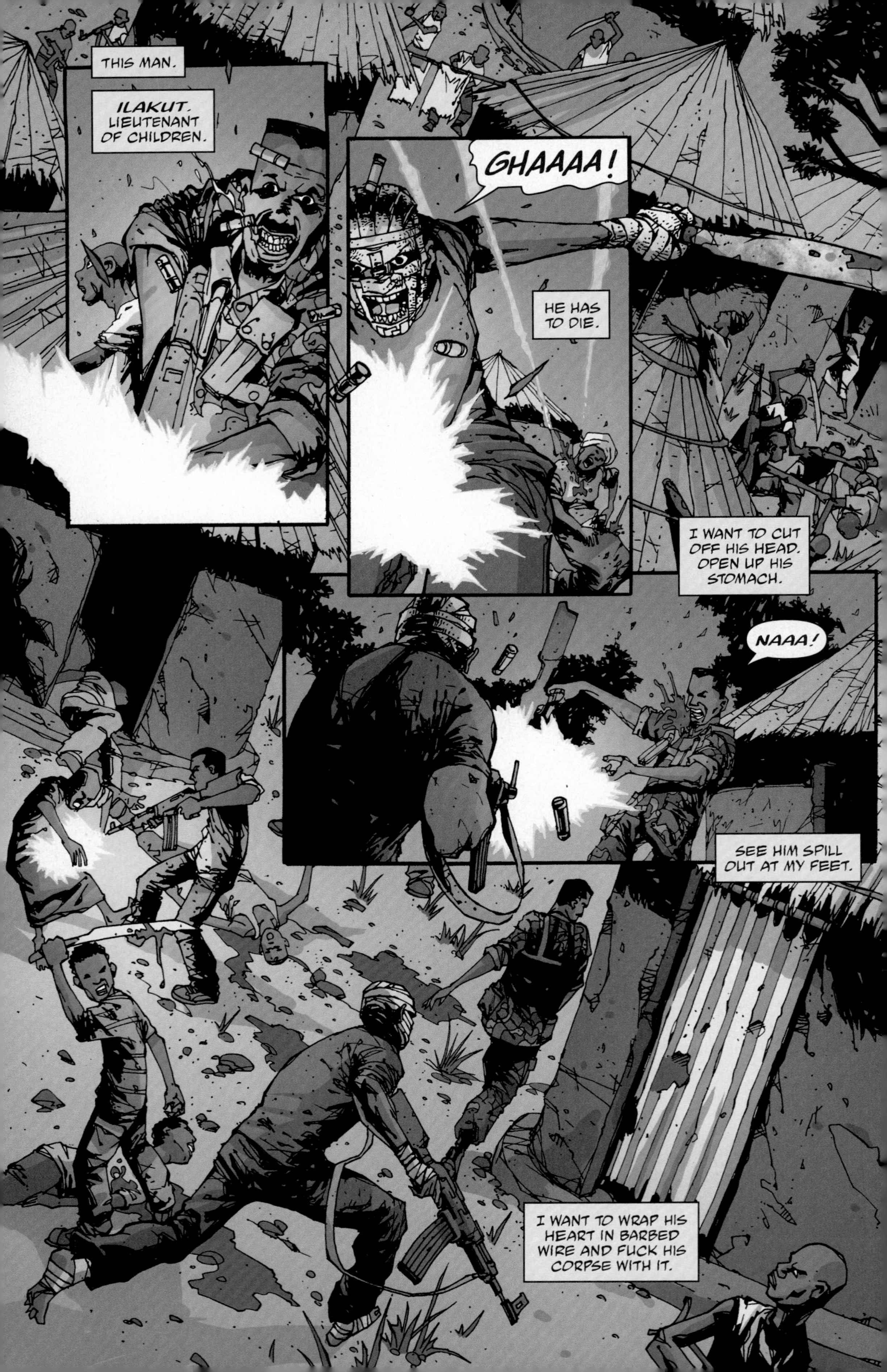
THIS MAN.
ILAKUT. LIEUTENANT OF CHILDREN.
GHAAAA!
HE HAS TO DIE.
I WANT TO CUT OFF HIS HEAD. OPEN UP HIS STOMACH.
NAAA!
SEE HIM SPILL OUT AT MY FEET.
I WANT TO WRAP HIS HEART IN BARBED WIRE AND FUCK HIS CORPSE WITH IT.

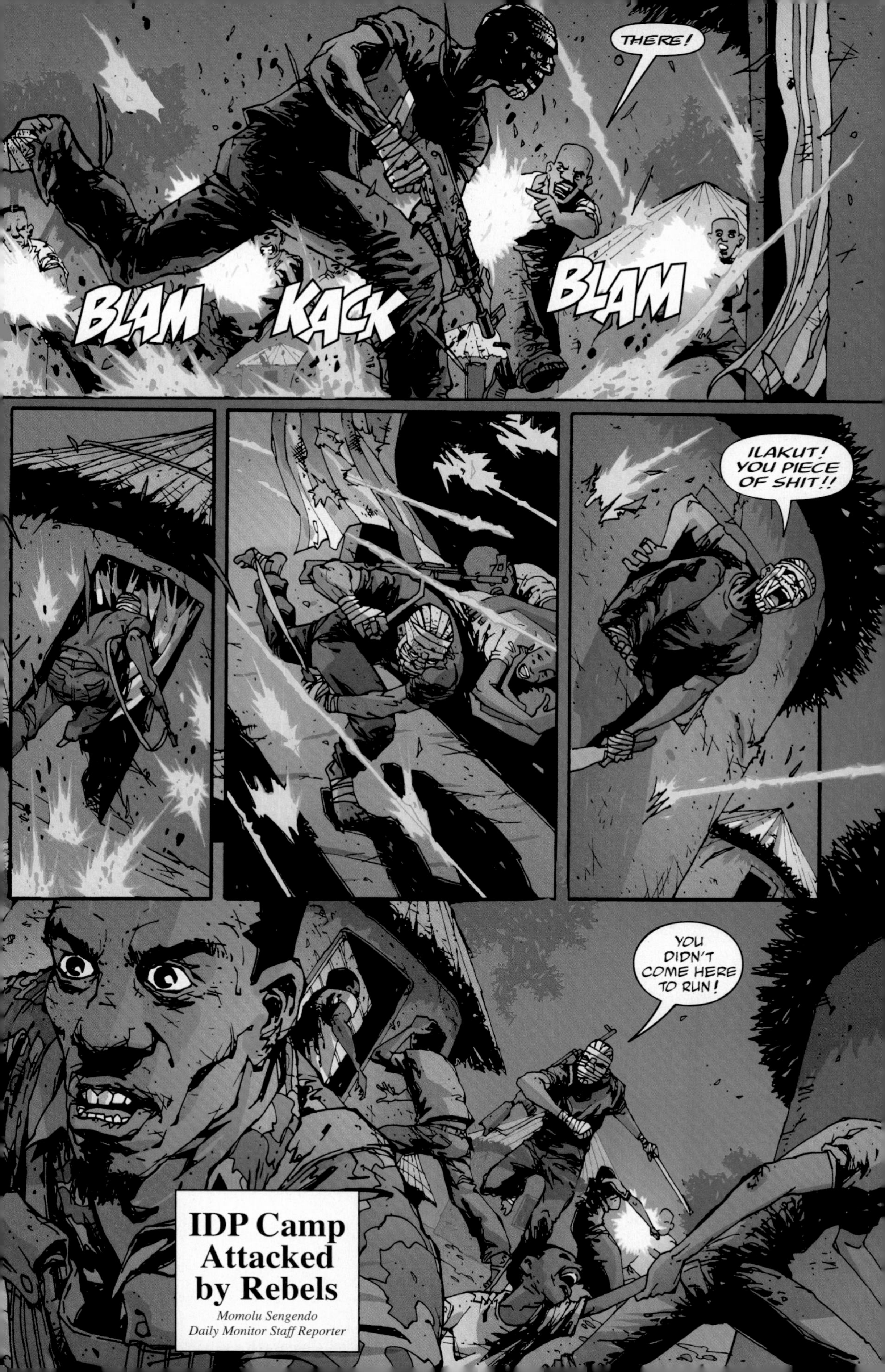
THERE!
BLAM
KACK
BLAM
ILAKUT! YOU PIECE OF SHIT!!
YOU DIDN'T COME HERE TO RUN!
IDP Camp Attacked by Rebels
Momolu Sengendo
Daily Monitor Staff Reporter

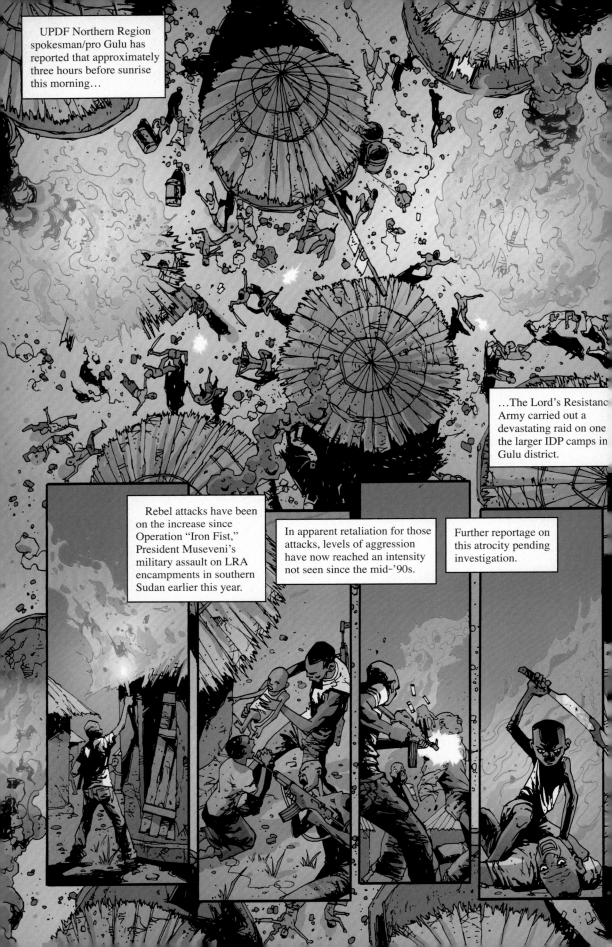

UPDF Northern Region spokesman/pro Gulu has reported that approximately three hours before sunrise this morning…

…The Lord's Resistance Army carried out a devastating raid on one the larger IDP camps in Gulu district.

Rebel attacks have been on the increase since Operation "Iron Fist," President Museveni's military assault on LRA encampments in southern Sudan earlier this year.

In apparent retaliation for those attacks, levels of aggression have now reached an intensity not seen since the mid-'90s.

Further reportage on this atrocity pending investigation.

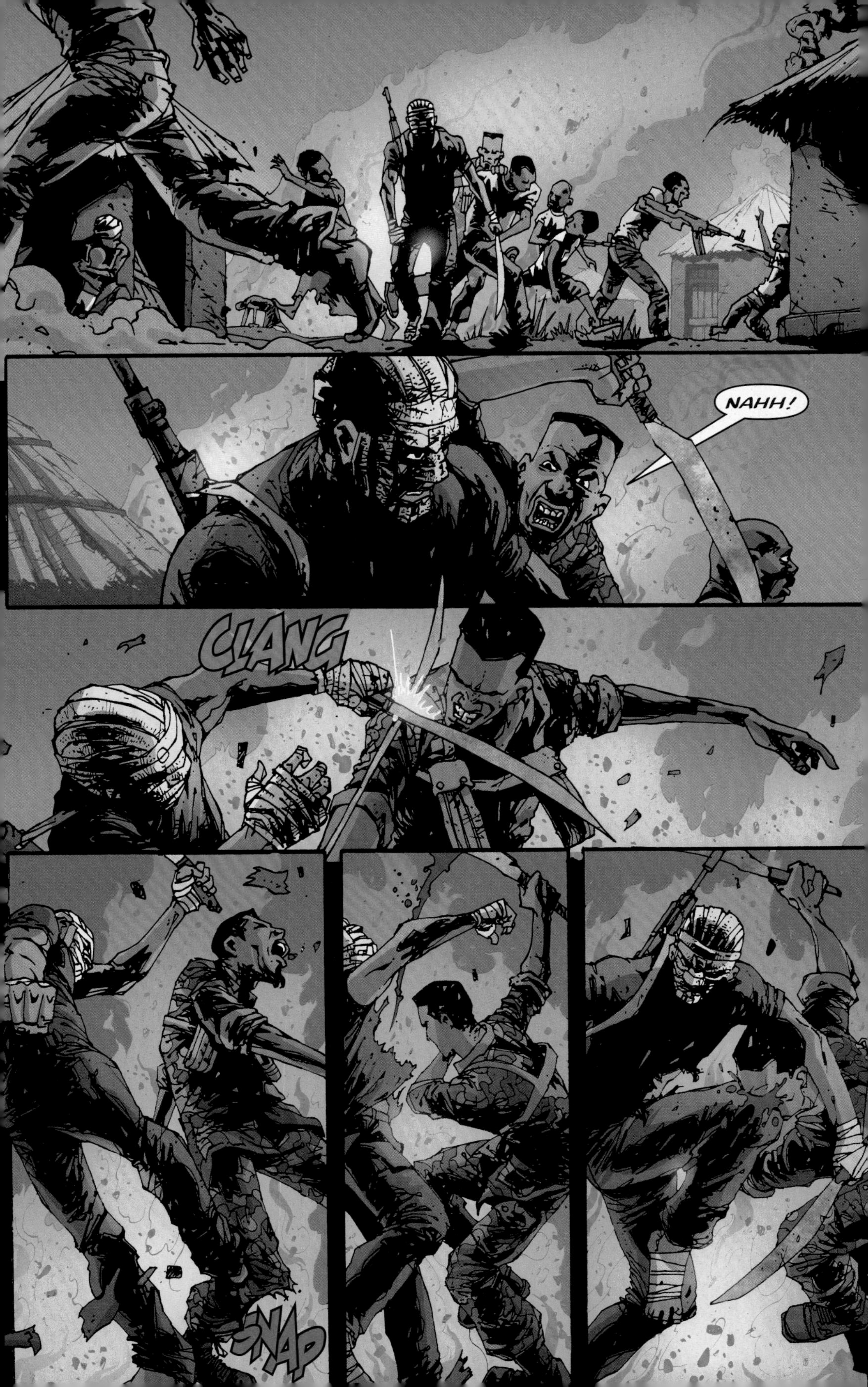
NAHH!
CLANG
SNAP

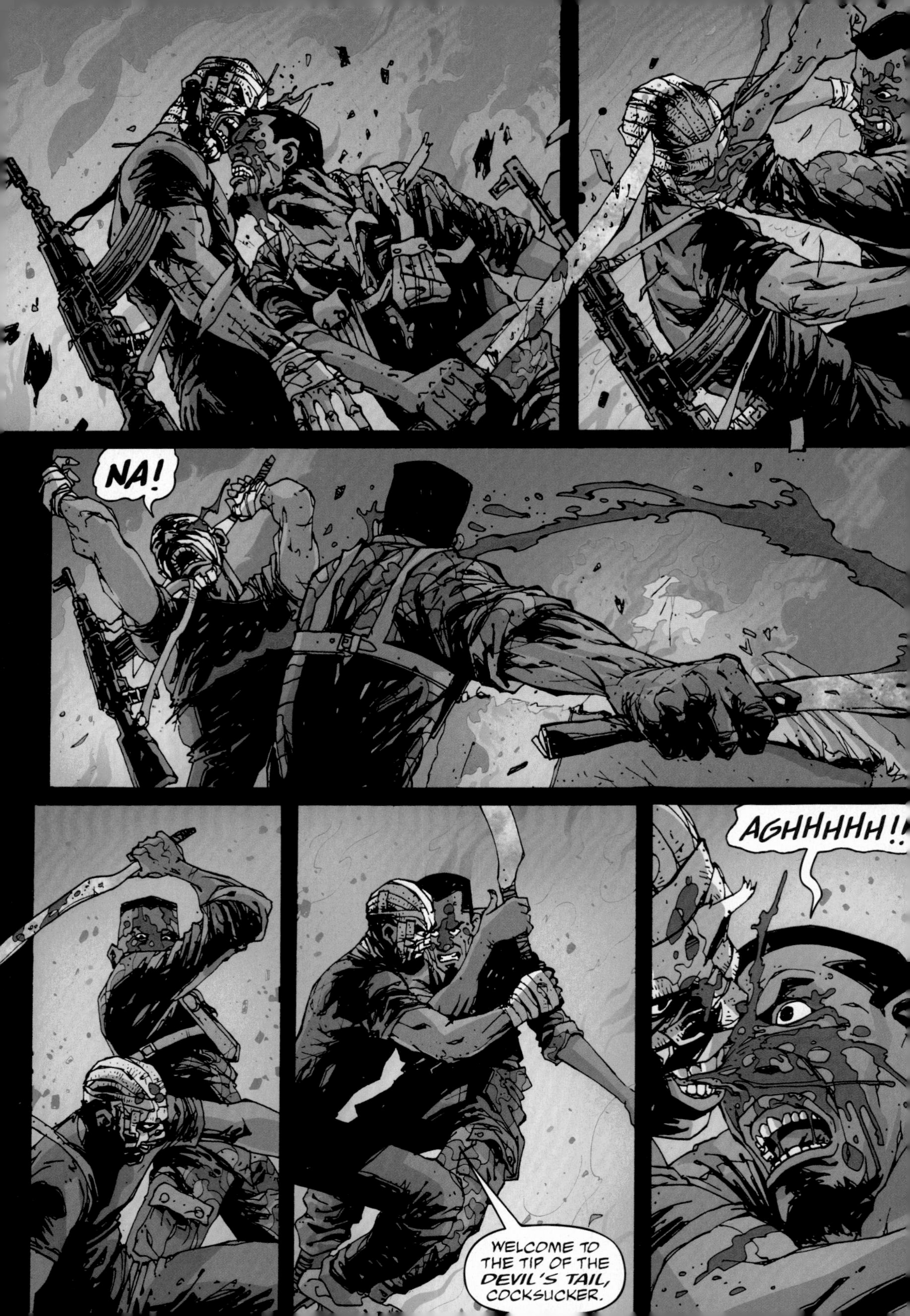
NA!
WELCOME TO THE TIP OF THE DEVIL'S TAIL, COCKSUCKER.
AGHHHHH!!

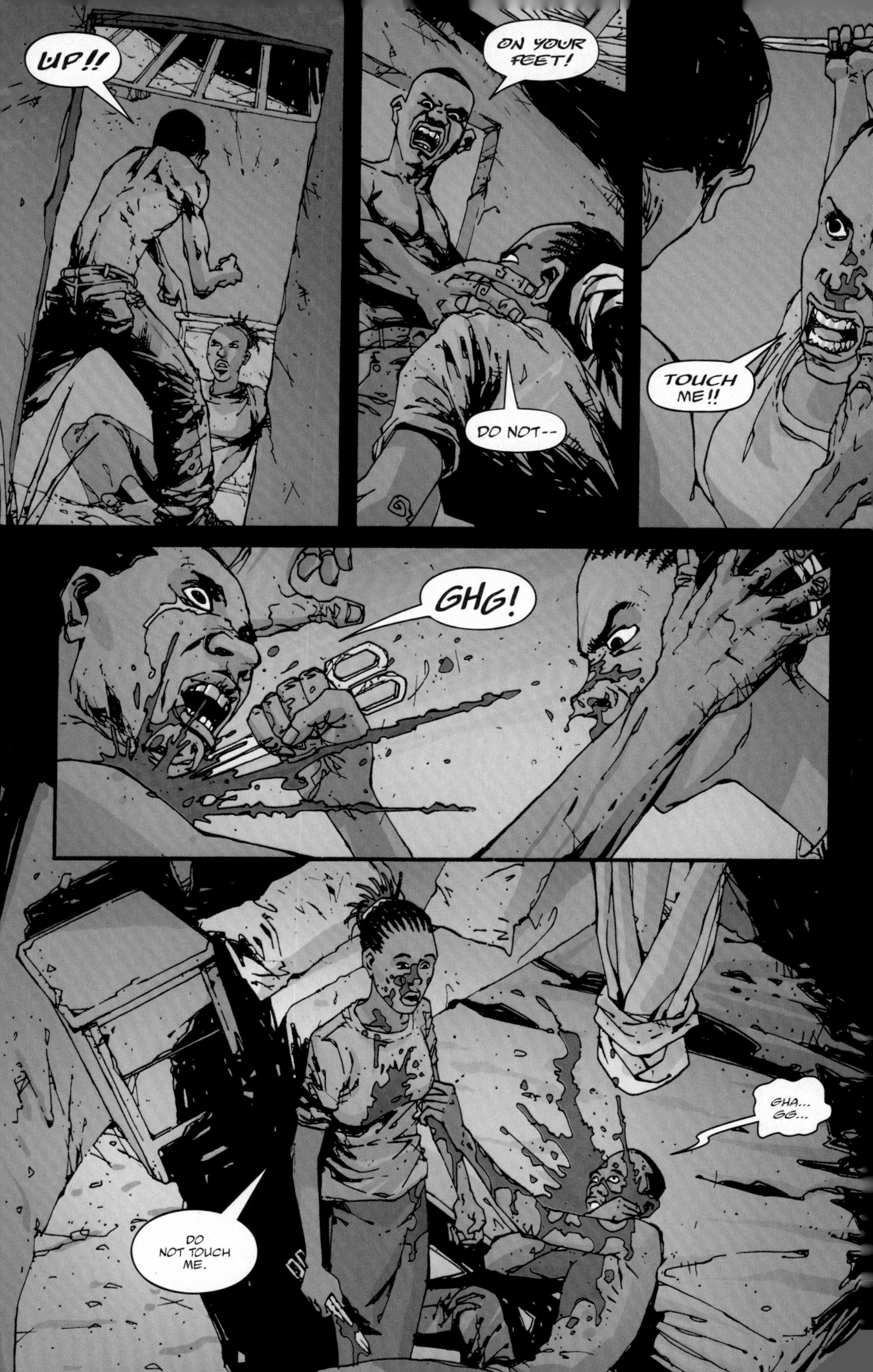
UP!!
ON YOUR FEET!
DO NOT--
TOUCH ME!!
GHG!
GHA... GG...
DO NOT TOUCH ME.

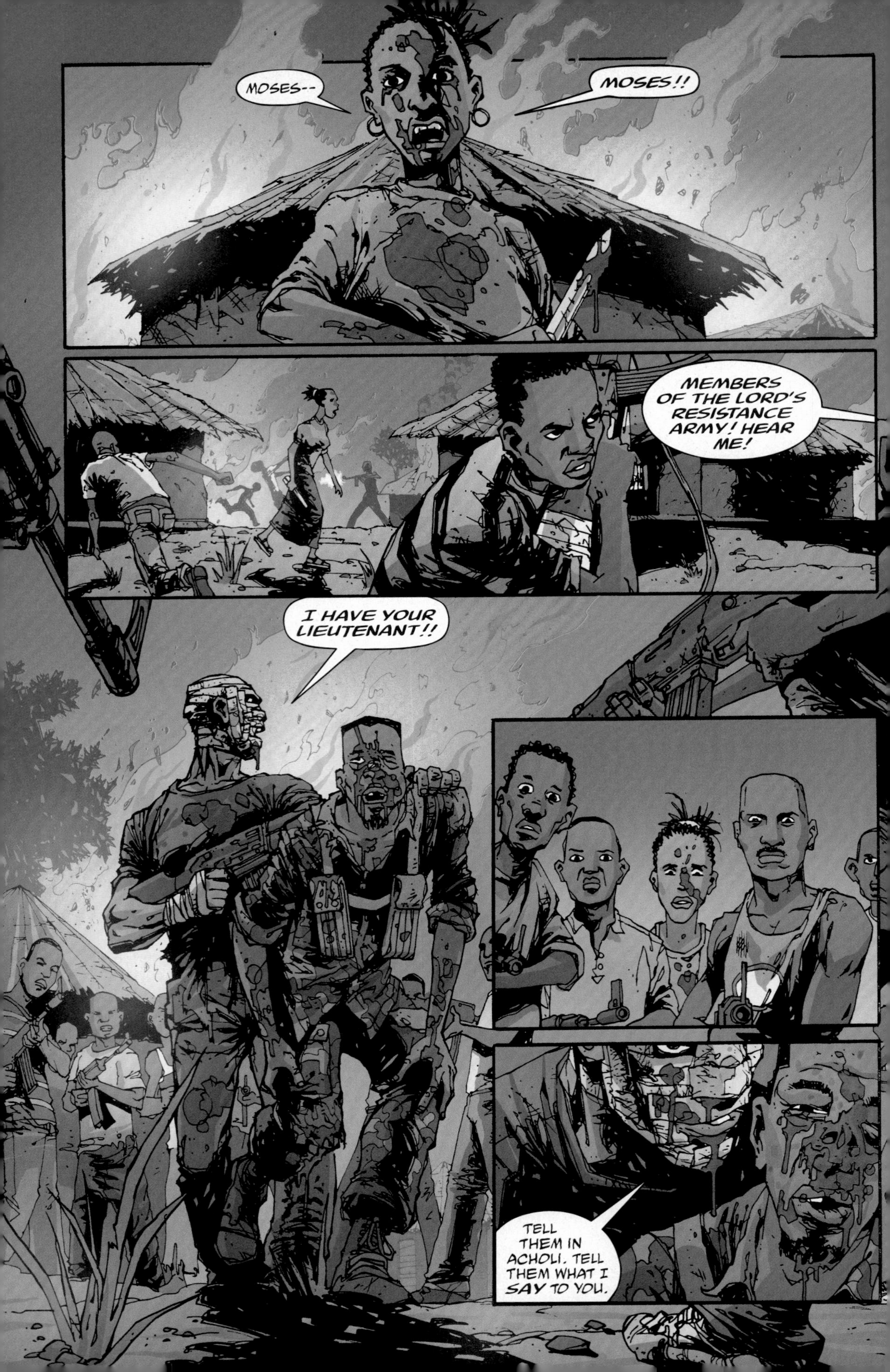
MOSES--
MOSES!!
MEMBERS OF THE LORD'S RESISTANCE ARMY! HEAR ME!
I HAVE YOUR LIEUTENANT!!
TELL THEM IN ACHOLI. TELL THEM WHAT I SAY TO YOU.

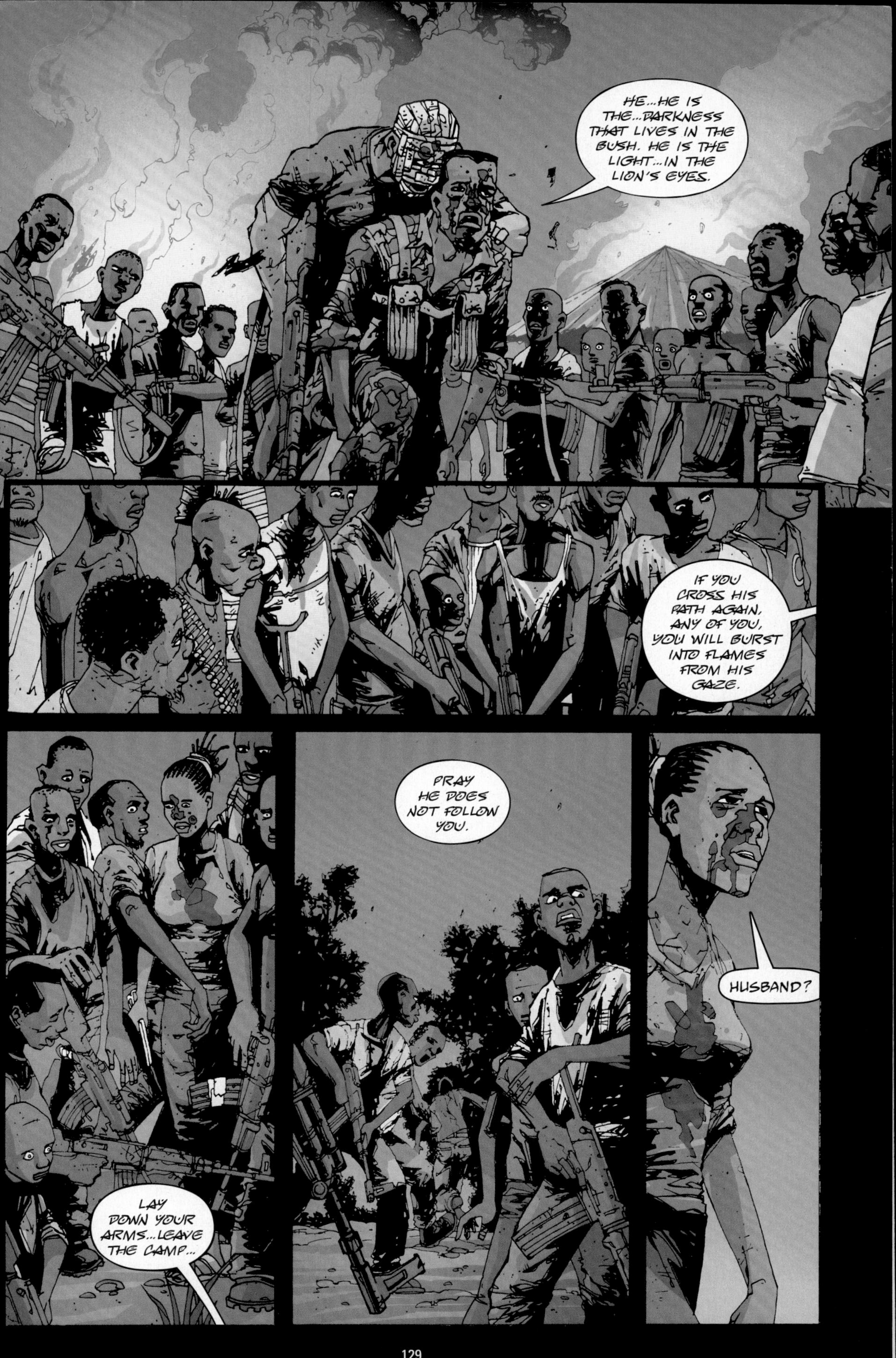
HE...HE IS THE...DARKNESS THAT LIVES IN THE BUSH. HE IS THE LIGHT...IN THE LION'S EYES.
IF YOU CROSS HIS PATH AGAIN, ANY OF YOU, YOU WILL BURST INTO FLAMES FROM HIS GAZE.
LAY DOWN YOUR ARMS...LEAVE THE CAMP...
PRAY HE DOES NOT FOLLOW YOU.
HUSBAND?

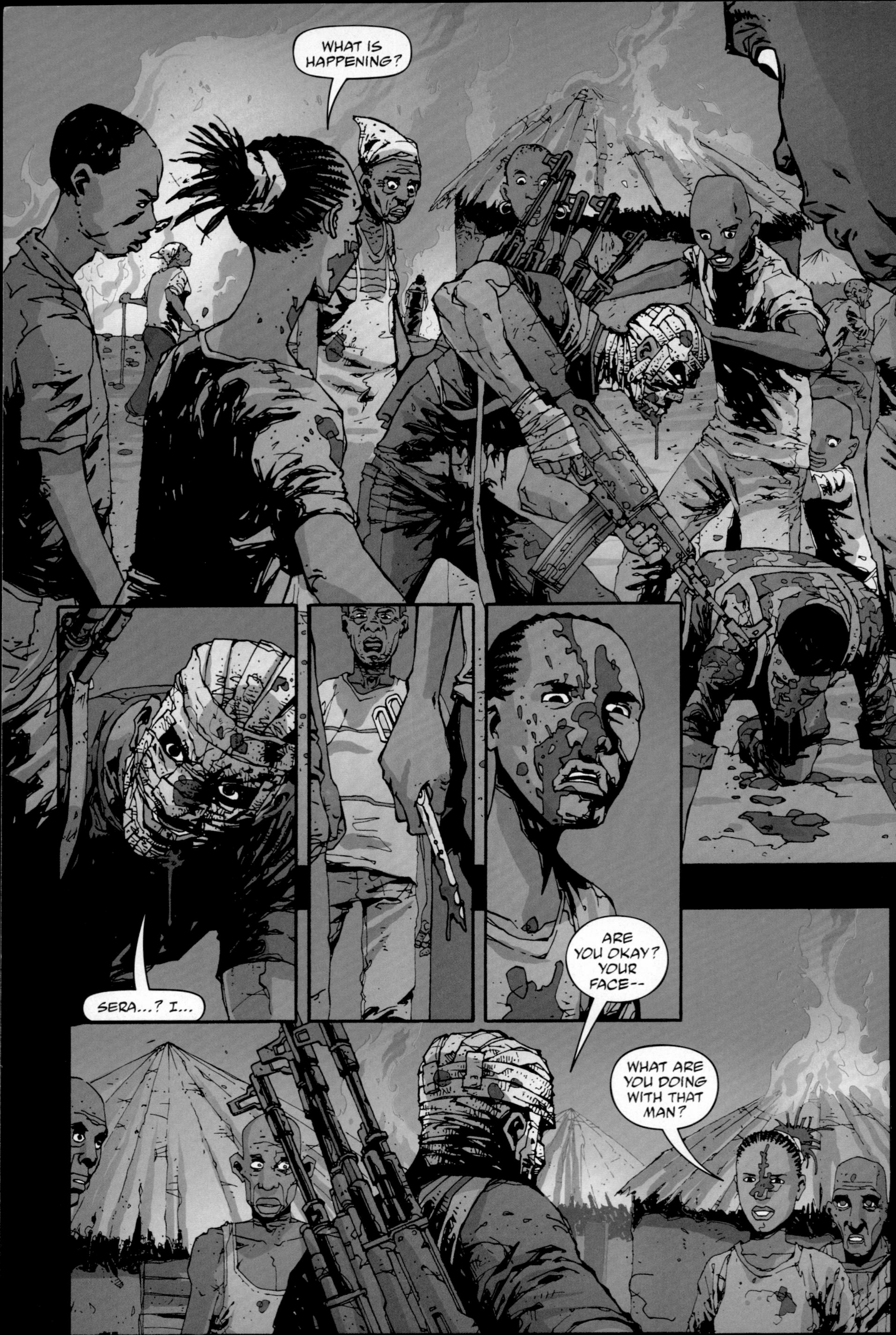
WHAT IS HAPPENING?
SERA...? I...
ARE YOU OKAY? YOUR FACE--
WHAT ARE YOU DOING WITH THAT MAN?

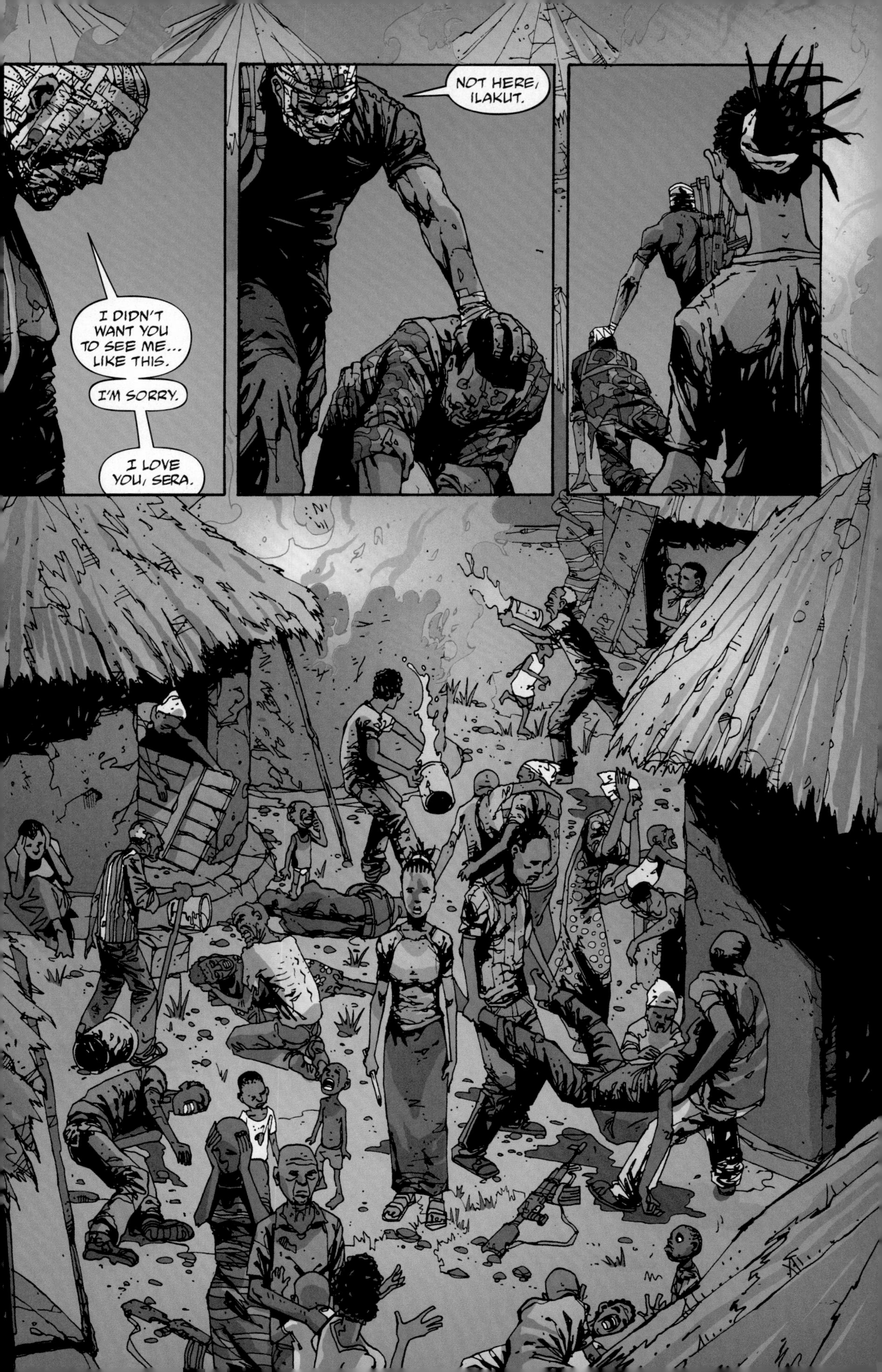

I DIDN'T WANT YOU TO SEE ME... LIKE THIS.
I'M SORRY.
I LOVE YOU, SERA.
NOT HERE, ILAKUT.

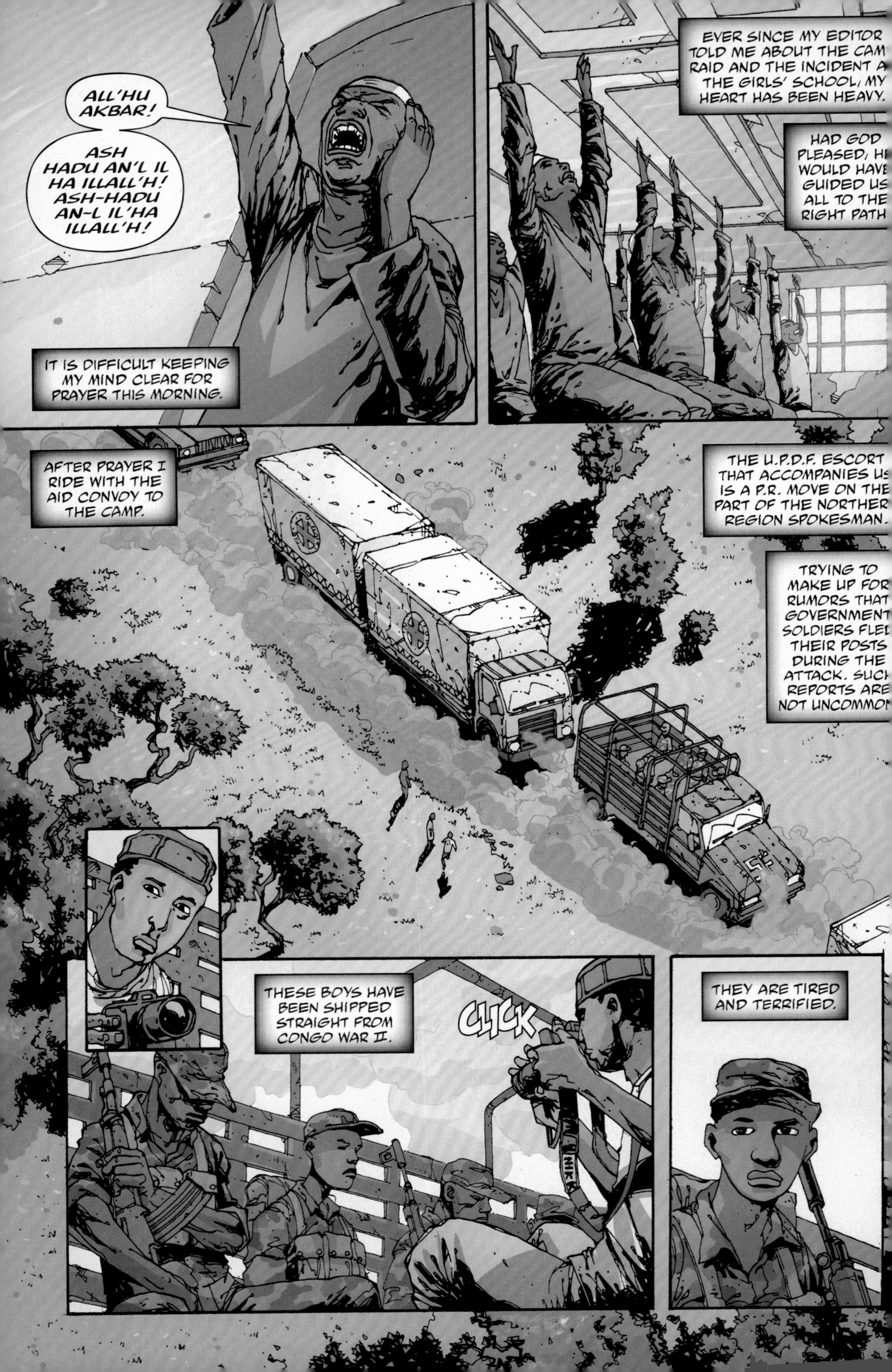
ALL'HU AKBAR!
ASH HADU AN'L IL HA ILLALL'H! ASH-HADU AN-L IL'HA ILLALL'H!
IT IS DIFFICULT KEEPING MY MIND CLEAR FOR PRAYER THIS MORNING.
EVER SINCE MY EDITOR TOLD ME ABOUT THE CAMP RAID AND THE INCIDENT AT THE GIRLS' SCHOOL, MY HEART HAS BEEN HEAVY.
HAD GOD PLEASED, HE WOULD HAVE GUIDED US ALL TO THE RIGHT PATH.
AFTER PRAYER I RIDE WITH THE AID CONVOY TO THE CAMP.
THE U.P.D.F. ESCORT THAT ACCOMPANIES US IS A P.R. MOVE ON THE PART OF THE NORTHERN REGION SPOKESMAN.
TRYING TO MAKE UP FOR RUMORS THAT GOVERNMENT SOLDIERS FLED THEIR POSTS DURING THE ATTACK. SUCH REPORTS ARE NOT UNCOMMON.
THESE BOYS HAVE BEEN SHIPPED STRAIGHT FROM CONGO WAR II.
CLICK
THEY ARE TIRED AND TERRIFIED.

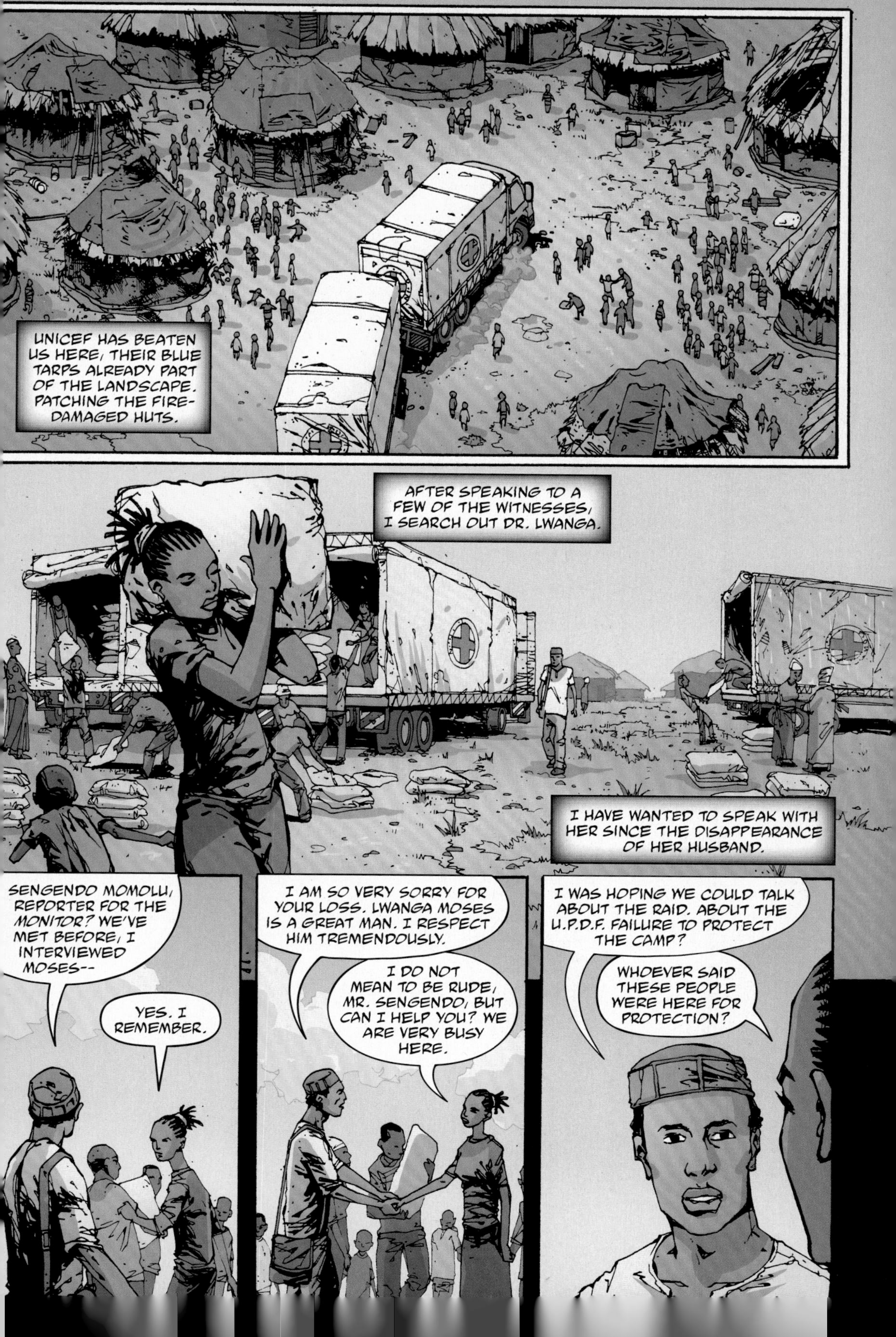
UNICEF HAS BEATEN US HERE, THEIR BLUE TARPS ALREADY PART OF THE LANDSCAPE. PATCHING THE FIRE-DAMAGED HUTS.
AFTER SPEAKING TO A FEW OF THE WITNESSES, I SEARCH OUT DR. LWANGA.
I HAVE WANTED TO SPEAK WITH HER SINCE THE DISAPPEARANCE OF HER HUSBAND.
SENGENDO MOMOLU, REPORTER FOR THE MONITOR? WE'VE MET BEFORE, I INTERVIEWED MOSES--
YES. I REMEMBER.
I AM SO VERY SORRY FOR YOUR LOSS. LWANGA MOSES IS A GREAT MAN. I RESPECT HIM TREMENDOUSLY.
I DO NOT MEAN TO BE RUDE, MR. SENGENDO, BUT CAN I HELP YOU? WE ARE VERY BUSY HERE.
I WAS HOPING WE COULD TALK ABOUT THE RAID. ABOUT THE U.P.D.F. FAILURE TO PROTECT THE CAMP?
WHOEVER SAID THESE PEOPLE WERE HERE FOR PROTECTION?

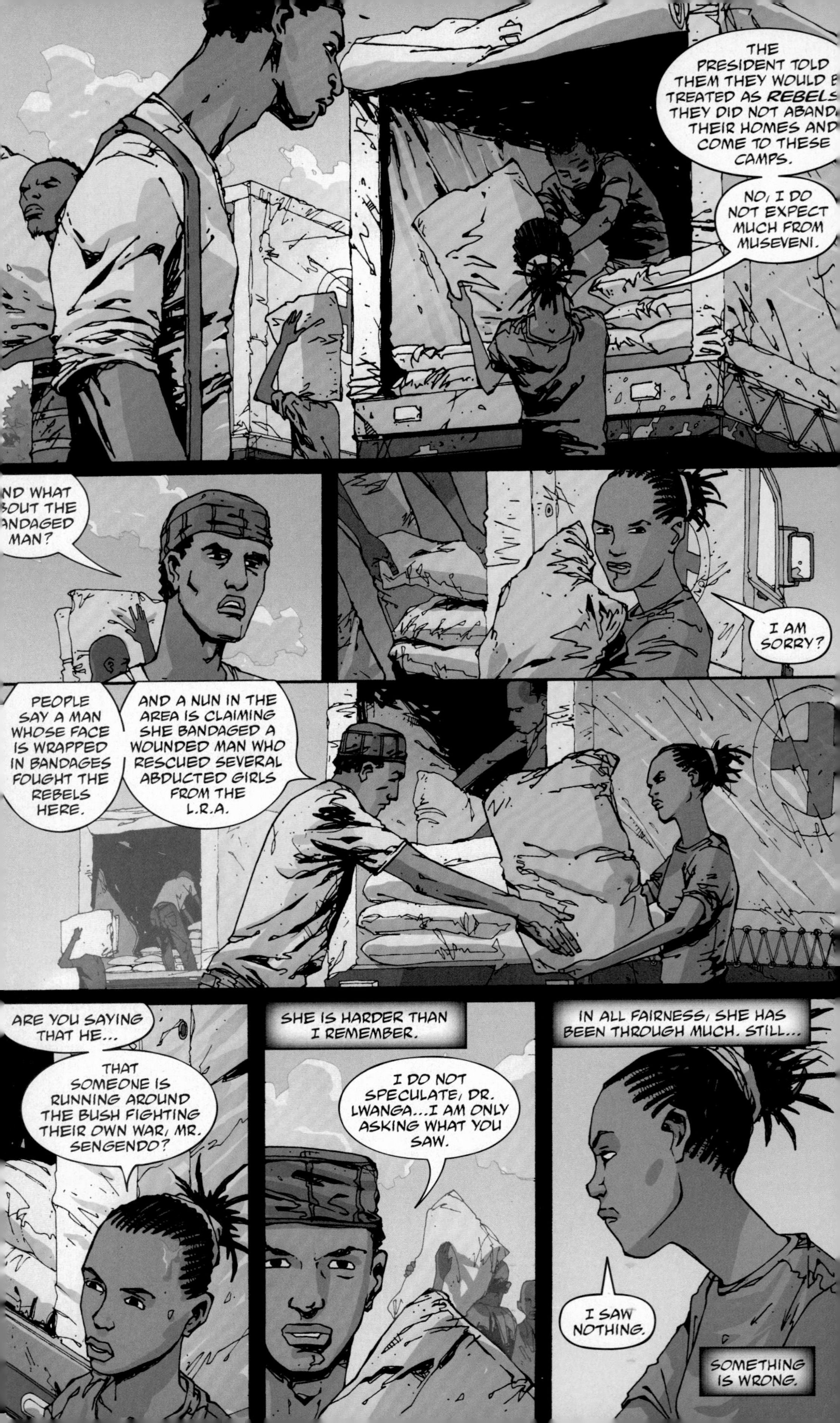
THE PRESIDENT TOLD THEM THEY WOULD B TREATED AS *REBELS* THEY DID NOT ABAND THEIR HOMES AND COME TO THESE CAMPS.
NO, I DO NOT EXPECT MUCH FROM MUSEVENI.
ND WHAT BOUT THE ANDAGED MAN?
I AM SORRY?
PEOPLE SAY A MAN WHOSE FACE IS WRAPPED IN BANDAGES FOUGHT THE REBELS HERE.
AND A NUN IN THE AREA IS CLAIMING SHE BANDAGED A WOUNDED MAN WHO RESCUED SEVERAL ABDUCTED GIRLS FROM THE L.R.A.
ARE YOU SAYING THAT HE...
THAT SOMEONE IS RUNNING AROUND THE BUSH FIGHTING THEIR OWN WAR, MR. SENGENDO?
SHE IS HARDER THAN I REMEMBER.
I DO NOT SPECULATE, DR. LWANGA...I AM ONLY ASKING WHAT YOU SAW.
IN ALL FAIRNESS, SHE HAS BEEN THROUGH MUCH. STILL...
I SAW NOTHING.
SOMETHING IS WRONG.

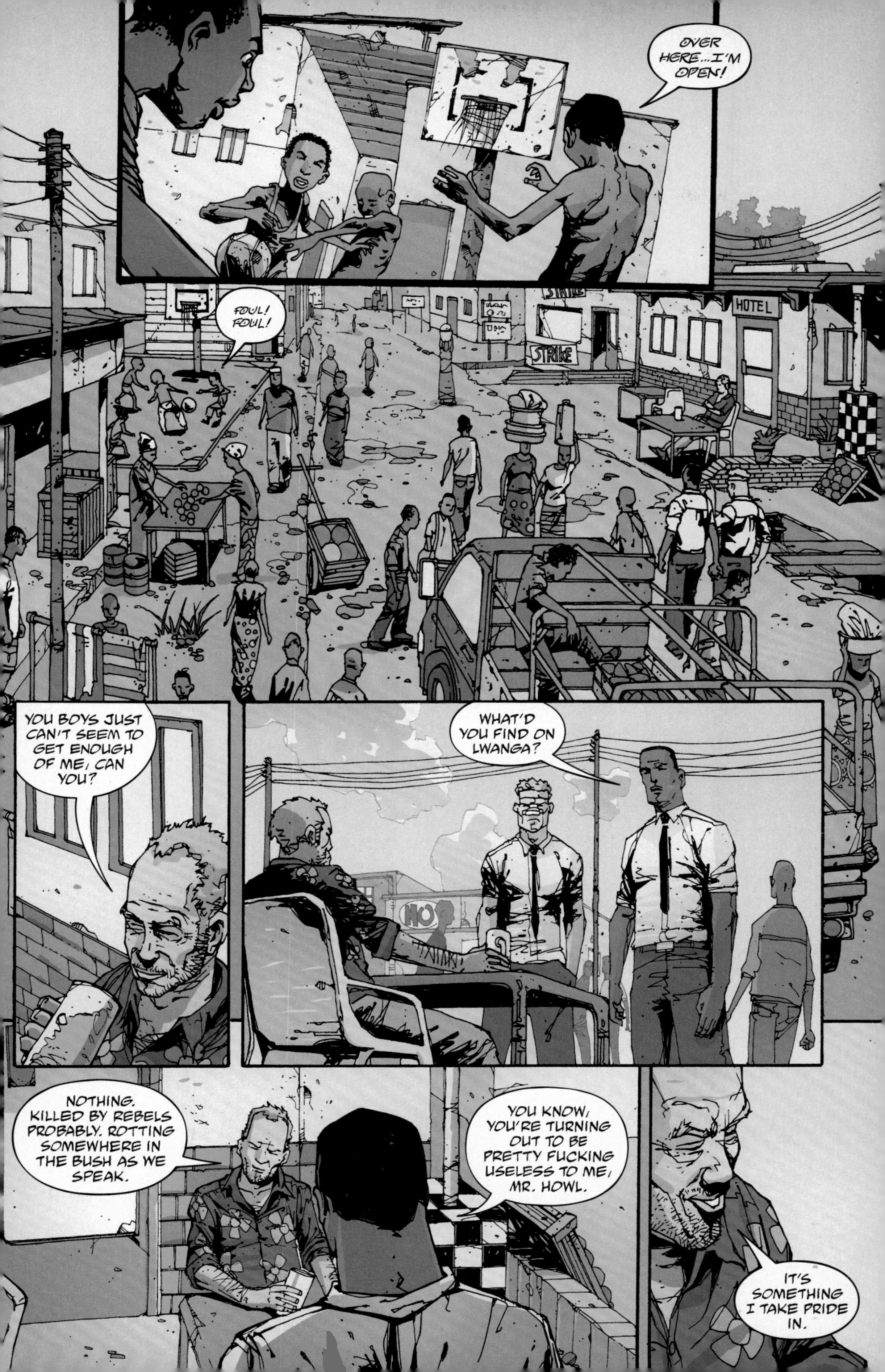

OVER HERE...I'M OPEN!
FOUL! FOUL!
HOTEL
STRIKE
STRIKE
YOU BOYS JUST CAN'T SEEM TO GET ENOUGH OF ME, CAN YOU?
WHAT'D YOU FIND ON LWANGA?
NO
NOTHING. KILLED BY REBELS PROBABLY. ROTTING SOMEWHERE IN THE BUSH AS WE SPEAK.
YOU KNOW, YOU'RE TURNING OUT TO BE PRETTY FUCKING USELESS TO ME, MR. HOWL.
IT'S SOMETHING I TAKE PRIDE IN.

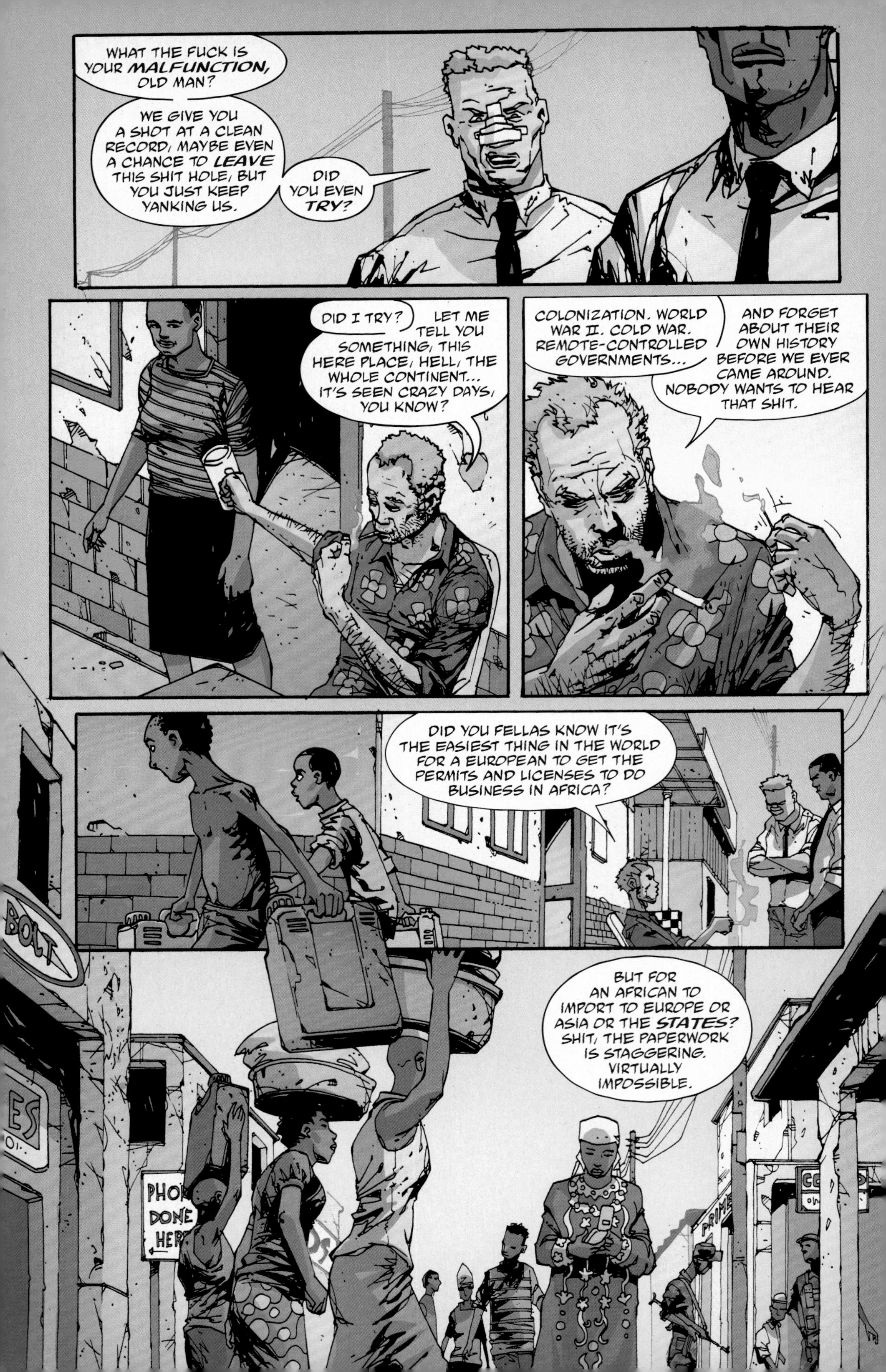
WHAT THE FUCK IS YOUR MALFUNCTION, OLD MAN?
WE GIVE YOU A SHOT AT A CLEAN RECORD, MAYBE EVEN A CHANCE TO LEAVE THIS SHIT HOLE, BUT YOU JUST KEEP YANKING US.
DID YOU EVEN TRY?
DID I TRY?
LET ME TELL YOU SOMETHING, THIS HERE PLACE, HELL, THE WHOLE CONTINENT... IT'S SEEN CRAZY DAYS, YOU KNOW?
COLONIZATION. WORLD WAR II. COLD WAR. REMOTE-CONTROLLED GOVERNMENTS...
AND FORGET ABOUT THEIR OWN HISTORY BEFORE WE EVER CAME AROUND. NOBODY WANTS TO HEAR THAT SHIT.
DID YOU FELLAS KNOW IT'S THE EASIEST THING IN THE WORLD FOR A EUROPEAN TO GET THE PERMITS AND LICENSES TO DO BUSINESS IN AFRICA?
BOLT
BUT FOR AN AFRICAN TO IMPORT TO EUROPE OR ASIA OR THE STATES? SHIT, THE PAPERWORK IS STAGGERING. VIRTUALLY IMPOSSIBLE.

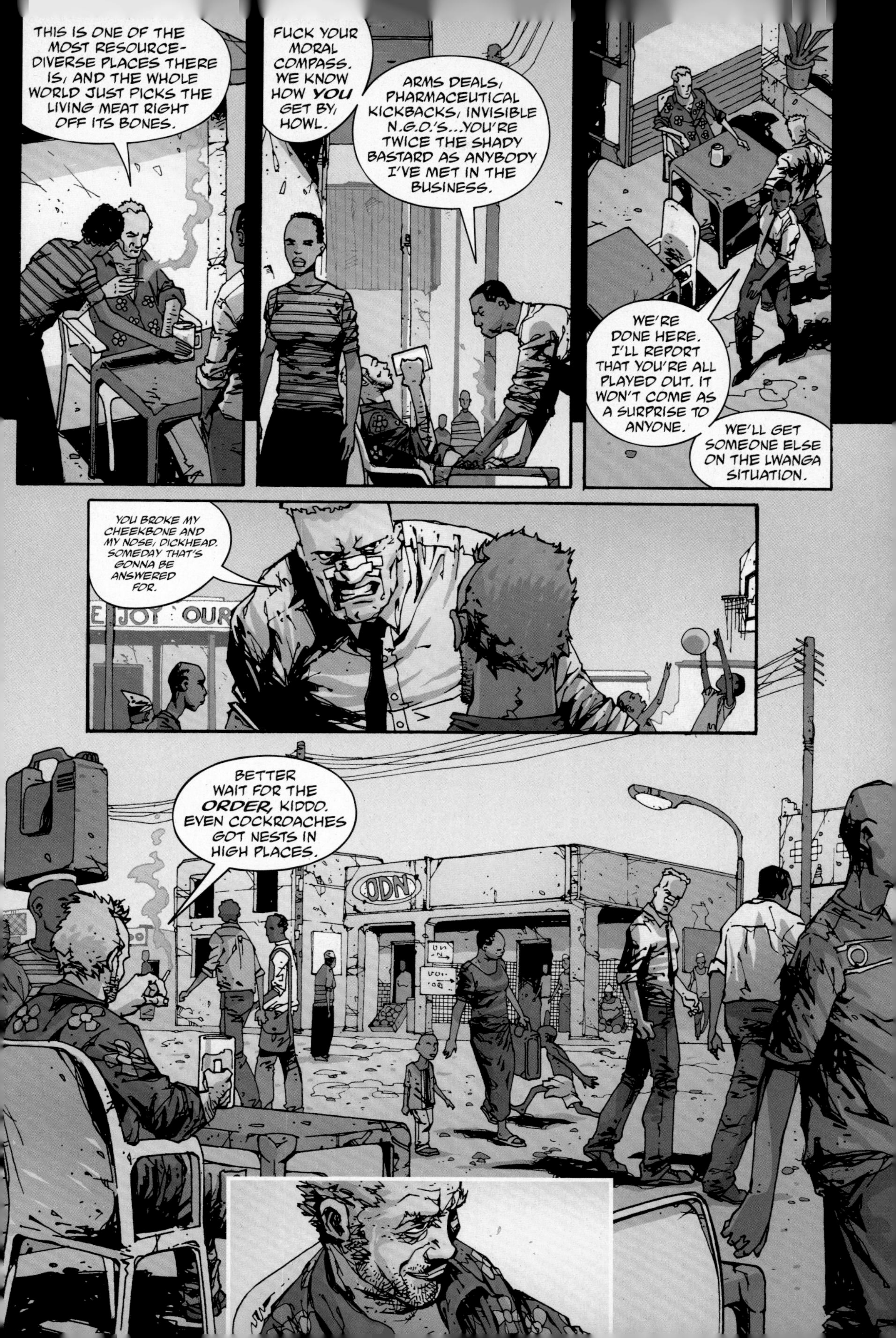
THIS IS ONE OF THE MOST RESOURCE-DIVERSE PLACES THERE IS, AND THE WHOLE WORLD JUST PICKS THE LIVING MEAT RIGHT OFF ITS BONES.
FUCK YOUR MORAL COMPASS. WE KNOW HOW YOU GET BY, HOWL.
ARMS DEALS, PHARMACEUTICAL KICKBACKS, INVISIBLE N.G.O.'S...YOU'RE TWICE THE SHADY BASTARD AS ANYBODY I'VE MET IN THE BUSINESS.
WE'RE DONE HERE. I'LL REPORT THAT YOU'RE ALL PLAYED OUT. IT WON'T COME AS A SURPRISE TO ANYONE.
WE'LL GET SOMEONE ELSE ON THE LWANGA SITUATION.
YOU BROKE MY CHEEKBONE AND MY NOSE, DICKHEAD. SOMEDAY THAT'S GONNA BE ANSWERED FOR.
ENJOY OUR
BETTER WAIT FOR THE ORDER, KIDDO. EVEN COCKROACHES GOT NESTS IN HIGH PLACES.
ODN

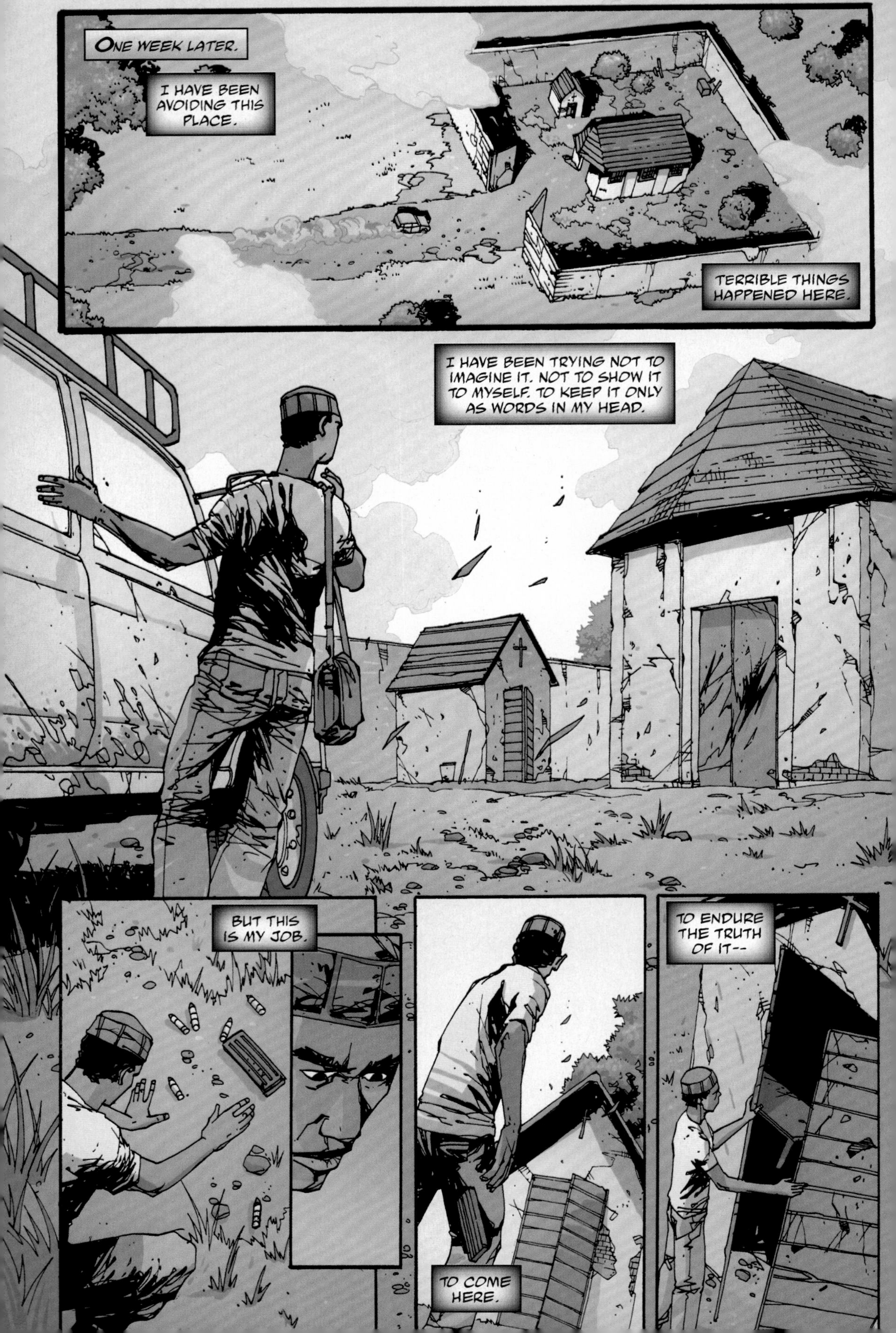
ONE WEEK LATER.
I HAVE BEEN AVOIDING THIS PLACE.
TERRIBLE THINGS HAPPENED HERE.
I HAVE BEEN TRYING NOT TO IMAGINE IT. NOT TO SHOW IT TO MYSELF. TO KEEP IT ONLY AS WORDS IN MY HEAD.
BUT THIS IS MY JOB.
TO COME HERE.
TO ENDURE THE TRUTH OF IT--

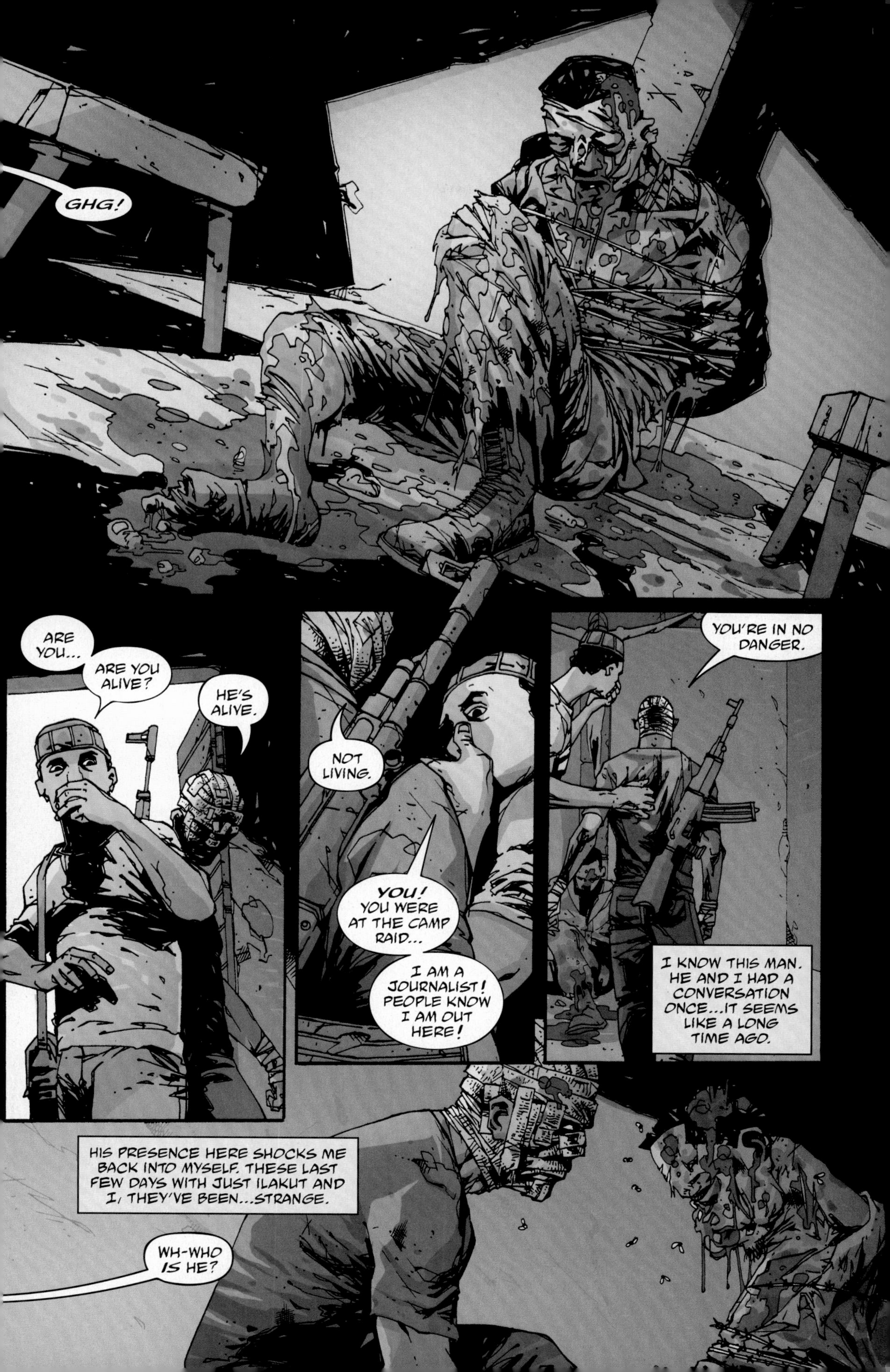
GHG!
ARE YOU...
ARE YOU ALIVE?
HE'S ALIVE.
NOT LIVING.
YOU! YOU WERE AT THE CAMP RAID...
I AM A JOURNALIST! PEOPLE KNOW I AM OUT HERE!
YOU'RE IN NO DANGER.
I KNOW THIS MAN. HE AND I HAD A CONVERSATION ONCE...IT SEEMS LIKE A LONG TIME AGO.
HIS PRESENCE HERE SHOCKS ME BACK INTO MYSELF. THESE LAST FEW DAYS WITH JUST ILAKUT AND I, THEY'VE BEEN...STRANGE.
WH-WHO IS HE?

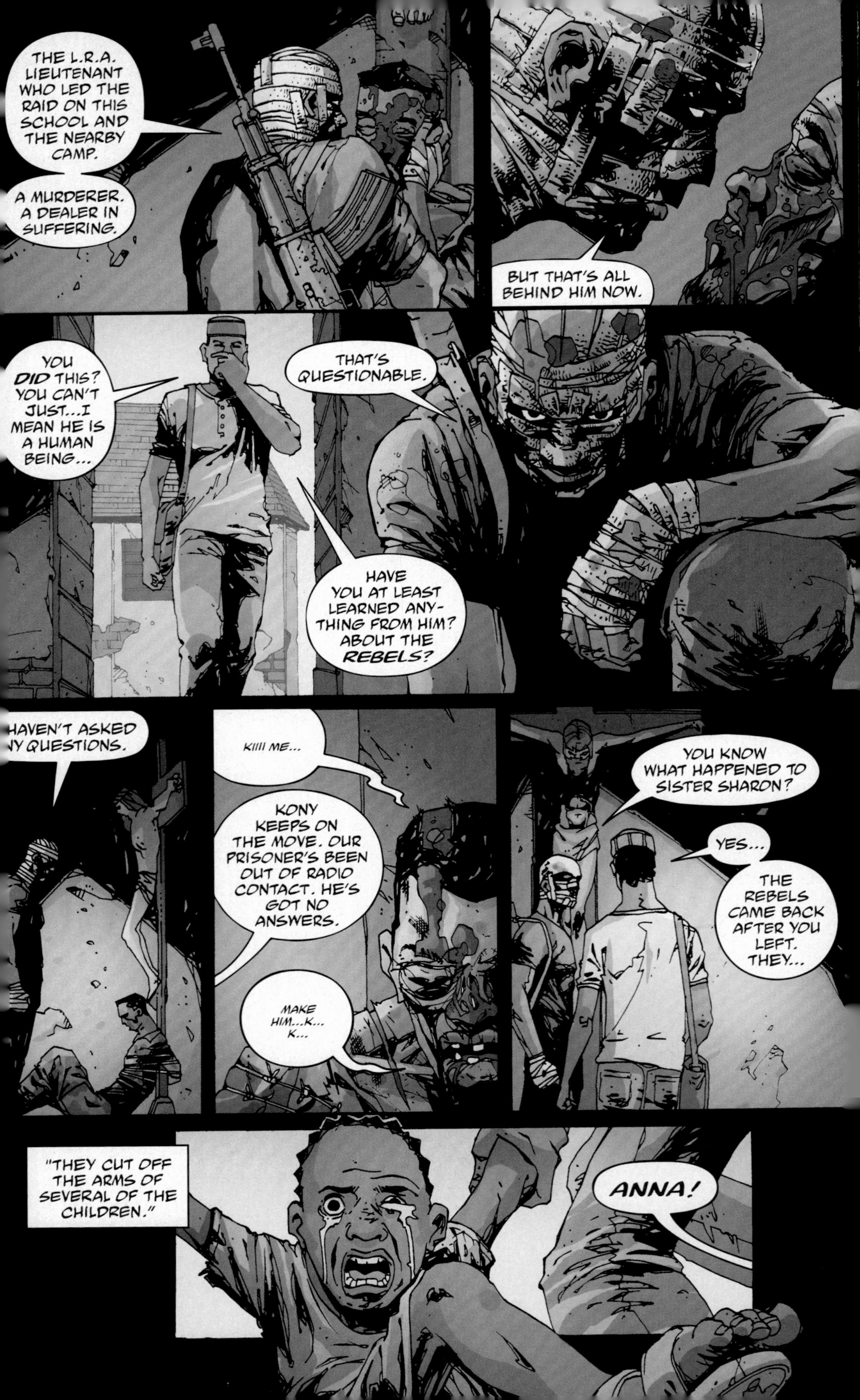
THE L.R.A. LIEUTENANT WHO LED THE RAID ON THIS SCHOOL AND THE NEARBY CAMP.
A MURDERER. A DEALER IN SUFFERING.
BUT THAT'S ALL BEHIND HIM NOW.
YOU DID THIS? YOU CAN'T JUST...I MEAN HE IS A HUMAN BEING...
THAT'S QUESTIONABLE.
HAVE YOU AT LEAST LEARNED ANYTHING FROM HIM? ABOUT THE REBELS?
HAVEN'T ASKED NY QUESTIONS.
KIIII ME...
KONY KEEPS ON THE MOVE. OUR PRISONER'S BEEN OUT OF RADIO CONTACT. HE'S GOT NO ANSWERS.
MAKE HIM...K... K...
YOU KNOW WHAT HAPPENED TO SISTER SHARON?
YES...
THE REBELS CAME BACK AFTER YOU LEFT. THEY...
"THEY CUT OFF THE ARMS OF SEVERAL OF THE CHILDREN."
ANNA!

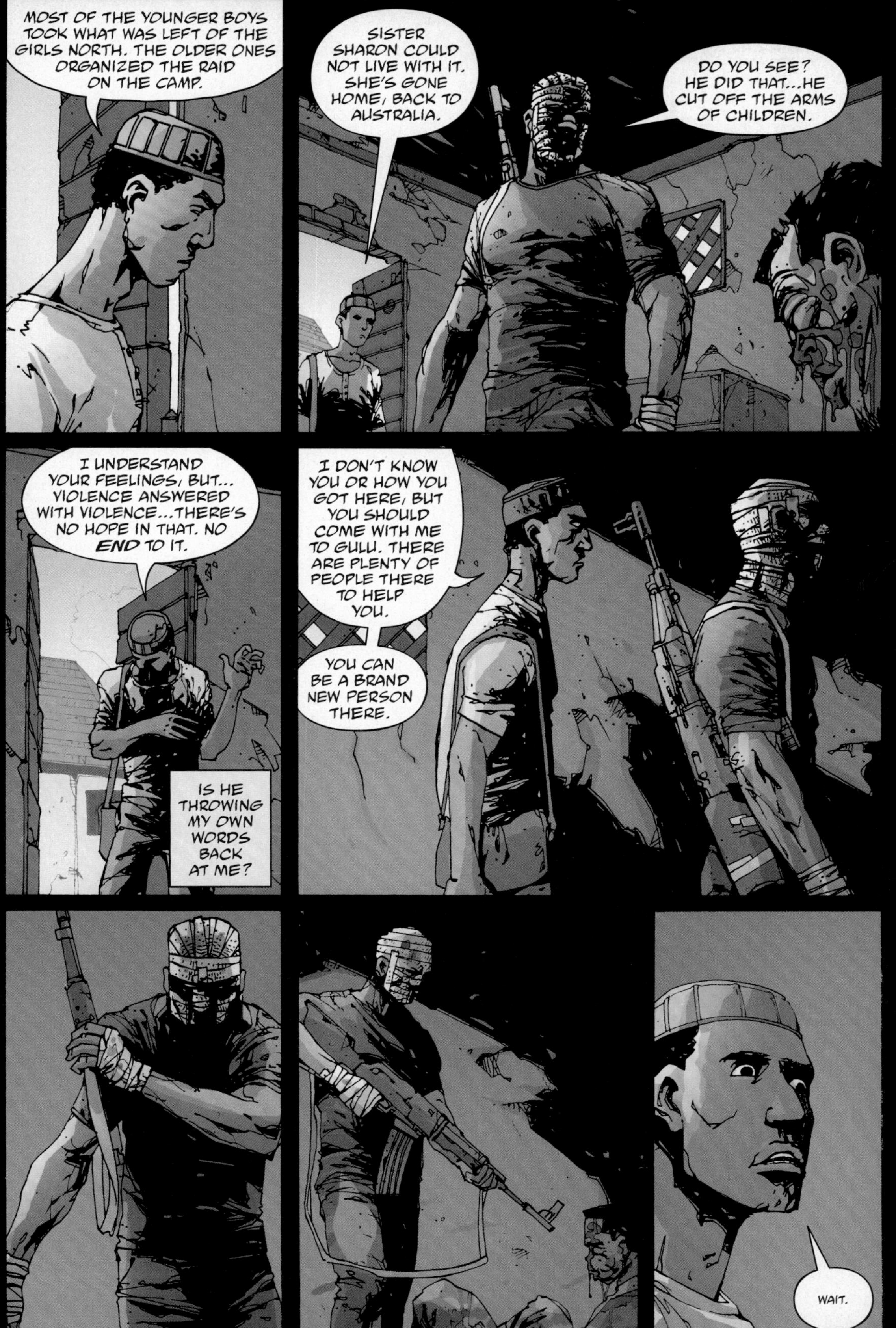
MOST OF THE YOUNGER BOYS TOOK WHAT WAS LEFT OF THE GIRLS NORTH. THE OLDER ONES ORGANIZED THE RAID ON THE CAMP.
SISTER SHARON COULD NOT LIVE WITH IT. SHE'S GONE HOME, BACK TO AUSTRALIA.
DO YOU SEE? HE DID THAT...HE CUT OFF THE ARMS OF CHILDREN.
I UNDERSTAND YOUR FEELINGS, BUT... VIOLENCE ANSWERED WITH VIOLENCE...THERE'S NO HOPE IN THAT. NO END TO IT.
IS HE THROWING MY OWN WORDS BACK AT ME?
I DON'T KNOW YOU OR HOW YOU GOT HERE, BUT YOU SHOULD COME WITH ME TO GULU. THERE ARE PLENTY OF PEOPLE THERE TO HELP YOU.
YOU CAN BE A BRAND NEW PERSON THERE.
WAIT.

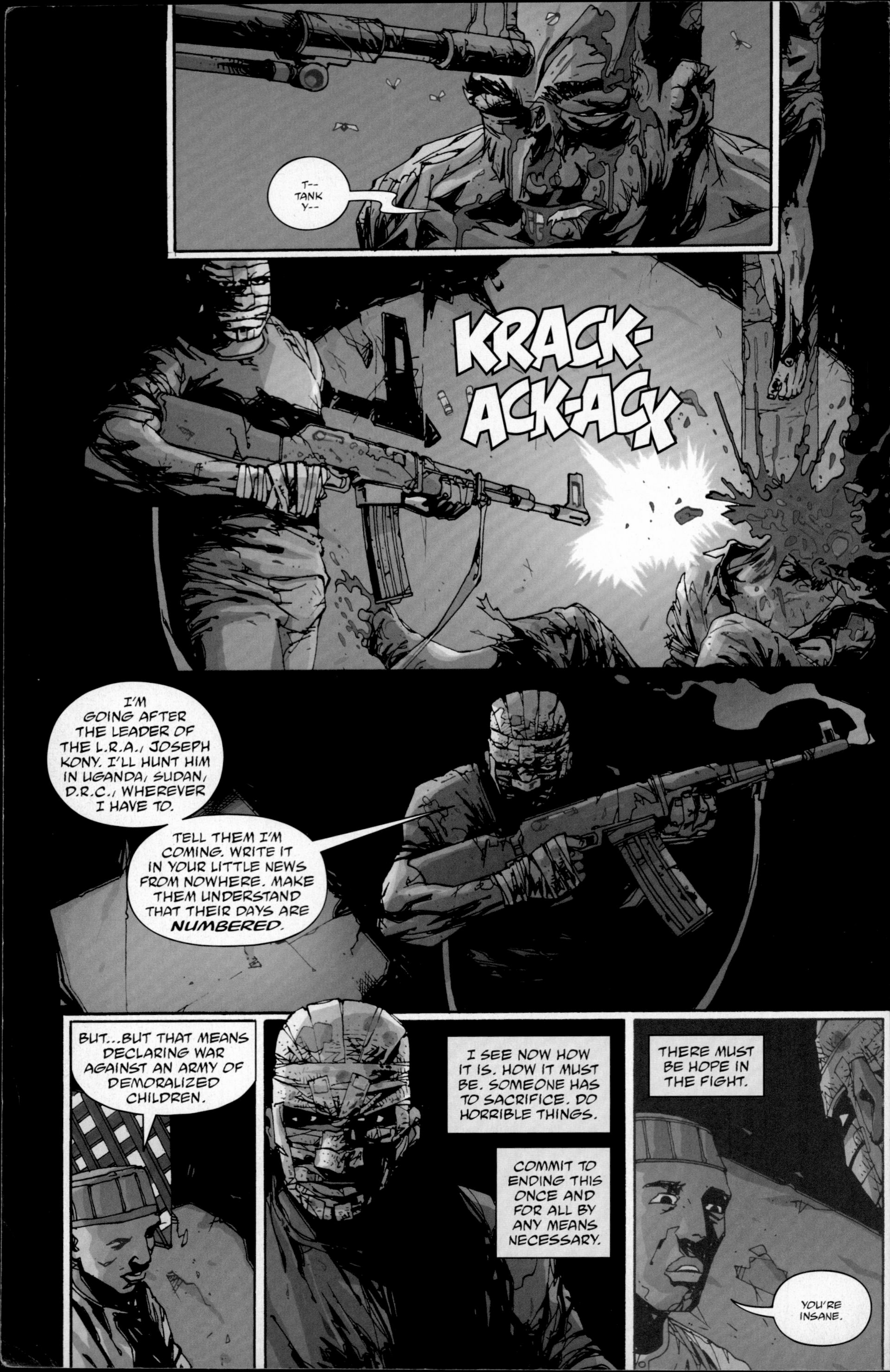
T--
TANK
Y--
KRACK-
ACK-ACK
I'M GOING AFTER THE LEADER OF THE L.R.A., JOSEPH KONY. I'LL HUNT HIM IN UGANDA, SUDAN, D.R.C., WHEREVER I HAVE TO.
TELL THEM I'M COMING. WRITE IT IN YOUR LITTLE NEWS FROM NOWHERE. MAKE THEM UNDERSTAND THAT THEIR DAYS ARE NUMBERED.
BUT...BUT THAT MEANS DECLARING WAR AGAINST AN ARMY OF DEMORALIZED CHILDREN.
I SEE NOW HOW IT IS. HOW IT MUST BE. SOMEONE HAS TO SACRIFICE. DO HORRIBLE THINGS.
COMMIT TO ENDING THIS ONCE AND FOR ALL BY ANY MEANS NECESSARY.
THERE MUST BE HOPE IN THE FIGHT.
YOU'RE INSANE.

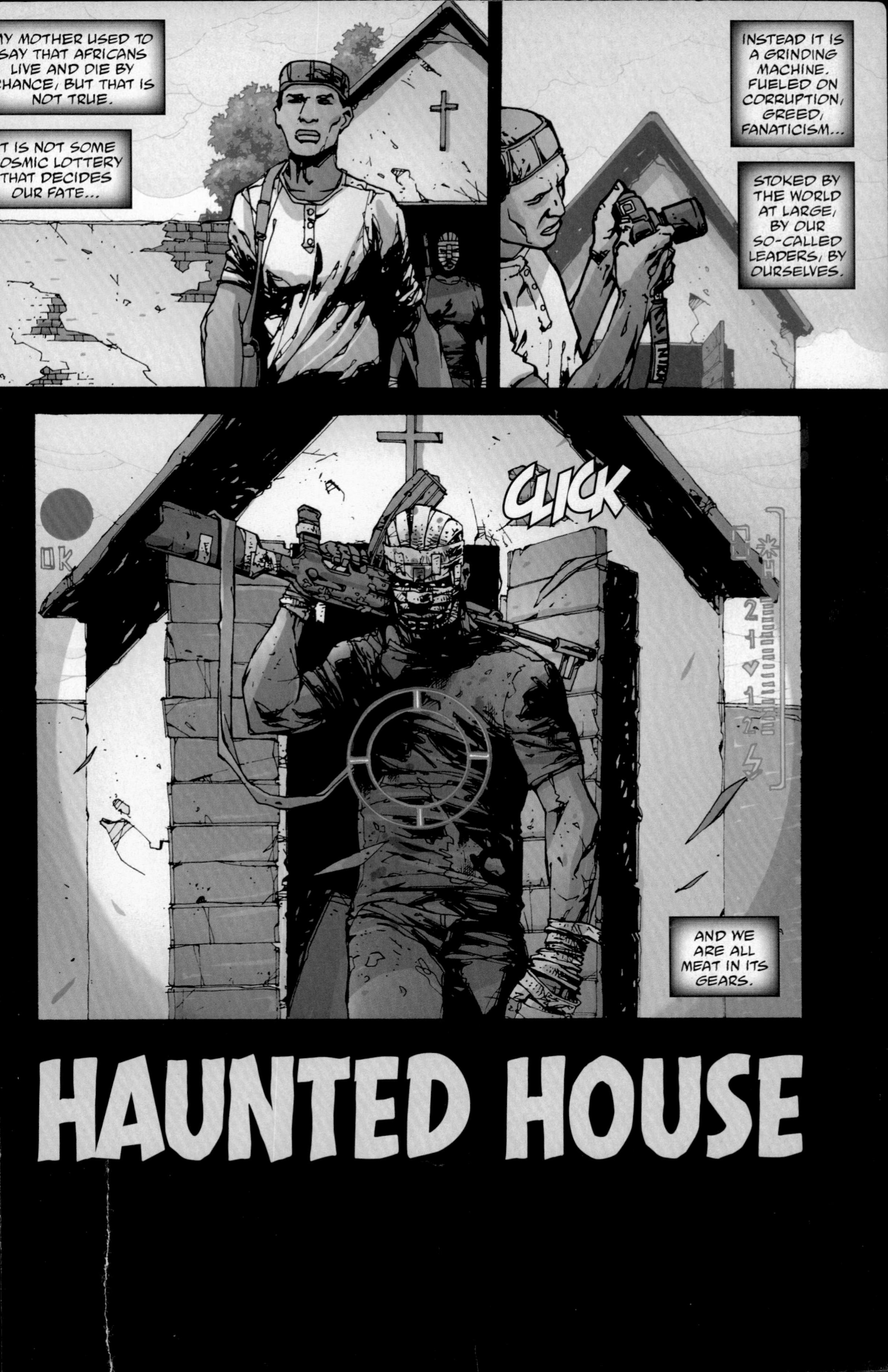
MY MOTHER USED TO SAY THAT AFRICANS LIVE AND DIE BY CHANCE, BUT THAT IS NOT TRUE.
T IS NOT SOME OSMIC LOTTERY THAT DECIDES OUR FATE...
INSTEAD IT IS A GRINDING MACHINE. FUELED ON CORRUPTION, GREED, FANATICISM...
STOKED BY THE WORLD AT LARGE, BY OUR SO-CALLED LEADERS, BY OURSELVES.
CLICK
OK
AND WE ARE ALL MEAT IN ITS GEARS.

HAUNTED HOUSE

GLOSSARY

ABDULKADIR YAHYA ALI: Prominent Somalia peace activist. Killed by gunmen in 2005.

ACHOLI: People from the districts of Gulu, Kitgum and Pader in northern Uganda and Magwe County in southern Sudan.

BUGANDA: The largest kingdom in present-day Uganda. They have primary rule over most administration and government. Conflict between the Acholi, Lango and Baganda people dates back to before British occupation.

DEMOCRATIC REPUBLIC OF THE CONGO (DRC): Third largest country by area in Africa. Formerly a Belgian colony.

GULU: Second-largest town by population in Uganda (119,430 in 2002). Located in Acholiland. The center of operations for the UPDF's war with the LRA. Host to more NGO's than almost any other town in the world.

HOLY SPIRIT MOVEMENT, THE (HSM): Ugandan rebel group in operation from 1986-1987. Led by Alice Auma, a spirit-medium. Left a number of smaller groups that subscribed to her doctrine that Jesus will reign on earth for 1,000 years. The most persistent eventually became the LRA.

INTERNALLY DISPLACED PERSONS (IDP'S): People forced to flee their residence who have crossed no international border. Not, technically, refugees, and not afforded the same rights as such under international law.

INTERNATIONAL RESCUE COMMITTEE (IRC): Non-sectarian relief and humanitarian aid org. Helps those fleeing racial, religious and ethnic persecution.

JOSEPH KONY: Leader of the LRA. Proclaims himself the "spokesperson" of God and a medium, primarily of the Christian Holy Spirit, which Acholi believe represents itself through many manifestations.

KAMPALA: Capital of Uganda. Largest city (population 1,208,544 in 2002). Travel guides say that, like Rome, Kampala is built on seven hills; this is inaccurate.

KHARTOUM: Capital of Sudan and of the Khartoum State. Government has been accused of supporting terrorism and the LRA.

LAURENT-DÉSIRÉ KABILA: President of DRC from 1997, when he overthrew Mobutu, until his assassination in 2001. Succeeded by his son Joseph Kabila Kabange.

LORD'S RESISTANCE ARMY (LRA): Christian guerrillas in northern Uganda and southern Sudan. They desire to establish a theocratic state based on the Ten Commandments. Accused of widespread human rights violations: murder, abduction, mutilation, sexual enslavement and forcing children into combat roles.

MAKERERE UNIVERSITY: Uganda's largest university. After Ugandan independence, it was a focal point for African nationalist culture.

MÉDECINS SANS FRONTIÈRES (MSF, DOCTORS WITHOUT BORDERS): Secular humanitarian aid NGO. Operates in war-torn regions and developing countries facing endemic disease.

NIGHT COMMUTERS: Children who nightly sought safety from LRA abduction in villages or shelters. In 2005, Amnesty International placed the number at nearly 30,000. The current cease-fire has halted the Night Commuter phenomenon.

NOAH'S ARK CHILDREN'S MINISTRY: Religious nonprofit that provided aid and shelter to the Night Commuters.

NON-GOVERNMENTAL ORGANIZATION (NGO): Legal organization created by private orgs or people with no representation of any government.

POSHO (UGALI): Cornmeal product. A staple starch of many African meals, especially in Southern and East Africa. Comfort food.

PRESIDENT YOWERI MUSEVENI: President of Uganda since 1986. Previously a rebel leader, who had himself been accused of abducting children into combat service. He ushered in prosperity in the south but did little to quell war in the north, and may have done things to exacerbate it, until recently.

SECOND CONGO WAR (AFRICA WAR II, AFRICAN WORLD WAR): War in DRC From 1998-2003. World's deadliest conflict since World War II. Fighting continues in the east.

UGANDA PEOPLE'S DEFENCE FORCE (UPDF): Armed forces of Uganda. National army.

UNITED NATIONS CHILDREN'S FUND (UNICEF): Provides humanitarian and developmental assistance to children in developing countries.

WORLD FOOD PROGRAMME (WFP): Food aid branch of the United Nations. World's largest humanitarian agency. Provides food to 90 million per year.

For more geography, history and information, go to joshuadysart.com